Expanding Your IBM PC

Material from the following IBM publications was reproduced by permission.

BASIC *Manual*, 2nd Ed. 1982. pp 44, 45, 55
Guide to Operations (Diskette) 1981. pp 44, 59, 60–71
Guide to Operations Display 1982. pp 45–47, 55
Guide to Operations (Memory) 1981. pp 10–12, 22, 28, 32, 43, 227, 228
Guide to Operations Switch Setting 1983. pp 14, 29, 159
Option Instructions Color/Graphics Adapter 1983. pp 31, 53, 227
Option Instructions Display and Printer Adapter 1983. pp 24, 30

Note to Authors

Do you have a manuscript or software program related to personal computers? Do you have an idea for developing such a project? If so, we would like to hear from you. The Brady Communications Company produces a complete range of books and applications software for the personal computer market. We invite you to write to David Culverwell, Publishing Director, Brady Communications Company, Inc., Bowie, MD 20715.

Publishing Director: David Culverwell
Acquisitions Editor: Chris Williams
Production Editor/Text Design: Barbara Werner
Art Director/Cover Design: Don Sellers
Assistant Art Director: Bernard Vervin
Manufacturing Director: John A. Komsa

Typesetter: Automated Graphic Systems, White Plains, Maryland
Printer: Fairfield Graphics, Fairfield, Pennsylvania
Typefaces: ITC Novarese (text), Universal Monospace (program)

EXPANDING Your IBM PC

A Guide for the Beginner

Bil. Alvernaz

Brady Communications Company, Inc.
A Prentice-Hall Publishing Company
Bowie, Maryland

Expanding your IBM PC

Library of Congress Cataloging in Publication Data

Alvernaz, Bil.
Expanding your IBM PC.

Includes index.
1. IBM Personal Computer. 2. IBM Personal Computer XT. I. Title. II. Title: Expanding your I.B.M. P.C.
QA76.8.I2594A45 1984 001.64 84-12342
ISBN 0-89303-445-2

Prentice-Hall International, Inc., *London*
Prentice-Hall Canada, Inc., Scarborough, *Ontario*
Prentice-Hall of Australia, Pty., Ltd., *Sydney*
Prentice-Hall of India Private Limited, *New Delhi*
Prentice-Hall of Japan, Inc., *Tokyo*
Prentice-Hall of Southeast Asia Pre. Ltd., *Singapore*
Whitehall Books, Limited, Petone, *New Zealand*
Editora Prentice-Hall Do Brasil LTDA., *Rio de Janeiro*
Prentice-Hall Hispanoamericana, S.A., *Mexico*

Printed in the United States of America

85 86 87 88 89 90 91 92 93 94 95 1 2 3 4 5 6 7 8 9 10

Limits of Liability and Disclaimer of Warranty

The author and publisher of this book have used their best efforts in preparing this book and the procedures contained in it. These efforts include the development, research and testing of the theories and procedures to determine their effectiveness. The author and publisher make no warranty of any kind, expressed or implied, with regard to these procedures or the documentation contained in this book. The author and publisher shall not be liable in any event for incidental or consequential damages in connection with, or arising out of, the furnishing, performance, or use of any product mentioned or any procedure suggested in this book.

DEDICATION

To

Diana and Ian:

For sharing a life of writing—the quest for goals, which sometimes seemed unreachable, in a long series of quiet victories, along with some loud disappointments—and, all with absolutely no guarantees. For believing in me and inspiring me at so many points when the pursuit could easily have lost its luster and magical attraction.

CONTENTS

FOREWORD

Personal computing has been entering the lives of more and more of us, in surprisingly rapid steps. While computer professionals have always known how wonderful and how frustrating working with computers can be, it's been a relatively recent discovery for most people. The wonderful part of computing we don't need any help with, but the frustrating part can be difficult indeed, and calls for all the help that we can get. That's where this book by Bil. Alvernaz can be a lifesaver.

Setting up a computer and equipping it with the right mixture of software and hardware options is a very complicated business. While computer enthusiasts, like myself, tend to relish the task of setting up a computer, ordinary folks—who are more interested in getting something useful done than in playing with a high-tech toy—can find it quite daunting.

When I put my heels on the desk and start thinking about what computers, and other smart and complicated tools, are doing in our society as a whole, I find myself coming to a startling conclusion. There is a story that I like to tell that illustrates the matter in a nutshell.

I have some in-laws who recently bought themselves a microwave oven. Now these folks are quite ordinary, college- educated middle class Americans, neither smarter nor dumber about technology than the average citizen. I was talking with them after they had been using—or trying to use—their microwave for a few months. It turned out that they had never really learned how to make it work. Of course they could turn it on and they could do simple microwave cooking, but they never were able to figure out, let alone master, the extra features that they had paid so much for. Programming the darned thing to defrost, cook, warm, hold, cook for time or cook to temperature—it was all too much for them.

Their experience with the microwave oven taught me a lesson that I've been pondering ever since. One side of the lesson is important, but doesn't have anything to do with the readers of this book: the frightening idea that everyday gadgets—like cars and TV sets—are becoming more complex than the average person can deal with. What does that say about the future lives of the half of our population that, by definition, is below average?

The other side of that lesson does concern us. It is that even talented people are faced with an awesome complexity in integrating a tool like a personal computer into their lives. It's not that you and I don't have the intelligence and skills needed to find our way out of the PC Woods—it's that we don't have the time to spare to do it ourselves. That's what this book is about, of course: finding our way more quickly and efficiently out of the confusing tangle of possibilities.

Pathfinder Bil. is giving us the quick way to our goal. Thank Heavens.

Eventually, the folks who create such wonders as personal computers will learn how to make them relatively simple to understand and use. That day hasn't come yet, though, and until then, we can turn to guides like this book to make the journey easier and more fruitful.

Peter Norton

Santa Monica, California
Fall 1984

PREFACE

Heading Toward Enlightenment

When I bought my IBM PC, I really had no idea what I was doing. I just knew about the advantages of word processing and felt confident of my decision.

That was in the "old days" of 1982 when the PC came with single sided disk drives, and the cost of a color monitor and graphics board seemed astronomical when tacked on to the price of the basic system. I was sure that 64KB RAM was plenty of user memory.

I really didn't grasp the significance of what I was doing. I thought I was just taking a step or two up from my correcting Selectric typewriter to make writing less of a mechanical effort. Not to worry about numbering pages or dread proofing and rewriting—well, I thought that was about all there was to it.

When I began using my PC, I started to learn what it all meant—things like RAM, ROM, memory, expansion slots, and so on. It overwhelmed me somewhat at first, but I kept at it until I reached "enlightenment."

That was the point at which I discovered that I not only understood a lot about the PC, but I could add memory if I wanted to. Or I could add my own expansion board. Or, when I mustered up all of my courage, I could even upgrade my system from single sided disk drives to double sided disk drives.

The joy of it all was in discovering that the PC didn't blow up when I slipped off its cover. There was no blue smoke pouring out of my PC's "entrails." The only strange noise I heard was the sound of my heart pounding. The sweetest part of all was that moment after I had put everything back together and saw that the PC worked just fine.

Today, my PC is much, much different from the machine I bought two years ago. It has been "expanded" in ways I never even imagined when I carted all of the boxes home. I used my PC to write this book, without any secretarial help or assistance (except the work done by my wife, Diana). I composed at the keyboard, going from outlines to drafts and finally to finished copy for the publisher.

The PC I used to write this book has two double sided disk drives, an IBM color monitor to go with my IBM green screen, a Paradise Multidisplay Card (for effortless switching back and forth between both screens), a Tecmar multifunction expansion card, 448KB RAM (with a 300KB phantom disk drive), a Sysgen II-20 (20 megabyte fixed disk), a Hayes Smartmodem 1200, an Epson RX-80 FT printer, a Diablo 630 ECS printer, a Speech Synthesis unit, a Dvorak-configured keyboard along with a QWERTY keyboard, Curtis PC Monitor Pedestals and a TUCK-IT keyboard drawer.

The programs I use on a regular basis include:

- Wordstar (version 3.3 for word processing)
- The Word Plus (superb spelling checker and counter)
- Punctuation + Style (for cleaning up)
- The Norton Utilities (utility programs everyone should have)
- PC-FILE III (a data base with power and simplicity built in)
- VisiCalc (it's old but it still meets all my needs)
- PC-TALK III (superb for communications and so reasonable in price)

I used all of them (except VisiCalc) in working on this book and, on a regular basis, for most of my other writing. Those programs have become "old friends." And when I combine all of that with the PC (my best friend), well, there's just no stopping me.

Writing and rewriting (mostly rewriting) a full length book like this is no small task. The wonders of word processing made much of the "process" effortless and, to be honest, many times fun. Despite all of the work, the PC never even worked up a sweat.

You, too, can do it!

You can go as far as you want in expanding your PC. It all depends on your needs and one other important factor . . .

Attitude. That's the key for unlocking your potential and the potential of your IBM PC. Sure, you can have things done in your local computer store, but you really can do it yourself. In the process you will learn a lot, have some fun, discover a new world, feel genuine self-satisfaction, and save a considerable amount of money.

There are people who would probably be better off letting the computer store or someone else add on to their PCs. But even for someone who doesn't want to do the work, this book outlines and shows just what needs to be done, including how to do it. It all helps you understand more about your PC and what makes it work.

Analogies Only Go So Far

To explain how it works, the computer has been compared to automobiles, stereos, and many other items. While most analogies (including the ones in this book) are helpful, they fall a little short in helping "mere mortals" understand the concepts involved. There really never has been anything like a computer before, and that is what scares the hell out of someone when he or she gets down to taking the cover off the PC.

Yes, a computer is like a stereo unit when it comes to adding "things" on. Yes, a computer is like a car, with more memory giving you more "power." B*ut*, just how you add things on and where you put them is a different matter.

Step-By-Step

I kept specific notes on my feelings and fears as I discovered the inner workings of my PC. While I had no idea that one day I would use those notes to write this book, I wanted to keep a fresh perspective of what it was like as I carefully worked my way through such a new world. Sure, there are fears, but you can handle it. That's the whole point of the "step-by-step" approach in this book.

How This Book Was Written

I combined all of my notes with my experience of teaching seminars and classes about the IBM PC. Such experience, plus my previous writing about the PC for related magazines, also developed my perspective toward the person reading and, more importantly, using this book.

I have read far too many books about the IBM PC which have left me with more questions and confusion than I had before reading them. Much thought has gone into the layout, structure, and philosophy of *Expanding Your* IBM PC. It's written to be used as a tool by the beginner for getting the most out of the IBM PC, as you "do it yourself."

My wife, Diana, played an important role in the writing of this book. Besides constantly checking for clarity and readability, she read the book from the perspective of only knowing how to turn on the PC and use it (with no programming or technical expertise). Through draft after draft of this book we refined it to be sure it was as complete as possible, ensuring the maximum benefit for the reader.

We also wanted whatever was included to be easily understood by the non-technical person. Nothing made it into *Expanding Your* IBM PC until it got Diana's certified seal of approval . . . and she was a real "stickler" on behalf of each person who would one day be reading this book.

Steps, Tips, Pointers, and Instructions

Just about anyone who can follow instructions is capable of adding on to his or her IBM PC. That's really what this book is all about. All steps, tips, pointers, and instructions have been carefully checked and rechecked to assure they are clear, understandable, and easy to follow.

I wasn't trained in computers; I learned on my own. By reading such magazines as PC *Magazine*, PC *Tech Journal*, PC *World*, PC *Week*, *Softalk*, *Byte Magazine*, *InfoWorld* and *Business Computing*, I picked up information in bits and pieces. There was no magic involved, just a great deal of reading, asking a lot of questions and, with a positive attitude, trying things out. I didn't have a source or point of reference like this book. I just kept notes on 3 × 5 cards—lots and lots of 3 × 5 cards.

It was like so many things which you need to just "jump in" and try. From the confusion in the beginning comes knowledge and understanding. You really can do it if you try.

Bil. Alvernaz

P.O. Box 21632
Santa Barbara, CA 93121
MCI Mail #207-8825
Fall 1984

ACKNOWLEDGMENTS

Thanks to:

Chris Williams Who had the original vision, who believed in me, encouraged me, sealed the agreement with a handshake and was/is a true friend.

David Culverwell A strong presence beyond leadership, bordering on mystic qualities.

Barbara Werner The person (and wizard) who, along with many other talented people at the Brady Communications Company (especially the art department), "pulled it all together" for *Expanding Your* IBM PC.

Peter Norton Someone who has reached the heights toward which we should all aspire; while keeping it all in perspective.

Alvin and Dorothy Alvernaz The two people who have always been a constant source of encouragement and support.

Bernie Shepard Professor of Journalism who passed along not only the skills and wisdom, but the depth to handle it all objectively.

George Armstrong A true professional, setting solid-gold examples by his actions, who is more than just friend. Someone who believes in me almost as much as I believe in him.

Wayne Holder For programs which remove so much of the mechanical drudgery, pain, and heartache of writing.

Tom Sheldon A source of information, a computer whiz, and a friend.

Edward Asner For encouragement and emotional support over the years.

Ken Bronstein The ink man, who really does make it all look so good on paper.

Those who reviewed and edited this book—the final product shines and sparkles because of the efforts of many people.

And . . .

Barbara Brubaker, Jim Button, Sara Hadley, Sam Katzen, Carol Wilkins

INTRODUCTION

This Book Was Written for You

This book is for the person with a limited computer background, and who has had an IBM PC or PC/XT for a while and now wants to add-on to it. It is also written for the person thinking about buying an IBM PC or PC/XT. This book can help you save a lot of money when purchasing a PC, if you're willing to consider the "do it yourself" option of opening up your computer and putting forth a little effort. It can save you quite a bit of money when you add on to your PC, too.

The design of the IBM PC makes expanding it so easy and simple that you can literally do it all yourself. You don't need any special skills to add on to your PC. You just need to know what to do.

The problem, until now, has been the lack of one single source or point of reference containing all of the necessary information. Well, it's all in here, outlined in a way to make everything as easy as possible for you.

Thinking about actually taking your PC apart brings up many questions, concerns, and doubts. Can I really do it myself? What tools will I need? How much work is involved? Can I hurt anything? How long does it take? Should I just let the store do it for me?

The purpose of this book is to answer those questions and more, while showing you how to expand your IBM PC or PC/XT. The text of this book will refer to the PC, but that really means the PC/XT (the fixed disk version of the PC), too. The differences between the PC and PC/XT will be explained where necessary. For the most part, the term PC will also imply PC/XT. IBM's portable computer, though different in many ways, is still a PC. Much of what is written in this book will apply to the portable PC, with differences noted as they occur.

Expanding Your IBM PC is more than just another how-to book, because it explains much of what everyone else assumed you already knew. Most manuals, books, and magazine articles have, at one point or another, not included certain steps or procedures in how-to guides, reasoning that readers already knew about them.

There are no such assumptions in this book. At points the text might seem too basic or too detailed, but the philosophy behind this book is to provide you with everything in the step-by-step process. If you see a step you already know how to accomplish, simply bypass it. However, it might not be too bad an idea to scan through even those steps you are sure of. You'll be surprised at how much you might have taken for granted.

Another purpose of this book is to show you how to save money when adding on to your PC or building it almost from scratch. You can purchase what is called a "no drive" PC and start from scratch by adding your own disk drives, diskette adapter, and everything else. If you are looking for a way to get a PC and save a lot of money doing it, then this book is for you.

It is possible to buy a PC which has only the chassis, the system board, the power supply, and a keyboard—a "no drive" system. It is very realistic to build such a PC from the ground up into anything you want it to be—for a whole lot less money than if you purchased the complete package from the computer store. Best of all, it isn't that hard to do. If you do build your own PC you will also need to include in your budget the cost of a monitor and a monitor adapter card.

You don't need any special skills besides being able to follow instructions and put pieces together. You will be surprised how easy it is to do it yourself, so much so that you will find yourself saying, "That's all there is to it?"

One of the underlying themes, running as a thread throughout this book, is confidence. By taking away the mystery of adding on to your PC, breaking it down into a step-by-step process, this book makes you feel more confident about doing it yourself. That's a subtle but significant aspect of *Expanding Your* IBM PC for people who never have done anything like this before. Confidence tends to make your fingers more nimble and sharpens your wit.

How To Use This Book

Use the table of contents or the index to find the subject you are looking for. When you turn to that section of the book you will find general information, along with a step-by-step guide. By carefully following the steps you will be able to add just about anything to your PC.

No two products, although similar, are ever quite the same, but the steps for installation fall into pretty much the same order. You must be sure to read the product's installation guide before doing anything else. This book will then explain the process of adding each product onto your PC.

Mark up this book! Write notes in the margins and circle key words. Underline and highlight those points or paragraphs you want to be able to find quickly when you refer back to the book. Put paper clips on those pages you want to get to quickly. Make it easy on yourself.

When you see a word or phrase you're not familiar with, chances are it will be listed in Appendix A, which is a glossary of terms.

Products and companies mentioned in this book are all listed in alphabetical order in Appendix B. If you're interested in knowing more about a product or company, you will find addresses and telephone numbers there. Appendix B is divided into two sections: one lists the companies, and the other one covers the products by category.

The products and companies referred to in this book were chosen because of the author's familiarity with them. Products were used as examples based on the author's practical work experience, background, expertise, and preference. Failure to mention a product is not a comment on its worthiness or usefulness. The author just cannot know about every product on the market.

Steps which are similar are repeated in different sections. This might seem a bit redundant, but it makes sense if you look at it from the standpoint of the user (that's you, remember). If you find yourself getting referred back and forth to different sections of this book where a certain procedure or step has already been covered, well, you'll spend most of your time flipping pages and keeping track of where you were.

The point here is to make things as easy as possible for you. The only times you will be referred to other parts of this book is when there is something that requires quite a few steps and illustrations. A good example of how that will work is with the initial step to adding on to your PC—when you pull off the PC's cover. The steps for that procedure are outlined in Appendix C.

Terminology

The words and phrases in the realm of computers can easily make the newcomer light-headed. IBM's standard terms are used as much as possible throughout this book. While other terms might be more popular, the reader will inevitably come face to face with the same terminology in IBM's documentation.

The list below outlines some of the key terms:

IBM TERM	COMMON TERM
Fixed Disk	Hard Disk
nKB User Memory or RAM	nK Internal Memory
Expansion Unit	Expansion Chassis Extender Unit
System Board	Mother Board
System Unit	CPU
Diskette Adapter	Disk Drive Adapter/Controller

Almost Like Holding Your Hand

There are many reasons why people have avoided the do it yourself option when it comes to expanding the IBM PC. Fear has a lot to do with it, but the poorly written manuals haven't helped matters any either. What most people like is a little hand holding. In other words, just about all of us want the detailed instructions on how to do something.

That's back once again to the whole point of this book. Say you want to expand the memory in your PC. You can find in that section of the book what you need to do. Once you know what is needed, you can follow the steps to do it. That's all there is to it for any aspect of expanding your PC: just simple steps to follow, which make it easier to understand your product's installation guide or manual.

So have some fun while you learn more about your PC . . . and, best of all, you will save a lot of money in the process.

1

1.1 It's a Lot Like a Rubber Band

Expanding your IBM PC is a lot like stretching a rubber band. A rubber band can be used to hold a bunch of 3 × 5 cards together; it can be wrapped around an inch thick folder of papers; or it can be looped around itself several times to hold a model in place until the glue dries. There are hundreds of uses for a rubber band. It all depends on how you want to use it. A rubber band is formless until someone does something with it.

In many ways your PC is like that rubber band. You can stretch its uses to the limit, loading it up with everything under the sun. Or you can use it only for one specific purpose like word processing or accounting. As you add on to your PC you are stretching it to do more for you. With more memory, a clock timer, another disk drive, or even the more efficient Dvorak keyboard, you increase the power of your PC as a tool each time you stretch it a little further.

1.2 No Magic Is Involved

As marvelous as the IBM PC is, there is no magic involved in how it does what it does. Contemplating everything a PC can do is enough to make the gray matter inside your skull ache. You really don't need to be concerned with all the details of how the PC functions internally, only how to make it do what you want. You don't need to be an engineer or have in depth training in math to add something to your PC.

Expanding your PC is as easy as snapping together the pieces of a child's toy. That might sound like an oversimplification, but all you will be doing is plugging in or connecting different pieces together. In some cases, you will flip switches to new settings. Actually, it's fun once you get past any fears you might have about doing it yourself . . . but there is no magic—it just seems like it.

1.3 Taking a Look Inside the PC

"Is that all there is?"

There are no wheels, gears or lights. No mice on a treadmill or tiny people. The PC is circuit boards and chips all arranged in space age order and predominantly green. There aren't many wires, either.

Figure 1.1 shows you what you will see as you look down on the PC, with the front of the unit facing you. The box in the back right hand corner is the power supply. The opening on top of the power is for the fan. The disk drives sit just in front of the power supply. If you only have one disk drive, it will be placed toward the middle of the chassis, with an open area to the right of it. If you have an IBM PC/XT there will be a floppy disk drive on the left and a fixed disk on the right.

On the left you will see what are called *expansion slots*. It is through these expansion slots that you will be able to connect your PC to other devices. You will fill expansion slots with adapter cards, which, in turn, will be connected to other devices.

There are five such slots on the IBM PC and eight on the PC/XT. On the PC/XT the three slots closest to the power supply are only able to hold short expansion cards or boards (i.e., ones that don't extend the length of the chassis). Most units have one or two expansion slots filled from the very beginning. A disk drive controller, needed for running the disk drive(s), takes up one slot.

Fig. 1.1: A view of the inside of the IBM Personal Computer

Another slot is used by the monitor adapter card, or board, with which you can run either a monochrome or color monitor (i.e., the screen you look at) or both. You can also run a printer with a monitor adapter card. IBM's cards are called the monochrome display and parallel printer adapter; and the color/graphics monitor adapter.

Everything you are looking at rests on what is called the mother board. That term might sound kind of funny, but it is from that board that your PC is controlled. Many manuals, including most of IBM's, refer to the mother board as the *system board*. In this book we will refer to it as the system board.

The system board is where the initial memory for your PC has been installed. The memory sockets (either filled or not filled with memory chips when you purchase the PC) are located on the front left side of the PC, near the speaker.

If you have a newer PC (manufactured after mid-1983), you can put 256KB (1KB = 1024 bytes or characters) of user memory on the system board. The older PCs only accommodate 64KB on the system board. This is a significant point you want to consider before you add any memory to your PC; if you can still add memory chips to the system board, then you might not need to purchase a memory expansion card. The way to tell which type of PC you have is explained in section 1.6.

The system board also contains the two switch blocks you will need to set. These tiny white switches, nested near the power unit across from the expansion slots, play an important role in directing what happens inside your PC.

Each time you change the configuration on your PC, especially in relation to memory, you will need to reset the switches. It is through the switch settings that the PC knows how much memory it is working with or what kind of monitor is being used.

The IBM PC/XT only has one set of these switch blocks because it can read how much memory you have on its own. So if you have a PC/XT, you won't have to worry about switch positions on switch block 2 (it isn't there). You will just be concerned about switch block 1 for different settings.

Whenever you are setting these switches you want to move them carefully with the tip of a pen to the correct settings. Improperly set switches can actually hurt the monochrome or color monitor or cause your PC to give you strange error messages.

The back of your PC (as shown in Figure 1.2) is where you will be plugging in everything from printers to keyboard to monitors. This is all covered in detail in other chapters.

1.4 A Typical PC

Most IBM PCs start out life rather modestly. A typical PC starter system of today looks something like this:

- Monochrome (green screen) Monitor
- Dual Disk Drives (Double Sided)
- System Unit (64KB User Memory)
- Standard IBM Keyboard
- Dot Matrix Printer

Fig. 1.2: The back panel of the IBM Personal Computer, where you will be making all of the connections.

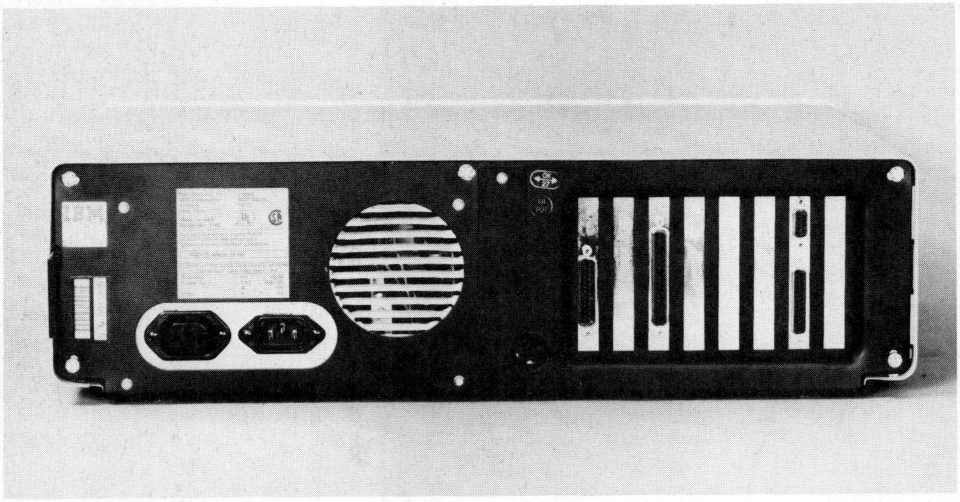

This package can be considered deluxe because there are a large number of IBM PCs out there with single disk drives, some of which are single sided. Many of the systems with two disk drives are single sided, also. A large number of PCs start out with 64KB memory, although the trend is towards starting with 128KB (which is much more realistic for business applications).

The amount of money one has to spend for a personal computer plays a big role in the setup one buys, but there are other factors too. This is the first computer purchase for many people who have a lot to learn. Other people may know something about computers, but still aren't sure what to get. With so much happening in the personal computer industry, consumers just do the best they can.

So, IBM PCs have arrived in households and offices across this country and around world far from loaded up with extras. Actually, that isn't as bad as it sounds, because when you first get an IBM PC you're not too sure what you ultimately want to do with it. As you discover more about the PC and decide how you want to expand, you can now do it yourself for far less money than you would pay retail.

1.5 Reasons for Expanding Your PC

Data bases, integrated software, and emulated (RAM) disk drives, all of which translate into the need for additional RAM (random access memory), are probably the most common and logical reasons for expanding your PC.

Within the last year more and more programs have been written to take advantage of all of the capabilities of the PC. That has meant an increased need for more internal memory (RAM) in the PC. At one time, 128KB was a lot of user memory, but today 256KB and up isn't considered exotic.

Programs which use additional internal memory don't need to keep going back to the disk drives for information or for different parts of the program. Each time the disk drive's red light is on the computer is *accessing* (reading from or writing to) the disk. That also means *time*. The more often the PC goes to the disk the more slowly the program works.

The newer programs reside in memory. In other words, when the PC needs information or instructions from the program it goes to its own internal memory. Doing that is lightning fast and results in the PC zipping in and out of memory to run your program(s).

The popular word processing program Wordstar is a good example of a program written for 64KB user memory. It constantly returns to the program disk for what are called overlay files. Each time you use any of the program's features it needs to go to disk, unless that overlay file happens to be in memory.

Because of this aspect of Wordstar, many people have gone to *emulated disks*. By creating a disk drive in your PC's internal memory you eliminate the mechanical whirling and clicking of accessing the disk. The emulated or phantom disk drive works like a regular disk drive but is much faster. And it reduces the wear and tear on your disk drive. To create an emulated disk drive you need something like 320KB or more of user memory to have enough room to do everything you want to do. (See Chapter 5)

Another benefit to having more memory with Wordstar is that you can move or copy bigger blocks of text from one area of a document or report to another. With 64KB user memory you can move only five or six paragraphs. As the user memory is increased so is the size of what you can move or even copy. While Wordstar will work just fine with 64KB it can take advantage of having more user memory.

Use of data base programs, which keep track of large amounts of information, like inventory and client lists, is another reason to add more memory to your PC. If your entire data base (the program and the data you are using) is in memory, the PC is lightning fast. Programs which do use the disk instead of internal memory for working are painfully slow.

The newer integrated programs have been designed to use more memory. With these programs, like the extremely popular 1-2-3 from Lotus Development Corporation, you have more than one program working for you at a time. With 1-2-3 for example, you can work on your electronic spreadsheet, use word processing and, when you need it, you can bring in a data base for sorting and other functions.

It's not unusual for an integrated program to use 320KB or more. In the months ahead we will see many such programs introduced. Thus, more PCs, perhaps even yours, will be needing a lot more memory.

If you have a PC with just one disk drive, you will benefit from increased memory for another reason: the more memory your PC has the less time it takes to copy a disk. With increased memory, the PC is able to hold more information in single chunks, cutting down on the time involved for making back-up copies, and eliminating the need for switching disks back and forth.

It's easy to get caught up in the status of having your PC loaded with a large amount of memory. Like in the days of the great horsepower races in automobiles, the amount of memory in PCs has become a big deal. Now instead of bragging about how much horsepower a car has, we brag about how much memory we crammed into the PC. For many people, loading a large amount of memory in the PC is equivalent to shooting ducks with cannons. The key point here is to get only what you need. Determine your needs and build your system from there. Remember that memory can be added 64KB at a time (or 16KB at a time on older PCs with less than 64KB). Your system can grow with you as your needs increase.

1.6 Which System Board Do You Have?

If you have decided to add more user memory to your PC, you first need to determine just when your PC was manufactured. If you have a PC/XT this doesn't matter; but if your don't, read on. The date you bought your PC is not the key factor here—when it was made is.

Figure 1.3 shows the rear panel of the PC. If there is a large white 'B' stamped on the unit between the power supply fan vent and the openings for the expansion slots, then the system board on your PC can be expanded up to 256KB. If there is no 'B' stamped there then you can only have 64KB on the system board, and more than likely that system board is already filled.

One other way to tell whether or not you have a new system board is to look inside the PC, in front of the expansion slot which is closest to the outside edge. If

Fig. 1.3: The back panel of the IBM Personal Computer, showing the white 'B'

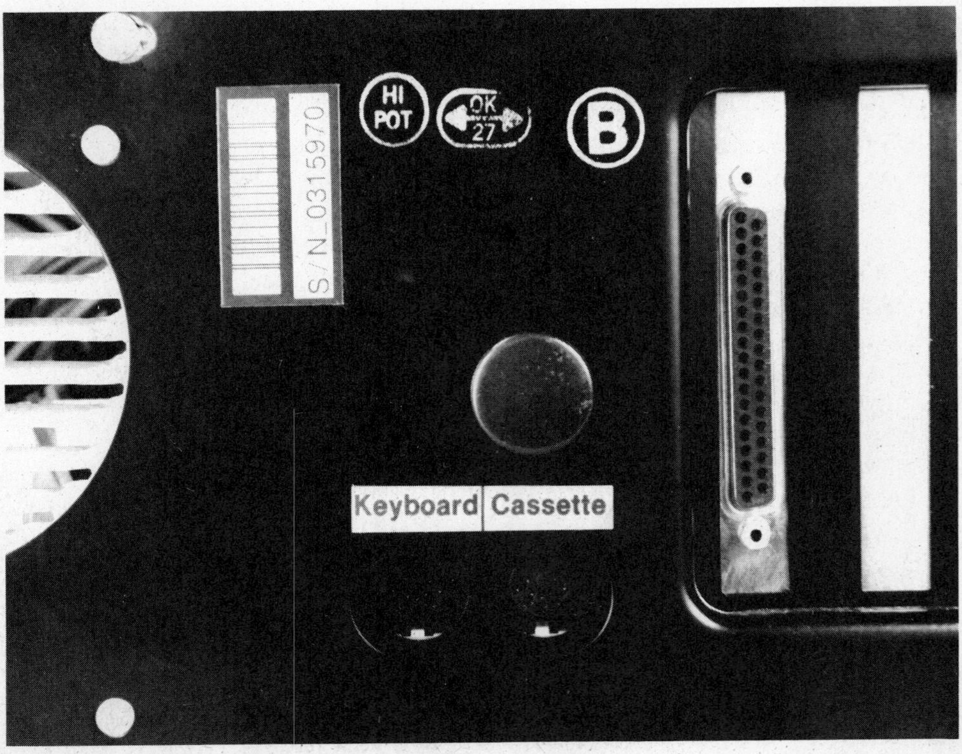

the identification stamp reads "64KB-256KB CPU" that means you can add up to 256KB to the system board. If the stamp reads "16KB-64KB-CPU," the maximum you can have on the system board is 64KB.

All of this is so important because without a system board expandable to 256KB, you need to add a memory adapter card to one of the expansion slots to add any large amount of memory. You must fill up the user memory on the system board first. This also saves your expansion slots for other things (most of which are covered in this book). At first look you might think you have plenty of expansion slots, but they can be used up in no time at all.

So, if you have a system board which can be expanded to 256KB, and you want that much memory, read the following sections. However, if you have one of the older system boards, then you will need to add more memory through the use of a memory card or a multifunction card. For that, see Chapter 2.

There is a way to upgrade an older PC's system boards. It will cost about $400, but after your current system board has been modified it will be brought up to the new standards and specifications. You should look closely at the value in relation to your need. You might be better off sticking with what you have or looking into the other option, which is an expansion unit (see Chapter 2). Such units give you more expansion slots more adapter cards, which can, of course, include memory cards and the multifunction cards upon which you can add significant amounts of memory.

1.7 Before You Get Started

There are a few more points you should be aware of before you open up your PC. If the difference between the older PCs and the newer ones wasn't enough to confuse you, IBM's new portable PC will. The portable PC not only has two half-height disk drives, it comes with 256KB memory (RAM) and its system board is expandable to 512KB (which should be enough for just about anyone).

If you have a portable PC, you need to follow the instructions in the User's Guide provided with it. Even the settings for the switch blocks are different (also outlined in the User's Guide). The information in this book is for the non-portable PCs.

The older PCs have what is called the *older revision board*. That refers to the system board. If you have less than 64KB on an older revision board, you must use different memory chips to upgrade it to its maximum of 64KB. The chips you want are labeled 4116 and rated from 250 nanoseconds (NS) down to 150 nanoseconds. Most chips are rated at 200 NS.

This is critical information, because if you plug a 4164 chip where a 4116 belongs (or vice-versa) *you could destroy all of the memory chips*. So, to make sure you don't end up with the wrong chips, here is what you need:

4164 200NS (*or faster*) Chips These are for the newer IBM PC which can have up to 256KB on the system board. These chips can also be used on the memory expansion boards which are placed in the expansion slots of the PC.

4116 200NS (*or faster*) Chips These are for the older IBM PCs (which were manufactured before to mid-1983 and do not have a white 'B' stamped on the rear panel), which can only accomodate 64KB on the system board.

Do not mix chips! The chips are not interchangeable.

1.8 What You Need To Expand the System Board

If you have a newer PC and want to expand the memory on the system board, read on. If you have an older PC, this section will not apply to you.

To expand the memory of your PC you will need to populate the system board. All that means is that you will stick little memory chips into specific spots. *The chips must be installed in a certain order*, so make sure you follow the instructions carefully. Adding user memory is done in increments of 64KB.

Adding memory dramatically illustrates how much money you can save by doing it yourself. The going rate for having someone else add 64KB of memory starts at around $150. If you buy the chips yourself you will pay as little as $45 for the entire set, depending on which kind of chips you buy. Are you even more interested now in doing it yourself?

The most economical way to buy memory chips is through the mail order houses. Pick up just about any computer magazine, (e.g., *InfoWorld*, PC *Magazine*) and you will see ads for memory upgrade kits. You will need nine chips for each 64KB of memory that you want to add. Many people think you only need eight chips, but the ninth chip is used for parity checking for that particular 64KB. Parity takes care of error checking.

The chips you want are labeled 4164 and work at a range from 250 nanoseconds down to 150 nanoseconds (NS). The speed of a chip is measured in nanoseconds and just means the time it takes to obtain a piece of information. The smaller the nanosecond number the faster the chip works. However, the faster the chip works the more it costs, too.

Normally, you will see the chips you want at either 200NS or 250NS. Chips purchased through mail order houses are already packaged and ready to go. However, it never hurts just to check when you are ordering to be sure you get exactly what you want. The place where you are purchasing the chips can usually help you determine which chips you will need. And remember that the lower the number of nanoseconds, the higher the quality.

You will need the following tools:

- One flat blade screwdriver (for removing the PC's cover)
- One 3/16" nut driver or wrench (for removing any expansion board that might be in your way). This tool will help keep the small screws from getting stripped.
- Insertion tool or tweezer-like module puller. This is used to put in the memory chips. Many people do this by hand, but the tool does make the process easier, especially when working on the system board.

Before you begin adding memory to your PC, you need to understand that *static electricity can spell doom for memory*. Avoid holding or playing with the memory chips. Don't touch them until you are ready to insert them on the system board. Leave them in the container or package they came in.

Static electricity is like an invisible bolt of lightning. When it hits memory chips—-and other kinds of chips, too—the high voltage actually either fuses the microscopic circuitry together or blows holes in it. Static charges can also erase portions of your floppy disks, too. See chapter 12.

Keep the following in mind:

- Stand on an anti-static mat or spray some anti-static spray on the floor where you will be standing when you install the memory.
- Wear shoes with rubber soles and don't wear any polyester clothes. Nylon socks should not be worn.
- When you do hold the memory chips, just hold the edges, and don't touch the tiny connector prongs.
- Touch the PC chassis frequently to discharge any residual charge. Do this in between inserting each chip.

Technicians touch the PC's power unit first (while the system is plugged in but not turned on). When you touch the power supply your body voltage is reduced to the static level of the computer. At that point you won't need to worry about static electricity hurting your chips. It's important to note that IBM designed the PC with high voltage completely isolated, so you really can't ever get to it anyway.

One of the best ways to be absolutely sure static electricity doesn't wipe out your chips is to have a static mat. You should actually do your work (i.e., putting in memory chips) on such a mat, touching it frequently so no static charge whatsoever can pass through to the chips.

You can't be too careful, even though you will hear of many people (including the technicians in the computer stores) just plopping in memory chips without any precautions or much concern as to static electricity. It's always better to do things as carefully and cautiously as possible so you don't have to do it all over again or spend a lot of time trying to find a bad chip once all of them have been installed.

1.9 Adding Memory Chips to the System Board

The entire process of adding memory to the system board, from start to finish, should take less than an hour. Don't try to set a new world's record here. It might take as long as a couple of hours, depending on your pace. Don't watch the clock, just carefully follow the steps and instructions outlined here for you.

Figure 1.4 shows the layout and details of the system board on an IBM PC. The first row of memory has already been installed for you at the factory. The rest of the memory is installed on the system board row by row, starting with the row next to the factory-installed memory and working towards the front of the chassis. This is clearly outlined in Figure 1.4 and is extremely important to the proper working of your PC after additional memory is installed.

To add memory chips to the system board:

STEP ONE: Unplug EVERYTHING attached to your PC. The monitor, the printer, the keyboard (and anything else attached to your PC) must all be disconnected. There

Fig. 1.4: The layout of the system board

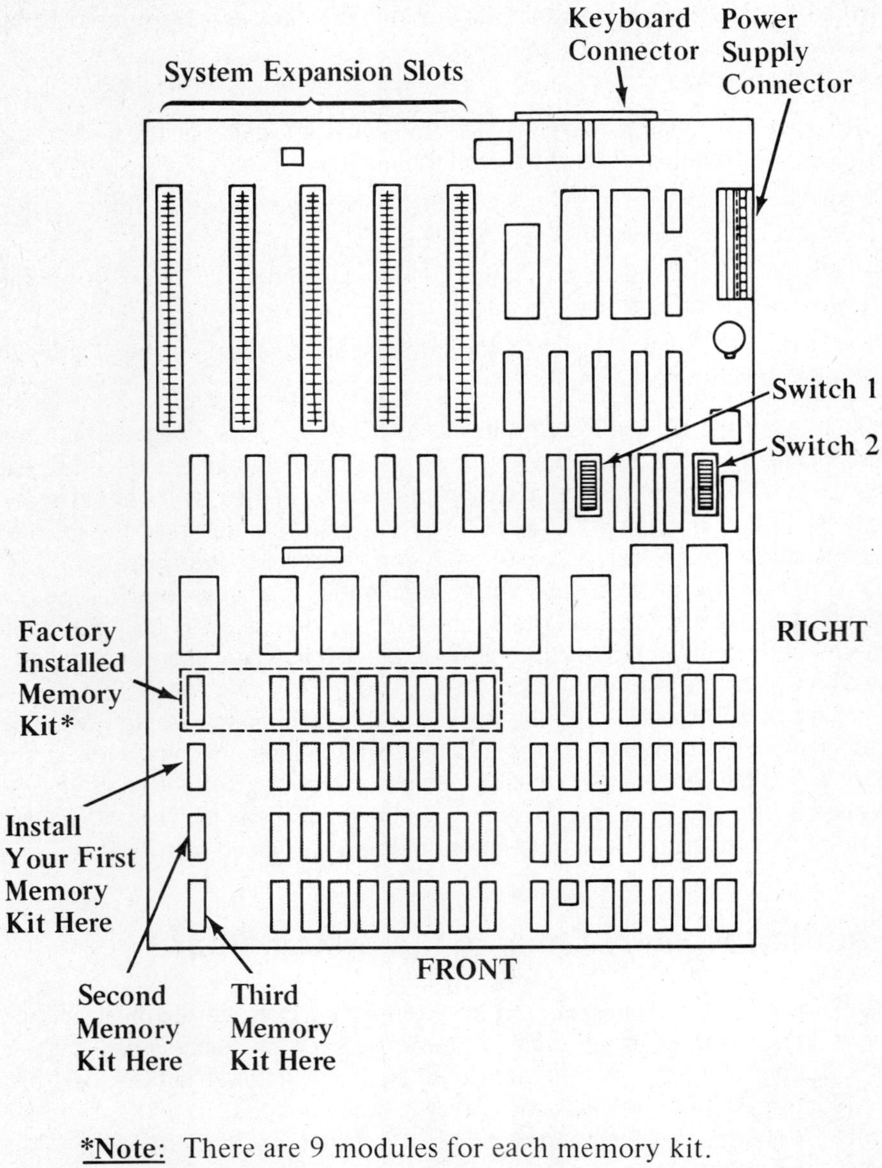

Courtesy of International Business Machines Corporation

should be absolutely nothing attached to the back of your PC when you are ready to take off the cover. You might want to mark the cable connections before you disconnect anything. This can be done with small pieces of masking tape. Use matching sets of letters or numbers so you can be sure you know where everything goes when it comes time to reconnect.

STEP TWO: Take the cover off your PC. (See Appendix C.)

STEP THREE: Remove any adapter cards or boards in the expansion slots. These need to be moved out of your way so you have enough working room while installing the memory chips. Each adapter card (or board) is held in place at the back of the panel by a small screw. Turn that screw counterclockwise to remove it. (Figure 1.5). Once you have removed the screw you can pull out the card (or board) by carefully lifting it up and out. Do this with each card in the expansion slots.

You clear the expansion slots because you will need all the room you can get to maneuver while putting in the tiny memory chips. The PC might not seem too cramped while you are looking at it, but once you get in there you will see the need for having as much room as possible. The boards or cards you just removed can be put back in

Fig. 1.5: Removing adapter cards from the expansion slots; notice closeup of screw to be removed

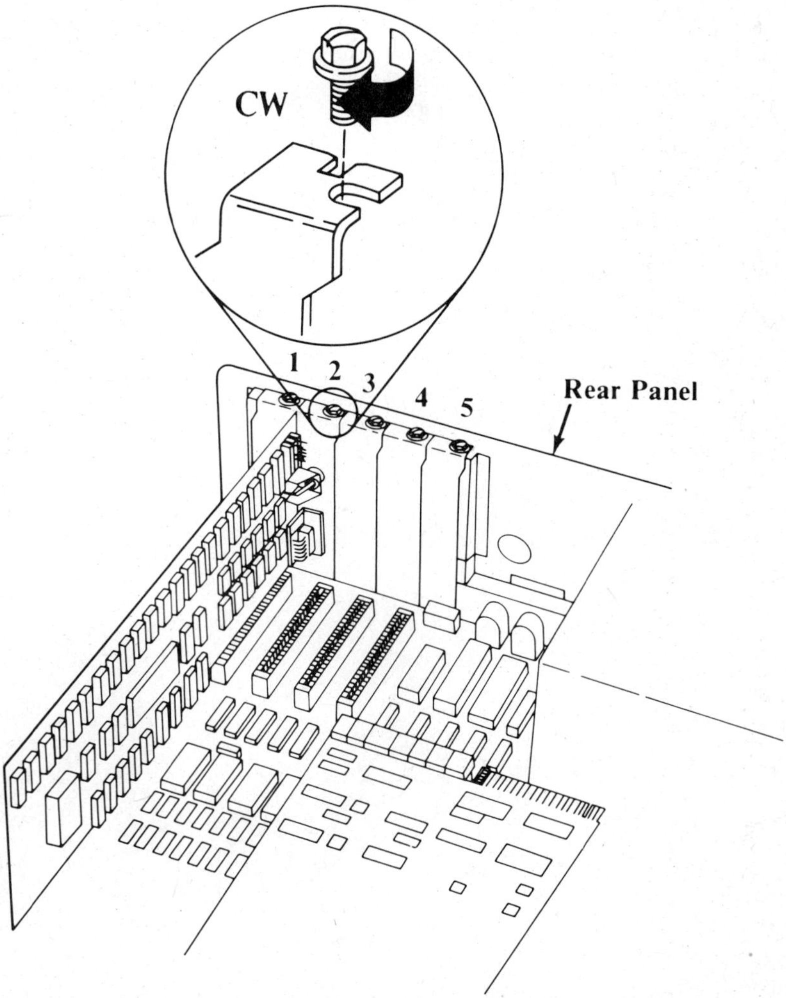

Courtesy of International Business Machines Corporation

any order, except that the diskette adapter needs to be as close as possible to the disk drive(s).

STEP FOUR: Take a look at Figure 1.4 again. You want to be sure of where to install the memory chips. If this is the first time you are installing memory and your system came with 64KB, you will be filling the row right next to the one already filled.

If you already have 128KB and are installing another 64KB, you will be filling the empty row of slots next to the two already filled. If you have 192KB, then there is only one vacant row left to fill, which will bring the total memory up to 256KB.

Once you decide on which row to fill you are ready to proceed. You will see that eight of the slots on the board are fairly close together, while the slot on the end closest to the outside edge is a little bit removed. *All nine slots must be filled with memory chips.* If you fail to do this the system will not function properly.

STEP FIVE: Each chip has a notch on one end (Figure 1.6). That notch must be facing the back of the computer when you install each chip. Also look at the chips already installed on the system board. All notches should be facing the same direction, without exception.

STEP SIX: Hold each chip lengthwise using an insertion tool or between your thumb and index finger. The pins (legs) of the chip will fit right into each socket. The pins often need to be bent inward just slightly to fit. Gently rock the chip back and forth, end to end, as you push it down into position on the socket. It will make a crunching sound as it slips right into place. Everything is okay; it's supposed to sound that way.

Be careful not to force it, and don't push too hard, because the chip's legs can bend easily. If that happens you might not be able to use that chip. And remember, the more you touch those legs, the more likely you are to create static electricity problems.

Fig. 1.6: Memory chip, showing circular notch, and connector (i.e., where the chip will be placed)

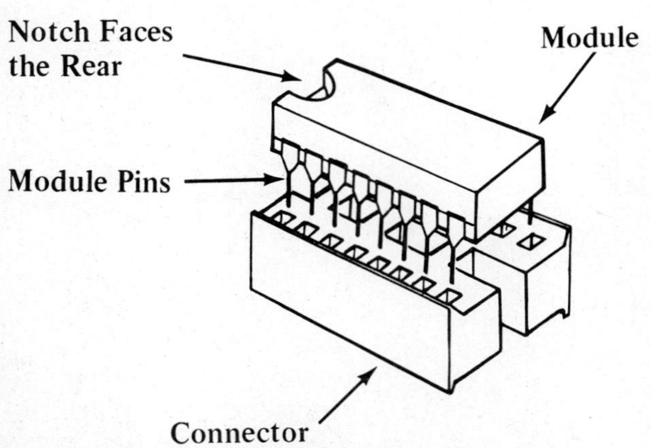

Courtesy of International Business Machines Corporation

Insert the rest of your memory chips the same way. When you are finished putting in the chips, go back and carefully push down on all of them (with your index finger) to be sure that each one is firmly in place. It is easy for a pin to bend undetected, so watch out for that.

STEP SEVEN: When all of the memory chips are installed you now need to reset the two blocks of white switches located near the power unit (see Figure 1.1). If you have a PC/XT there will only be one set of switches. Resetting lets the PC know under what conditions it will now be operating. It is through the settings on the two blocks of switches that you tell the PC how much memory it has.

There are eight switches on each block. On switch block 1 you will only be concerned with the third and fourth switches. From 64KB upward those positions on switch block 1 will be in the OFF position. On switch block 2 you will only be moving switches 1 through 5. The other switches on the switch blocks take care of other functions, including disk drives.

These switches are fragile. You must move them carefully to their new settings. The amount of memory you have in your PC determines how to set the switches. Figure 1.7 shows the different settings required for memory from 64KB to 640KB.

You can easily move the switches with the tip of a pen. Figure 1.7 shows how to set the positions on each switch block, with blackened areas to indicate the ON or OFF position.

Mark the position of all switches before you reset them. This is important because, if for some reason the new memory doesn't work, you can almost effortlessly return your system to the original configuration by removing the memory chips you just added and resetting the switches. Also, you will then be able to trouble-shoot the problem more easily if you have an idea of where you started. (See section 1.10.)

Set all of the switches exactly according to the list in Figure 1.7, for the total amount of memory in your system. The total amount of memory is determined by adding the memory you have on the system board to that on the memory card(s) in your expansion slots. You want to base switch settings on the TOTAL amount of user memory in your system.

STEP EIGHT: Put all of your cards (boards) back in their expansion slots. The order in which you replace them does not necessarily have to be the same in which you removed them. You do want to be sure that the diskette adapter (the one attached to the disk drives) is as close as possible to the disk drive(s).

Be sure that you tighten each screw holding the cards in place at the back of the PC. See Figure 1.5.

STEP NINE: Put the cover back on your PC. Reverse the steps outlined in Appendix C.

STEP TEN: Reconnect everything to the PC. With more memory inside your PC now it will take longer to come on once you flip the power switch. As the amount of the PC's memory increases, so does the length of time the PC takes to check everything when it starts up. It's not a great deal of time, but there will be a noticeable difference. If it's any longer than 85 seconds though, something is definitely wrong.

Fig. 1.7: Settings for system switch blocks from 128KB to 640KB

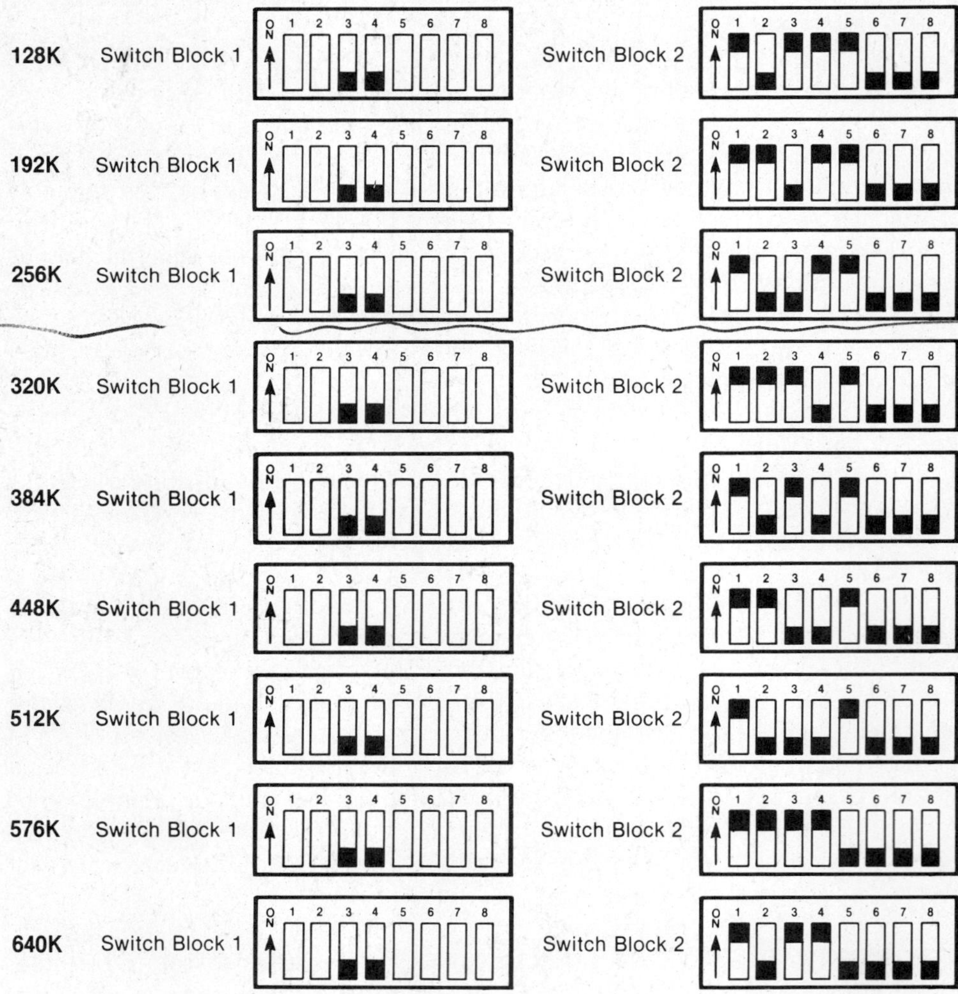

Courtesy of International Business Machines Corporation

STEP ELEVEN: Once your PC is put back together you should put your DOS disk in the A drive. Turn the system on. When you get the prompt A>, type CHKDSK. This is a quick way to see if everything is okay and if you have the new amount of memory you just installed.

CHKDSK stands for *check disk* and will give you a message display on the screen similar to the one shown below (which is for a system with 320KB RAM):

```
362996 bytes total disk space
102400 bytes in 31 user files
260596 bytes available on disk
```

```
->327680 bytes in memory
  295280 bytes free
```

The arrow points to the line which tells you how much memory you have in your PC. In this case with 320KB in memory you have 327,680 bytes of total memory. Remember that 'KB' is 1024 bytes, so 320KB is really 320 times 1024 which equals 327,680. Whatever amount of memory you have, the CHKDSK program will show you the exact number of bytes (which seems a little higher until you actually do the calculation). The last line of the CHKDSK screen refers to how much of the user memory (RAM) is not in use (i.e., the free space you have in which to work).

1.10 What To Do If You Have Problems

If you don't think you have the right amount of memory, once you have followed all the steps outlined in this section, then you should first redo the calculation at the end of STEP ELEVEN. Next, turn everything off, unplug everything but the system unit, and pull the cover off your PC again. Check the settings on the switches with those shown in Figure 1.7. More than likely one of the switch positions was set improperly. If that was the problem, put the PC back together and run the CHKDSK program again.

What if nothing works?! After you have checked your calculations and rechecked the settings on the switches, there is only one other area to check if you still have problems—the memory chips themselves. Be sure you used the right kind of chips. Be sure that you have installed them in the right row (see Figure 1.4). Be sure that each chip is pushed all the way into position. Be sure the notches on the chips are facing the back of the computer. Be sure all slots in the row are filled. Remember that you must fill all nine slots, including the one which is closest to the outside edge, a little bit away from the others.

Now, if you have done all of that and the amount of memory doesn't check out with CHKDSK, then you must assume you have one faulty chip (or more). At this point you will enter the trial and error phase of trouble-shooting the problem, because there is no clear-cut way to determine which chip (or chips) is bad.

Remove all of the chips you just installed. Put each chip back in its container. These containers will protect your chips against static electricity and any kind of mechanical damage. Reset the switches to their original positions. Put the PC back together (this is a lot of work, but unfortunately this is the only way to do it) and run CHKDSK again. The system should check out, which means you have a bad chip or two in the set you bought.

At this point you are faced with a decision. You can, through trial and error, put one new chip at a time in the current row you know is working. Then run CHKDSK each time until you find the culprit. This can take some time, but will assure that you find the problem chip(s). You can even check out two at a time if you want.

The decision you face is this: You can go through all the checking or you can return the chips to the vendor and ask for new ones. It depends on the amount of time you have and how much trouble-shooting you want to do. You will need to return at least one chip anyway, so you might want to return them all. You won't be able to add as much memory as you wanted until you get replacement chips, anyway.

If you find out that none of the chips are bad, you have a problem on the system board itself. This means that the computer store where you bought your PC will need to fix it. Don't let such a problem frustrate you or keep you from adding other things to your PC. It's not much of a consolation, but such problems as faulty system boards are truly rare with the PC . . . and remember that they are easily fixed.

2

Adding one or more adapter cards to the expansion slots of the PC will probably be one of the most common things done in the way of expanding the PC. Such cards bring graphics, additional memory and much, much more to any PC. As with most other aspects of adding on to the PC, putting in adapter cards does not require any special skills.

Adapter cards are the long, rectangular objects with chips, switches, and circuitry on them, attached to your PC by a series of gold fingers. You add adapter cards to the PC by inserting them in expansion slots. See Figure 2.1.

IBM designed the PC to allow you to expand it in hundreds, if not thousands, of different ways. Those expansion slots are there to be used as you do more with your PC. Such flexibility allows you to tailor the way you originally set up your PC system, and then to expand it as your needs change. You connect devices to your PC through the adapter cards in the expansion slots. Then the PC can work with all of those devices together, using each one as you need it (or even using them in different combinations).

By plugging an adapter card into an expansion slot you are not only able to get more memory, but your PC can then talk to (interface) many devices, such as the printer, the screen, or a modem. The adapter cards are actually Input/Output interfaces (i.e., connections) between the PC and whatever you are using outside of the PC itself.

You can add an adapter card to any open expansion slot, because each time you turn your PC on it reads those slots to see what you have hooked up. Whatever is there will be used by the PC as it works. With some adapter cards you will need to flip tiny switches near the power unit to specifically direct what the PC should be doing.

Adapter cards come in all sizes, lengths and colors. They perform dozens of different functions on the PC, from graphics to monitor control. Some perform only one function, others perform several. That's where the term multifunction comes from.

Fig. 2.1: Photograph of System Board of IBM Personal Computer; notice the location of the expansion slots

Courtesy of International Business Machines Corporation

2.1 Multifunction Adapter Cards

Multifunction cards have become popular because you can accomplish so much with one card, that is, with just one of the expansion slots on the PC. After a while you will see how quickly those expansion slots can be filled up and how important multifunction cards are. However, there are still reasons for single purpose cards, and those will be discussed later in this chapter.

A typical multifunction card (or board) is the TecMar PC-Mate shown in Figure 2.2. It has a serial port, a parallel port, a clock/calendar, utility software, and options for implementing password controls. The card is also socketed for memory expansion up to 384KB (in 64KB increments).

2.2 Aspects of Multifunction and Single Purpose Adapter Cards

The whole purpose of an adapter card is to allow you to do more with your PC. As your needs increase, the adapter cards are the secret to flexibility in shaping what

Fig. 2.2: TecMar PC-Mate Multifunction Board

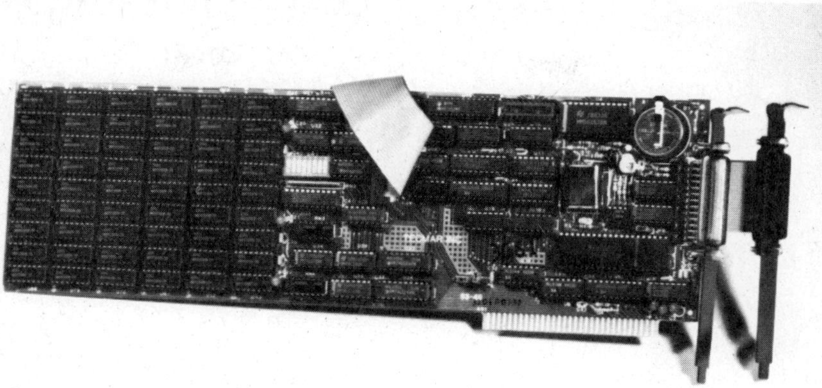

Courtesy of Tecmar, Inc.

you do with your PC and how you do it. Since everyone has different needs and therefore different ideas on how to do things, there will be a wide variety in terms of how PCs are expanded.

While one person might only have one purpose for expansion—say memory, another person might have two or three needs—more memory, a serial printer, and a clock/calendar. It's true that you can combine your needs with multifunction cards, but that will cost more, too.

Originally, adapter cards to add more memory to your PC were expensive ($500 to $700 for 256KB), and added memory was all you got. Today you can get much more on a multifunction card, including the option of adding more memory, for much less money. Many PC owners already have a multipurpose card and now want just one other feature (like an internal modem or an extra serial port)—so the need for single purpose adapter cards is still quite valid. The PC/XT model has three short expansion slots which are perfect for single purpose cards.

The brief listing below outlines many of the uses for adapter cards, which can be applied to single purpose or multifunction cards.

Clock/Calendar through which your PC will automatically put the correct time/date stamp on all of your files;

Diskette Adapter coordinates and controls your floppy disk drive(s);

Game Card allows you to use a joy stick instead of keyboard controls to play games;

Graphics Card controls graphics aspects from color monitor to light pen;

Fixed Disk Controller like the diskette adapter for floppy disk drive(s), this card orchestrates the fixed disk;

Memory user memory can go to 512KB (or more) on multifunction and single purpose adapter cards;

Password Control allows for restricted use of software;

Serial Input/Output Port used for controlling a modem, serial printer, plotter, or other serial device;

Utility Software gives you options like RAM spoolers (which allow you to print while using another program) and electronic disks.

2.3 Differences Between the PC and PC/XT Models

The IBM PC and the fixed disk version of the PC called the PC/XT are different in many ways besides their disks. When you add memory to a PC/XT there is less to worry about in terms of flipping switches (explained further on in this section). The PC/XT was designed to read how much memory is installed, without being instructed through switch blocks as is the PC.

The PC/XT also has a serial port already installed, which comes in handy for specific kinds of printers and, what is probably one of the serial port's most popular uses, for connecting modems (i.e., hooking the PC to other computers via telephone lines). If you want such an option on a PC you have to pay extra for it.

One of the most significant differences between the PC and the PC/XT is that the PC/XT has three extra expansion slots on the system board. This means that with a PC/XT you get more room to add adapter cards. That's the good news. The bad news is that four slots are used up from the minute you get the PC/XT—one for the fixed disk controller, one for the floppy diskette adapter, one for that serial port (which is attached to an adapter card) and another one for a monochrome display/parallel printer adapter card.

Of course, you still have four slots open at that point, whereas on a regular PC you would only have one left. However, there is another aspect to those eight expansion slots on the PC/XT. Three of those slots are for shorter adapter cards, like the ones used for graphics or single functions. There just wasn't enough room to squeeze in eight full sized adapter cards, so IBM did the next best thing.

The eight expansion slots are all the same size. It's just that the three expansion slots closest to the power unit are the ones destined not to be used for full length adapter cards because other things are in the way.

You can put an adapter card in any open expansion slot, so long as there is room for it and it fits. (*Note*: On the PC portable this is not true for the last expansion slot.) For example, if you are installing a diskette adapter, it will work in any open slot. However, you need to plan ahead because of the short cable from that card to the disk drive(s). The farther you install it from the disk drives, the more problems you will have when filling other expansion slots.

Once you have installed an adapter card you can always move it if and when you run into problems later on. The point here is that while an adapter card will work in any slot, you need to think about what you're doing in terms of future cards and/or eventual expansion on your PC.

One last point about the PC/XT's expansion slots: to get an extra three slots on the system board, IBM had to squeeze them just a little. That means you won't have as much room between the adapter cards, especially with some of the multifunction boards. You might find yourself putting some of the bulkier adapter cards on the outside edges. In fact, some of the older adapter cards were made to specification for the PC (before the PC/XT came out), so before you buy an adapter card you want to be sure it will fit in your PC/XT. This might never be a problem for you, but it's important to be aware of, considering how much adapter cards cost.

And if all of that weren't enough to be concerned about, there are two versions of the IBM PC (besides the PC/XT model). It's important that you are aware of the difference before you think about adding memory to an expansion card or buying an expansion card primarily to have additional user memory (RAM).

If you have an IBM PC manufactured after mid-1983, you will be able to put up to 256KB of user memory on the system board without adding an expansion card for more memory. PCs made before that time are limited to 64KB user memory on the system board. So before you do anything else you need to determine which PC you have.

The way to tell which model of the PC you have is to look at the back panel of your PC. If you see a large white letter 'B' with a circle around it stamped on your PC in the middle of the back panel's top portion, then you have one of the newer PCs (see Figure 1.3 in Chapter 1). Remember that when you bought your PC isn't important, the date it was made is. So even if you bought your PC in July or August (or later) of 1983 you might have gotten one manufactured earlier.

One model is just as good as the other. It's just that IBM continues to add enhancements with newer models. A newer model gives you the option of adding a significant amount of user memory before you ever need to add memory with an adapter card.

You must add memory chips on the system board of newer PCs before adding user memory with an expansion card. If you do have a newer PC, more than likely you can still add user memory to the system board (unless you had it loaded up with memory when you bought it). The adapter card with more memory won't function properly until the system board is completely filled up to 256KB. Chapter 1 shows you how to add memory to the system board.

You can upgrade your system board. It will cost about $400. Besides getting the 256KB worth of memory (RAM) on that new system board, you will get the added bonus of an 8088 micro processor that is timed to run properly with the 8087 math chip (if you have one).

There are companies who will upgrade your current system board to the new standards and specifications. With the cost being what it is you need to look closely at the value in relation to the costs.

2.4 Removing an Adapter Card from the PC

If you purchased your PC with an adapter card for additional memory and you now want to add memory to what you already have, you will first have to remove the adapter card. Even if you've just bought your adapter card and haven't yet put it in, you should skim over this section. It will help you become more familiar with this area inside your PC. Also, there will surely be a time when you want to remove at least one of your adapter cards.

Before doing anything about adding memory, you should see what memory chips you've got and where they are. It has been at this point that some people have found that they didn't even have adapter cards for memory.

First you need to remove the cover from your PC. (See Appendix C.) Figure 2.3 shows what you will see inside the PC.

Fig. 2.3: The system board of the IBM Personal Computer

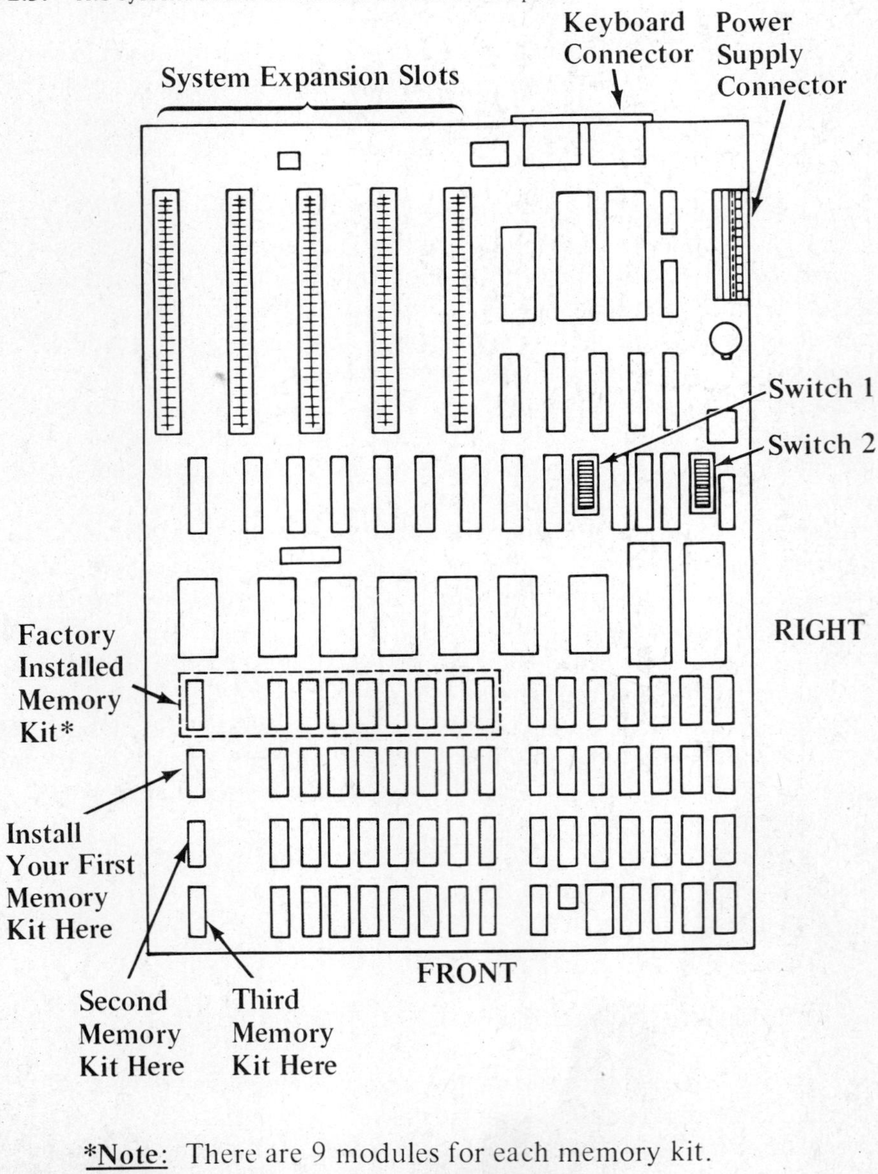

Courtesy of International Business Machines Corporation

Once the PC's cover is off you, look around a little bit, reviewing the following check list:

Check the adapter cards. Look over and review what adapter cards are already in expansion slots. One of the cards will be connected to your disk drive(s). Another adapter card will be used to connect your monitor and/or printer. Other expansion slots might be filled with adapter cards connected to other devices.

If you have an adapter card for adding memory, the memory chips or empty sockets (like in Figure 2.2) will all be in rows on the end of the adapter card closest to the front of the PC. This will be the adapter card you will remove to add more memory (if there is room for more chips on it).

Check the memory sockets on the system board. Look at the chips on the system board, which are located in the left front of the PC chassis. If you see that there is room to add more memory chips there, *you must do that first,* before you put memory chips on an adapter card. Adding memory chips to the system board sockets is covered on pp 9–13.

Zero in on the adapter card you want to remove. After checking out the memory sockets on the system board you want to go back to the adapter cards in the expansion slots. If the new memory chips are going to go on an adapter card, you want to be sure you are removing the right adapter card.

Your adapter card will have rows of sockets on the end closest to the front of the PC's chassis, next to the disk drives. Some of the sockets will already be filled. The adapter card you will add memory chips to is similar to the one in Figure 2.2.

Remember that, at this point, you might discover that you don't have an adapter card or that the switches haven't been set properly. This point is important because, often through error, oversight, or hurry, a PC ends up in someone's hands minus some of what it should have, or with switches relating to how much memory you should have not set properly. Any number of things can happen that you just don't know about. The point here is just to make you more aware of what you do and don't have inside your PC.

The steps for removing an adapter card. You will need a flat blade screwdriver or 3/16" nutdriver. A nutdriver is better because it prevents stripping of the small screwheads.

STEP ONE: Unhook any connections from the adapter card you are planning to remove. Those connections will be inside the PC, on the back panel. You want to be sure that the adapter card is free to be lifted out from the system board. If your adapter card has more than one connection (like a serial or parallel port), disconnect all of them.

STEP TWO: Remove the screw at the back of the rear panel on top of the adapter card you plan to pull out. Figure 2.4 shows this in detail. Your adapter card is attached to the PC through the socket, but held firmly in place at the top of back panel with this screw. Many people have tried, unsuccessfully, of course, to take out an adapter card without first removing this screw. Save yourself a lot of trouble, just take out the screw first. Set the screw down where you will be able to find it easily.

Fig. 2.4: Adapter card in expansion slot, with blowup of screw to be removed

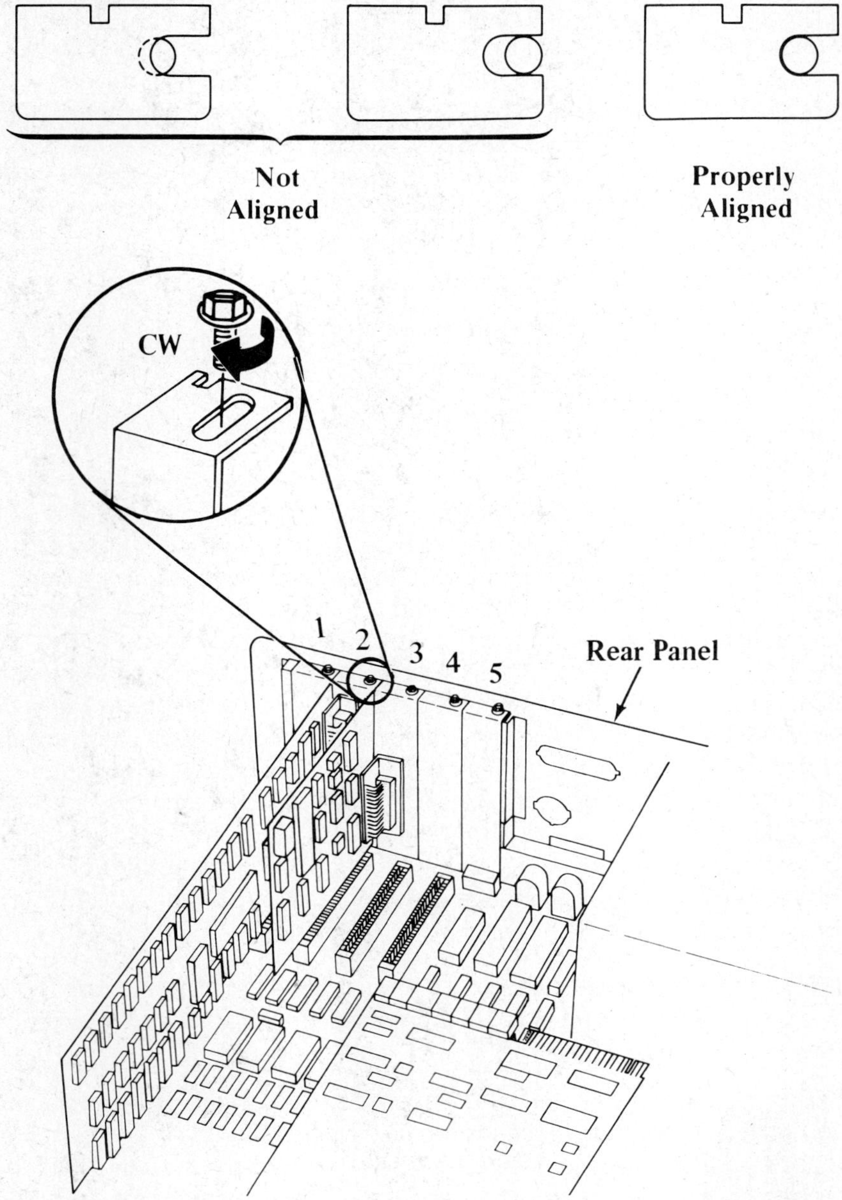

Courtesy of International Business Machines Corporation

STEP THREE: Hold the top of the adapter card firmly with both hands. Now pull upward, rocking the adapter card slightly back and forth. This helps the adapter card come upward. Remember that everything you're doing here is done *gently*. Don't force anything, and *go slowly*. The adapter card will slip right out of the socket if you carefully ease it upward.

STEP FOUR: Once you have removed your adapter card, set it down on a clean, roomy, and well-lit work area.

2.5 Adding Memory Chips to an Adapter Card

If you have an adapter card which already has the memory chips on it, then you can skip to the next section.

Here's what you will need:

Memory Chips The chips you want are labeled 4164 (4116 if you have an older PC) and work in a range of 250 nanoseconds (NS) down to 150. A chip is rated in terms of speed, the fastest time it can be cycled to obtain a piece of information. The lower the nanosecond number the faster the chip can work, but there is no advantage to installing a chip that is faster than the system clock.

With your IBM PC you will be able to use 4164 chips from 250NS to 150NS. Be aware that the faster a chip can go (i.e., the lower the number) the more it will cost.

You will need nine 4164 chips for each 64KB of user memory you add. (You increase your PC's memory (RAM) in increments of 64KB.) Eight of those chips will be dedicated to memory use. The extra chip controls parity for the other eight chips. Just be sure you have nine chips, instead of eight. Some chips come with their legs flat out, sideways, and need to have the legs made parallel. You must carefully bend the legs to the proper position.

Tools All you need to install memory chips is an insertion tool. It looks like a long pair of tweezers and costs about $12.00. Most people just use the thumb and index finger to put the chips in. It all depends on your preference.

Before you get down to the task of adding those memory chips to your adapter card, you should be aware of the only dangerous aspect of the entire procedure of working with memory chips. *Static electricity can wipe out not only the memory chips you handle, but other chips and even data on your floppy disks.* It has enough force to fuse together or blow holes in the microscopic circuitry inside a memory chip.

Take precautions when it comes to static electricity, especially when you're handling and installing memory chips. Keep the following in mind:

- Stand on an anti-static mat or spray anti-static spray on the floor where you will be standing when you install the chips.
- Avoid wearing polyester clothes. Don't wear nylon socks or tennis shoes. Leather-soled shoes are preferable.
- Don't take the memory chips out of their protective container until you are ready to use them. When you do handle them, hold them by their edges. Avoid touching the tiny connector prongs or legs.
- Touch the PC chassis or a metal lamp frequently to discharge any residual electricity. Keep your hands dry as you work.

Using a static mat as a work surface is one of the safest ways of protecting your memory chips from static electricity. A static mat keeps static charges from building up as you work. Or, you can use static spray purchased from just about any computer store and even from some office supply stores.

While it is true that many people (including technicians) almost haphazardly put chips into computers, it's always better to be as careful as possible just to be sure you have no problems.

Adding memory chips to your adapter cards shouldn't take longer than half an hour (depending on your pace and how much memory you are installing). Don't be in a hurry to do this, and do each step carefully.

To add memory chips to your adapter card:

STEP ONE: Prepare your work area. Have the adapter card, the memory chips, and the adapter manual, along with this book, right there on your work area. Review the manual which came with your adapter card before you get started.

STEP TWO: Determine which row of empty sockets to fill on your adapter card. This should be explained in the manual that came with the card. Figure 2.5 shows the TecMar manual example of which empty row to fill and the order in which to fill it. Be sure where to install the memory chips. If you put them in the wrong row you will have problems. So look over that section of your adapter card manual carefully before you proceed.

STEP THREE: You are now ready to install the memory chips. Each chip has a notch on one end. That notch must be facing the same direction as all of the other chips on the adapter card. See Figure 2.6. Also, be sure to check this in the product manual for your adapter card.

STEP FOUR: Place the memory chips into their sockets on the adapter card. Remember which direction you want the notch to face. Hold each chip lengthwise with an insertion tool or between your thumb and index finger.

The legs of the chip will fit right into each socket. Gently rock the chip back and forth, end to end, as you push it down into position on the socket. It will make a crunching sound as it slips right into place.

Be careful not to force it, and don't push too hard because the chip's legs can bend easily, making it unusable. And remember that the more you touch those legs the more chance you have to create static electricity problems.

Insert the rest of your memory chips the same way. When you are finished putting in the chips, go back and carefully push down on all of them with your index finger to be sure that each one is firmly in place.

STEP FIVE: With all of the memory chips installed you now need to set the switches on the adapter card and on the system board. If you have an IBM PC/XT you will not need to reset switches on the system board, but you will need to set the switches on the adapter card.

It's best to set the switches on the adapter card first. That way you won't forget to set them.

The manual for your adapter card or multifunction card will show you how to set switches on the card for the amount of memory your PC now has. Remember that

Fig. 2.5: TecMar adapter card (from manual), showing where memory chips go

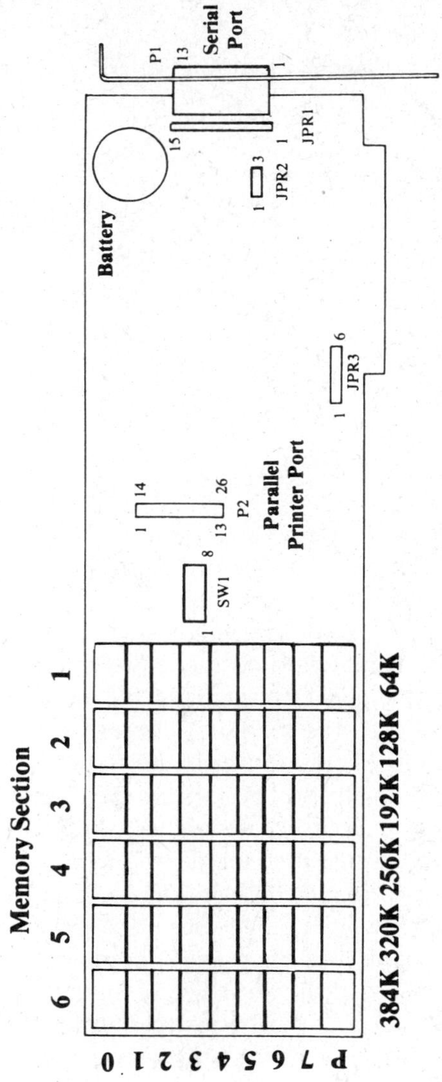

Courtesy of Tecmar, Inc.

you want to calculate the *total* amount of memory, including the memory chips on the system board.

The switches to set on your adapter card are very similar to the switches on the system board, which you will be setting next. You will either flip a switch to the ON or OFF position. Figure 2.2 shows the layout of the TecMar card, including the location of the block of switches to be set. Once these switches are set you will be ready to reset the switches on the system board.

STEP SIX: Now reset the switches on switch block 2 on the system board. If you have an IBM PC/XT you can skip this step because the PC/XT doesn't have switch

Fig. 2.6: Memory Chip, showing circular notch and connectors

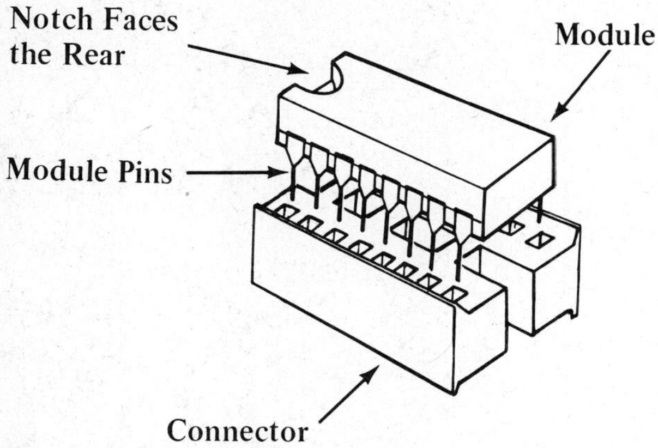

Courtesy of International Business Machines Corporation

block 2. The PC/XT can read how much user memory is installed each time you turn it on. The PC does not do this, so you need to physically set switch block 2 to tell it how much user memory it has to work with.

There are eight switches on each block. On switch block 1 you will only be concerned with the third and fourth positions (which are always in the OFF position with 64KB or more of memory). On switch block 2 you will only be moving positions 1 through 5 (see Figure 2.1). The other positions on both switch blocks take care of other functions, including the disk drives in the system.

These switches are fragile. You must move them carefully to their new settings. The amount of memory in your PC determines how to set the switches. Figure 2.7 shows the different settings required for memory from 64KB to 640KB.

You can easily move the switches with the tip of a pen. Figure 2.7 shows how to set the positions on each switch block, with blackened areas to indicate the ON or OFF position. If you see the black mark in the ON position then you will use the tip of your pen and push that switch DOWN. If you see the black mark in the OFF position then you will use the tip of your pen to push the switch DOWN on that side.

Mark the position of all switches before you reset them. This is important because if, for some reason, the new memory doesn't work, you can almost effortlessly return your system to the original configuration. Also, you will then be able to trouble-shoot for the problem.

Set all of the switches exactly as you see them listed in Figure 2.7 for the amount of memory in your system. The total amount of memory is determined by adding the memory on the system board to the memory on a memory board in one of your expansion slots. You want to set the switches based on the *total* amount of memory in your system.

STEP SEVEN: *Double check everything.* Be sure you have the switches flipped to the correct positions. Press down on each memory chip you installed to be sure it is firmly in place.

Fig. 2.7: Chart of settings for system switch blocks

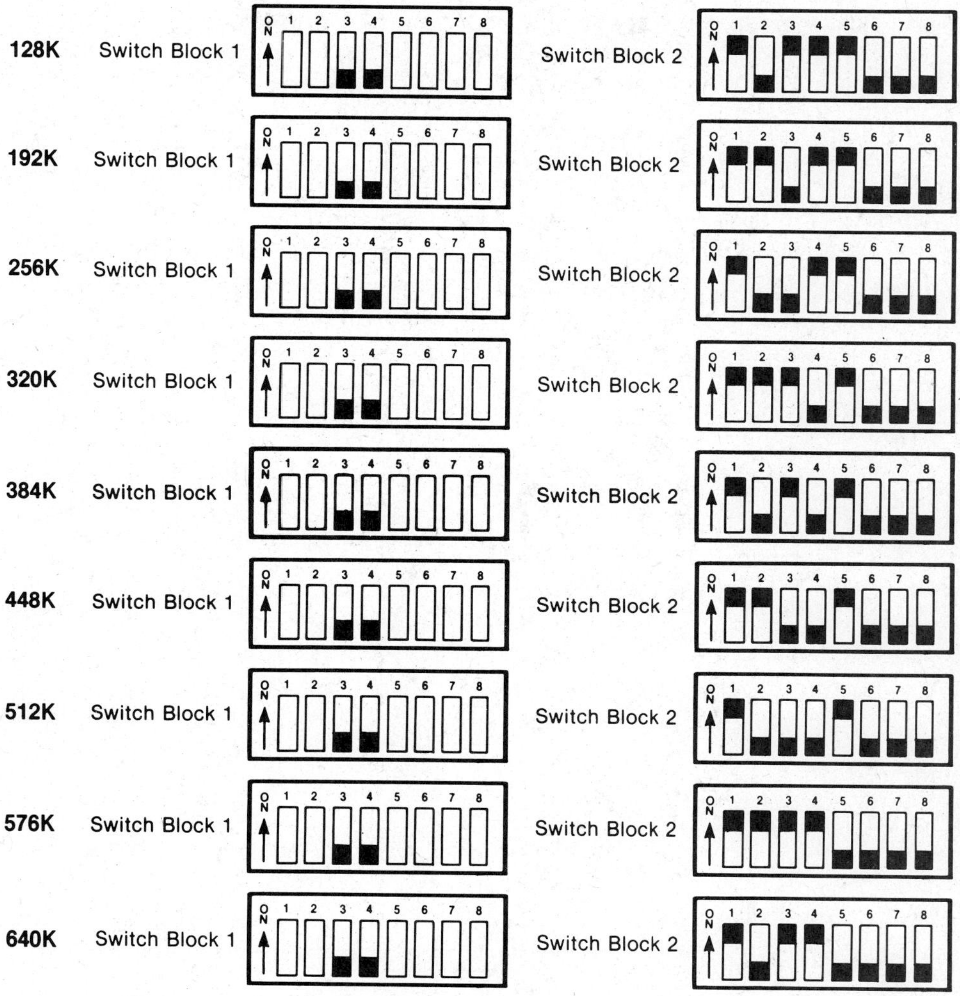

Courtesy of International Business Machines Corporation

After you have done all of your checking you are ready to put the adapter card in place on the PC.

2.6 How To Install an Adapter Card

If you are putting an adapter card in the PC for the first time, you should review sections 2.1, 2.2 and 2.3 of this chapter. Also review the manual which came with your adapter card.

To install an adapter card in the PC:

STEP ONE: Select which expansion slot you will place your adapter card in. (Refer to Figure 2.1.) You can place an adapter card in any open slot, so long as there is room for it (some cards are wider than others). Don't forget about cable connections, especially for multifunction cards, which connect to other areas inside the PC.

STEP TWO: Before placing your adapter card in an expansion slot, be sure that the flat metal strip attached to the rear panel of the PC and the screw on top of the back panel have been removed. (See Figure 2.4.)

STEP THREE: If you have a full length adapter card (i.e., one which goes from one end of the chassis to the other), you will see that there are mounts or holes for mounts on the front of the PC's chassis. (Figure 2.8.) Most adapter cards come with their own mounts or brackets. Such mounts slip right into the holes already in the PC chassis. After you have the mount or bracket in place you are ready to install your adapter card.

Fig. 2.8: Card support mount or bracket for IBM PC chassis

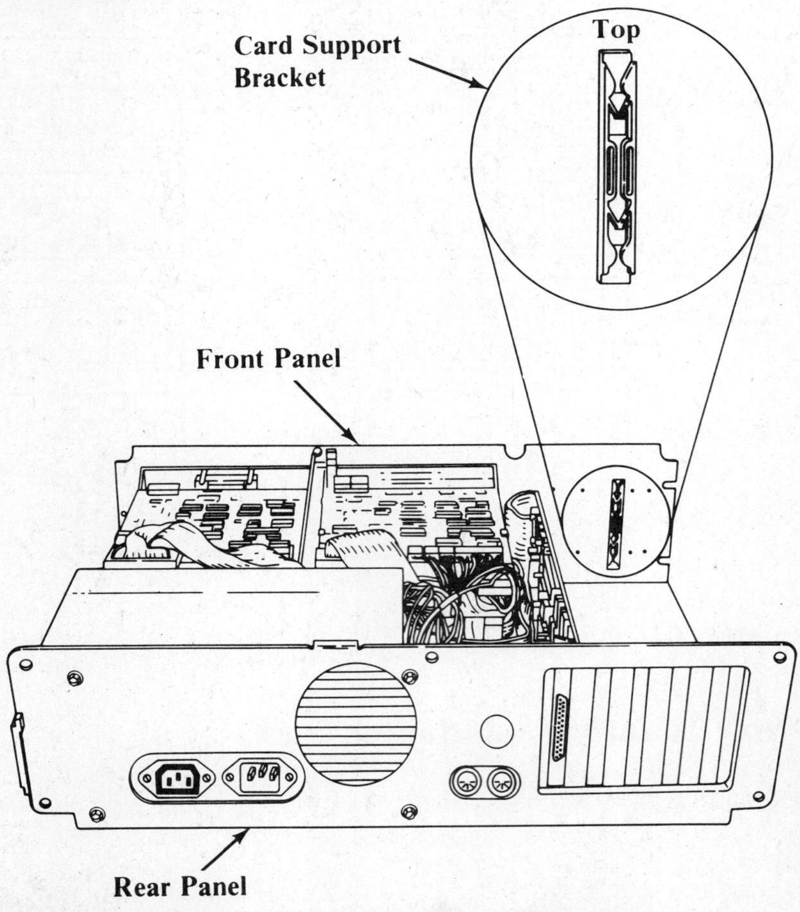

Courtesy of International Business Machines Corporation

STEP FOUR: You will now place the adapter card in the expansion slot you have selected. Hold the adapter card with both hands, as in Figure 2.9, and carefully push the card down into position on the expansion slot. The card's gold fingers will ease right into place, if you don't force it.

As the adapter card slides down into position, pay close attention to the mount on the front of the chassis (if your adapter card is long enough to reach). The adapter card should go right down in the middle of that mount. Be sure the other end of the adapter card is fitting down into position where the flat metal bar was removed at the back panel. All of this happens at once as the gold teeth slip down into the expansion slot.

STEP FIVE: Once the adapter card is in the expansion slot you are ready to screw the adapter card in position. The screw goes in at the top of the back panel. (Figure 2.10.) Align the hole in the adapter card with the hole in the back panel. (See Figure 2.10.)

STEP SIX: If your adapter card has an extra serial or parallel port to connect, be sure to arrange those internal cables and connections before you do anything else. Refer to your product's installation manual.

Fig. 2.9: Placing an adapter card down into position in the expansion slot

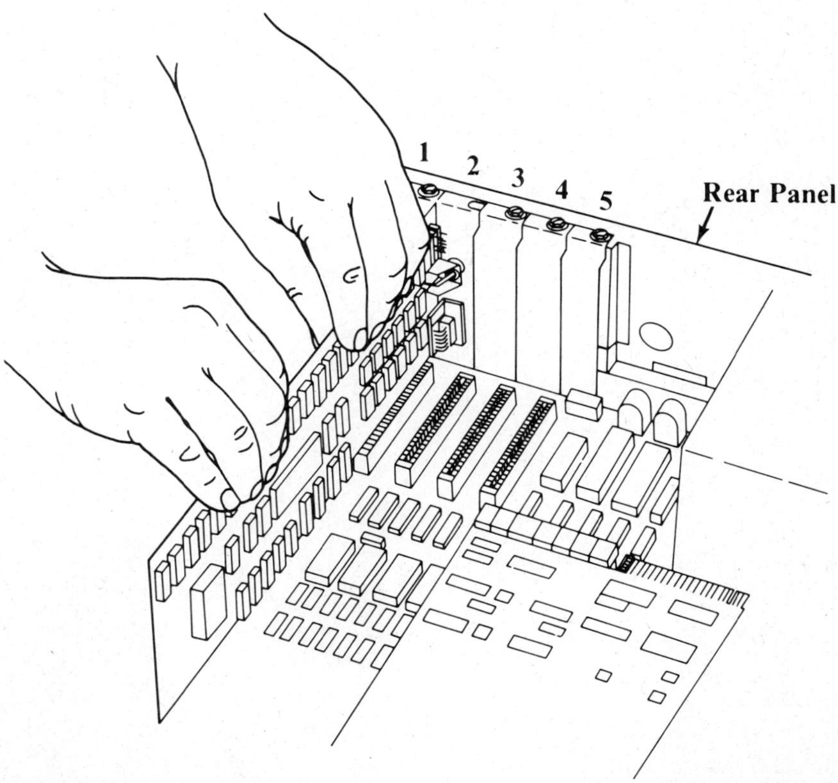

Courtesy of International Business Machines Corporation

Fig. 2.10: Adapter card in position; notice detail of how card should be aligned

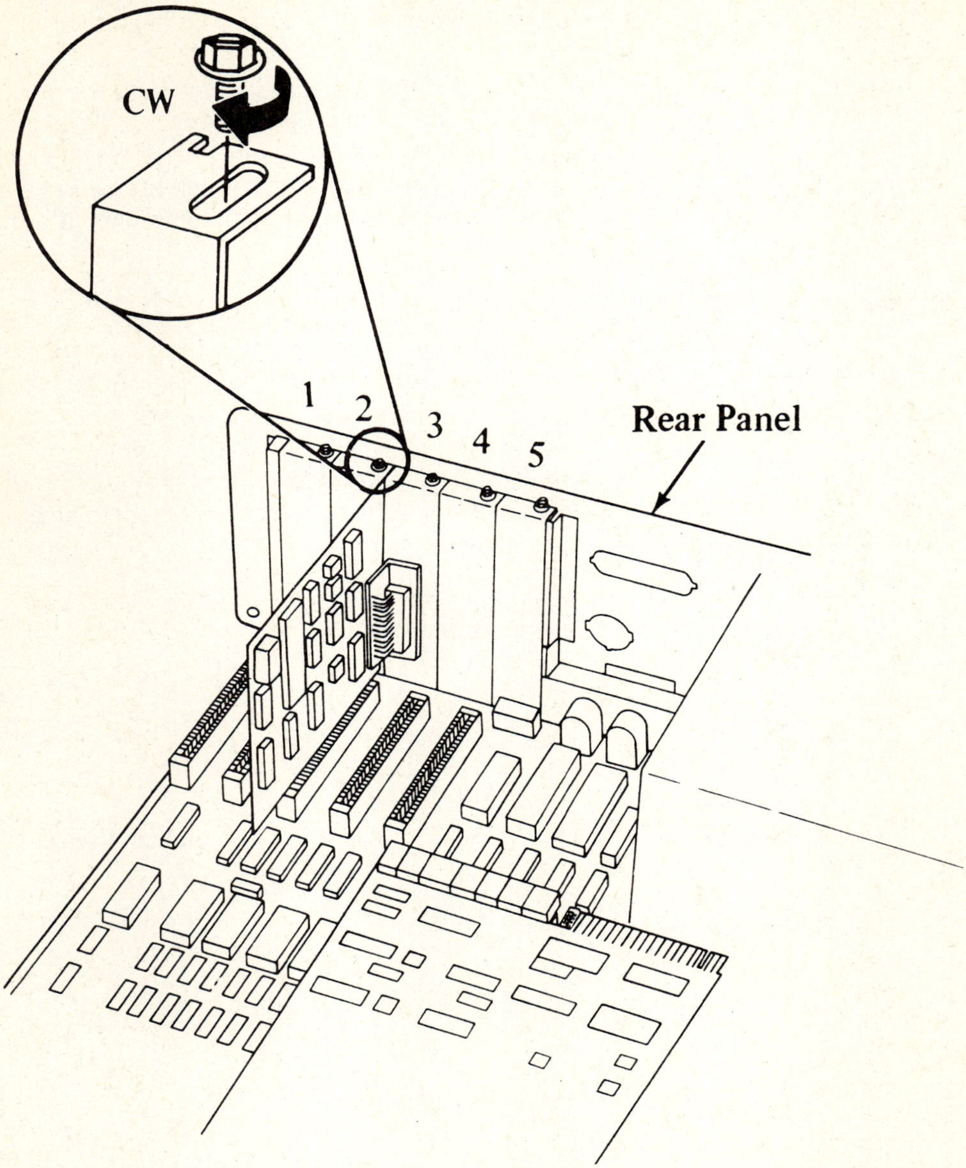

Courtesy of International Business Machines Corporation

STEP SEVEN: Put the cover back on your PC. See Appendix C.

STEP EIGHT: Now reconnect everything at the back of your PC. After you have completed this step you are ready to run a check to be sure you have the correct amount of memory in the PC. It is at this point that you might run into some problems or kinks. Section 2.7 should help you over the rough spots.

2.7 What To Do If Something Goes Wrong

Now that you have your new adapter card with all of that extra user memory (RAM) installed, you need to verify that you have done everything correctly and that the PC is working properly. It doesn't take long at all to run a check on the system.

Here are the steps to follow for checking out the system, followed by what to do if you have problems:

STEP ONE: Before turning on the PC, insert your DOS diskette in drive A (the one on the left hand side). After you do that you can move the power switch to the ON position.

If you have just installed memory chips, the first difference you will notice is that your PC will take a little bit longer to come on. This is normal. As the amount of the PC's memory increases, so does the length of time it takes the PC to check everything out when it starts up.

STEP TWO: When you get the prompt A>, type CHKDSK. This is a quick way to see if everything is okay and whether or not you have the amount of new user memory you have just installed.

CHKDSK stands for "check disk" and it will give you a message display on the screen similar to the one shown below (which is for a system with 320KB RAM, using DOS 2.0):

```
  362996 bytes total disk space
  102400 bytes in 31 user files
  260596 bytes available on disk

->327680 bytes in memory
  295280 bytes free
```

The arrow points to the line which tells you how much memory you have in your PC. In this case with 320KB in memory you have 327,680 bytes of total memory. Remember that a 'KB' is 1024 bytes, so 320KB is really 320 times 1024, which equals 327,680. The number of "bytes free" is how much room you have to work with in the user memory (RAM). Whatever amount of memory you have, the CHKDSK program will show you the exact number of bytes. The total number of bytes for disk space refers to a double sided disk formatted with DOS 2.0.

STEP THREE: If you don't think it's displaying the right amount of memory, first re-do the calculation. Next, pull the cover off your PC again (don't forget to unplug everything) and compare the settings on the switches with those shown in Figure 2.7. You also need to check the switch settings on your adapter card (yes, that probably means taking the adapter card out to look at it closely and carefully).

More than likely one switch position was set improperly. Check the adapter card manual again and review Figure 2.7 slowly. Don't panic at this point, and don't be in too much of a hurry just to somehow get it fixed. Remember that the switch settings on the adapter card are different from the switch settings for the system board. Don't confuse the two. If you do find the problem is in the switches, correct the switch settings, put the PC back together and then run the CHKDSK program again.

STEP FOUR: What if that doesn't do any good?! After you have checked your calculations and rechecked the settings on the switches (both on the system board and on the adapter card) the only other area to check is the memory chips themselves.

Be sure you used the right kind of chips. Refer to your manuals—both IBM and the one for you adapter card—for more detailed information on the specific kind of chips you need. Be sure that you have installed them according to the instructions in your adapter card manual. Be sure you filled in the correct row. The manual outlines and defines the order in which to fill empty rows.

Be sure the memory chips are pushed all the way into position. Be sure the notches on the chips are facing in the right direction. The circular notch on the end of each memory chip should be facing the same direction as all of the notches on the adapter card's other chips. Be sure all sockets in the row you worked on are filled. Remember that you must fill all nine sockets.

STEP FIVE: Now, if you have done all of that and the amount of user memory doesn't check out with CHKDSK, you must assume you have a problem with the PC itself. This is highly unlikely, but a possibility. It means that the computer store where you bought your PC will need to fix it. If you do have such a problem don't let it frustrate you or keep you from adding other things on to your PC.

It's not much of a consolation, but such problems are truly rare with the PC . . . and remember that it can be easily fixed. More than likely you have set a switch wrong (double check for that).

2.8 An Expansion Unit for More Slots

What many PC owners quickly find out is that five expansion slots aren't quite enough. Even with multifunction adapter cards, those expansion slots somehow seem to get filled up. The reasons for that are varied, but all have to do with the increased usage of a PC as the owner learns what it can really do.

Initially, a PC owner does word processing and, works with an electronic spreadsheet and probably a data base. Then as he or she learns the ins and outs of the PC and becomes more sophisticated using the PC, the adapter cards start going in. Modems, fixed disks, a second printer, plotters, graphics, and networking (linking two or more PCs together) all demand an expansion slot. If you have an external modem (see Chapter 8, section 8.2) you won't need an expansion slot if your adapter card has a serial port. There are ways to work around the limitation of five expansion slots (PC/XT owners are fortunate to have eight expansion slots).

One way is through switches, which allow you to switch back and forth between devices. In essence you have one connection to the PC (so only one expansion slot is used), but then from a switch you can redirect things to different devices. The use of switches is covered in more detail in Chapter 7.

Another option for dealing with the limitation of five expansion slots is an expansion unit. Through this you actually hook up another chassis to your PC. You use up one of the PC's expansion slots to do that, and in the process get as many as eight extra expansion slots.

Figure 2.11 shows the Dynaframe, an expansion unit with a fixed disk made by Vista Computer Company (notice the eight expansion slots in the cutaway photo). Figure 2.12 shows an expansion unit from I-BUS Systems, which gives you six more expansion slots.

Such devices, with their own power supplies, let you do what the switches do, but go beyond the built-in limitations of the switches. With switches you have no room for any adapter cards. The expansion units can give you as many as eight more adapter cards. That means you have virtually no limitation in terms of doing just about anything with your IBM PC. The best aspect of an expansion unit is that you usually can get a fixed disk along with the extra slots—if you want it. IBM also has made an expansion unit for the PC available for quite some time.

These steps for installing an expansion unit are based on the I-BUS Six-Pac unit, which has no fixed disk. Most expansion units will be added to the PC in a similar way. The procedures outlined here will give you a basic understanding of what needs to be done.

2.9 How To Install an Expansion Unit

The time involved for hooking up an expansion unit will vary, based on specific differences. However, you can figure about 45 minutes from beginning to end. You will need:

Fig. 2.11: Vista Computer Company's Dynaframe—cut away photo

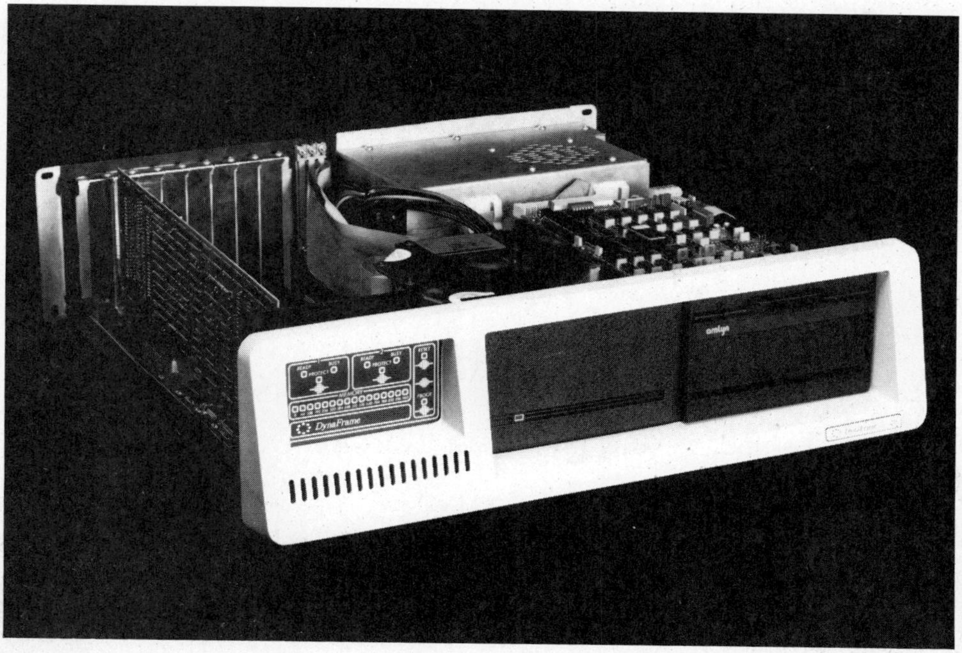

Courtesy of Vista Computer Company, Inc.

Fig. 2.12: I-BUS Systems' expansion unit

Courtesy of I-BUS *Systems*

- one flat blade screwdriver or 3⁄16″ nutdriver. Remember that the nutdriver keeps the screws from getting stripped and is probably better to use than a screwdriver;
- one Phillips screwdriver (if your expansion unit requires it);
- the manual for your expansion unit.

Review all of the steps in this section and the instructions in your expansion unit manual *before* you do anything else. You want to be as familiar as possible with everything you will be doing. There is nothing very difficult at all about what you are going to do, but if you leave out a step or get in a hurry you will certainly have problems.

STEP ONE: Turn the power off in your PC and in anything else attached to it. Unplug everything from the back of your PC. This includes the electrical cords and all connections (like those to the printer, monitor, and anything else you have attached to your PC).

STEP TWO: Place everything you will be working with on your table or work area. This includes the PC (which now is free of all connections), the expansion unit, the adapter card (which might be referred to an interface card), the connector cable for the expansion unit, and any tools you will be using.

STEP THREE: Be sure that your expansion unit is not plugged in. You don't want *anything* plugged into electrical outlets.

STEP FOUR: Remove the cover from your PC. (See Appendix C.)

STEP FIVE: Now place the adapter card (remember that the manual might be referring to it as an "interface card") in one your PC's expansion slots. If you need to refresh your mind on how to do this, take a moment now and review section 2.6.

Read the expansion unit manual closely before you install this adapter card, because you might be directed to put the card in a specific slot. The I-BUS unit requires that the adapter card be mounted in the extreme left slot of the PC. If you run into such a requirement and find that you already have an adapter card in the expansion slot they want you to use, then just move that card to another empty slot, if you have one. Otherwise, remove one of the adapter cards and set it aside for installation in the expansion unit. *However, it is important to keep all adapter cards with memory chips on them in one of the expansion slots on the PC's system board.* It's important that you install the adapter card where instructed. The reasons for such requirements are varied and sometimes complex, but can be as simple as a short connector cable.

STEP SIX: Once you have put the adapter card in place, you are ready to close up the PC. Be sure you have put the mounting screw (see Figure 2.10) back in place, too.

STEP SEVEN: Now connect the expansion unit to the PC. Take the connector cable and, following their manual, insert one end of the cable in the expansion unit and the other at the back of the PC, into the connection on the adapter card you just installed.

STEP EIGHT: At this point you are ready to reconnect everything to your PC. You shouldn't have any problems with your new expansion unit, but if you do, check the cable connections first. After that, check out the adapter card (which means taking the PC apart again) to be sure you installed it correctly and that it is in the proper slot (if there was a requirement to use a specific expansion slot).

If all of that checking fails to produce results, then you must go to the company that made your expansion unit to resolve the problem. Most companies resolve such problems quickly, so if this does happen to you . . . it's not the end of the world and certainly should not curtail your career of adding on to your PC.

Once you have your expansion unit up and running you will be ready to add more adapter cards as you need them. Adding adapter cards to your expansion unit is done the same way as adding adapter cards to the PC expansion slots (see section 2.6).

One expansion unit should be enough for adding all the adapter cards you need. However people have chained two or more expansion units to the PC. It all depends on just how many devices you have and how much you want to do with your PC.

3

When IBM first introduced the PC in August of 1981 there was no color monitor—only what has become known as the green screen. Other companies (Amdek and Princeton Graphics) were quick to produce color monitors which worked extremely well with all of the advanced capabilities of the IBM PC.

It wasn't until March of 1983 that IBM released its own high resolution color monitor. It seemed that once again IBM had let other companies develop the market before venturing into it. Color was a very important step for the IBM PC, but with IBM releasing a high quality color monitor at a very reasonable price (under $700), well, that sort of legitimized color graphics for the IBM PC.

Color graphics will open up a whole new world for you. You can go with IBM's monitor or any of the other outstanding monitors on the market today. A color monitor brings your PC's screen display to life. Even word processing programs like Wordstar are more interesting in color. Color adds dimension (color screens are usually a little bigger than the monochrome ones) and excitement . . . and fun.

You won't find a primer on graphics in this chapter: it will be more like a compass to help point you in the right direction. Many options will be outlined, along with a how to guide that will generally assist you in getting things set up. Specific examples of products will be used, but you need to evaluate your own needs and circumstances before making a decision as to which product(s) will fit in best with your system.

3.1 Getting Started with Graphics

The starting point with graphics is the monitor. A monitor can either be color or monochrome (i.e. green, black and white, or amber). It is possible to have graphics on a monochrome monitor (see section 3.5). Anything you will be doing in graphics with your PC hinges on a graphics adapter card (which goes in one of the expansion slots inside your PC). It is the software which causes your screen (and printer) to display the graphics.

Programs like 1-2-3, Visicalc IV, and Supercalc 3 create graphics to go with spreadsheets. Other programs, such as Fast Graphs, expand the possibilities of the graphics you create and of the way you create them. You can write your own programs, too: see section 3.4. In fact, writing your own programs opens up a whole new realm of experimenting and exploring for you and your PC.

You can also have graphics on a monochrome monitor. Instead of different colors for the graphics, you will have various shades of green. **A note of caution:** Do not connect a monochrome monitor directly to a color graphics adapter card.

Choosing color graphics means you will have three basic options:*

Television: Color graphics on your television set will not be as good as you may have been led to believe. If you are considering hooking your PC up to a television, first have a look at a PC already set up that way. The colors really aren't very good or all that clear. Worst of all, if you want an 80 column screen, you can pretty much forget about it with a television set; the 40 column screen will look okay. You'll also need to keep your PC disk drives at least 12 inches away from the television because of the powerful electromagnetic fields the television generates.

For approximately $50 you can buy an RF (radio frequency) modulator which you can use to hook up your PC to a television set. The output from the color graphics adapter card in your PC will actually transmit—in much the same way that a radio station does—signals to the television set. The result will be color graphics on the television screen.

Composite Monitor: Color monitors all produce colors with similar technology. There are still three individual beams as with television monitors, but the signal is combined so that it can be sent on one pair of wires between the PC and the monitor. The electron beams are flashed or sprayed from an electron gun at the back of the monitor to the screen. How this is done determines the clarity of the images on the screen. With a composite monitor the signals that drive the electron beams which hit the screen as colored dots are combined in a composite video signal—thus the name composite monitor.

Composite monitors range in cost from $200 to $500 and produce medium-resolution graphics. The images on the monitor will not be extremely sharp, as they would be with an RGB monitor. When choosing a monitor it is best to view it first, taking a look at the programs you intend to use. Many people feel that composite monitors are more than sufficient to meet their graphics needs.

RGB *Monitor*: The RGB stands for Red, Green and Blue. An RGB monitor, like the one made by IBM for the PC, provides the highest resolution and sharpest clarity for images displayed on the screen. This kind of monitor is considered the top end of the scale for graphics use; a television screen is at the bottom.

All color televisions use three electron guns—one red, one green and one blue—to fire electrons which end up as colored dots on the screen. Variations of color are produced by different combinations from the three electron beams. The RGB monitor allows the PC to control each beam individually to create such clarity in the graphic representations. Of course, the cost will be higher for an RGB monitor.

---

*For a complete explanation of what they are and how they work see *The Graphics Generator* by Larry Joel Goldstein (Robert J. Brady Company, 1983).

Both RGB and composite video monitors can handle 80 column screens very well. In fact, both can be used for word processing, electronic spreadsheets, and data bases without any problem. The combination of colors you decide to use will determine how hard or easy it will all be on your eyes.

Here's what to look for in a color monitor:

Are the letters or images fuzzy? If what you see is fuzzy and you know you don't need glasses, then you might want a higher resolution monitor. Remember that as the resolution goes up, so does the price. An RGB monitor like the one made by IBM has 640 horizontal pixels (dots) and 400 vertical lines. That's a lot of colored dots. However, you can get over 1,000 pixels per line and more than 1,000 lines on certain monitors (the cost will be somewhere around $5,000 or higher), and then the resolution is impeccable. But you can get very a acceptable color monitor for under $1,000. *Note:* The stock IBM PC cannot drive the 1000 × 1000 monitor.

How does an 80 column screen look? If you plan to do spreadsheets and word processing you will need a color monitor that can handle it. As you look at the screen keep in mind that this is what you will be looking at on a regular basis, if and when you buy it.

How many colors does it produce? It's true that the graphics card you put inside your PC will determine most of this. However, you want to be sure that the monitor you're getting can handle everything coming from the graphics card.

What is the quality of the color produced by the monitor? Unless you're 100 percent happy with the colors produced by the monitor, don't buy it. Take a close look at the reds, greens, and browns.

Is the monitor compatible with your system? What you want to look for here is how well the monitor will work with your system—especially in relation to the graphics card you have or intend to buy. It is always best to have a demonstration on a PC system set up exactly as the one you use.

How reliable is the company? Will the company manufacturing the monitor be around a year or two from now when you might need replacement parts or repairs? Check with people who have its products to see how they feel about them and also how well those products work.

For how long is the warranty? While you're looking at the owner's handbook and installation instructions, take a look at the warranty. It's better to find out all the details at this point, instead of running into a surprise or two if problems develop.

3.2 Step By Step to Graphics

Setting up your PC for graphics isn't that hard. You will need a few tools and some specific items—all of which are outlined below. While this step by step guide is specifically for the IBM Color Display, much of it will apply to other monitors. You should carefully read over the product manual and installation guide for the particular color monitor you plan to add to your system.

Tools needed:

- 1 small flat head screwdriver
- 1 medium flat head screwdriver

Items needed:

- 1 color monitor
- 1 color graphics card
- 1 cable (for connecting monitor to PC)

To hook up and install a graphics adapter card and color monitor:

STEP ONE: Turn off your PC and remove the cover. (See Appendix C.)

STEP TWO: Install the color graphics adapter card in one of the empty expansion slots on the system board of the PC. IBM recommends using expansion slot number 2 (which is the second slot in from the outside edge of the PC). Actually, you can put the graphics adapter card in any open slot. Perhaps IBM's reason for this recommendation is that the connector cable will be closer to the outside edge, allowing you to have your color monitor a little further away from the System Unit.

If you need help installing the graphics adapter card, turn to Chapter 2, section 2.6. That section tells you step-by-step how to install an adapter card.

STEP THREE: Once the graphics adapter card is in position you can set the proper system switch on switch block 1. Figure 3.1 shows the location of the two switch blocks on the system board of the PC, between the power supply and the expansion slots. You will only be concerned with switch block 1.

Set switch block 1 according to the positions shown in Figure 3.2. Notice that there are settings for color (40 and 80 column) and monochrome. The monochrome setting also allows you to have more than one monitor; for example, one color and one monochrome monitor. Set switch block 1 to correspond with your system configuration.

STEP FOUR: Replace the cover on the PC. (See Appendix C.)

STEP FIVE: As you hook up all of the cables and power cords, connect the color monitor as shown in Figure 3.3. Notice that the power cord for the color monitor goes into a wall outlet. This is especially important if you plan to continue using a monochrome monitor (which plugs directly into the PC itself). After everything is connected you are all set to give it all a try.

STEP SIX: Notice that the power control, the brightness control, and the contrast control are on the front of the monitor (Figure 3.4). To adjust the vertical hold or vertical size (the actual size of the letters and images on the screen) use the two knobs on the back of the color monitor (see Figure 3.5). This layout should be similar for most color monitors.

Fig. 3.1: Switch blocks 1 and 2 on the system board.

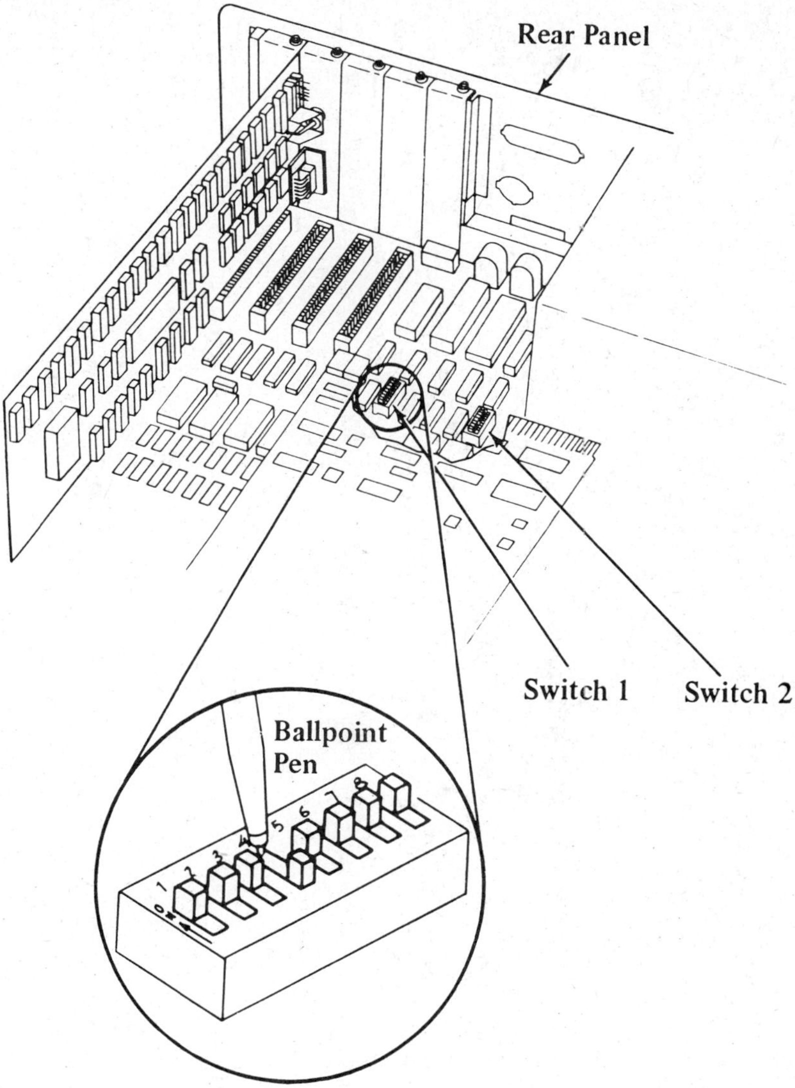

Courtesy of International Business Machines Corporation

If you experience any problems, retrace your steps. More than likely you missed a step or did something incorrectly. If, however, you find that everything has been done properly and there is still a problem, contact the store that sold you the monitor. Problems seldom come up, and most people find that as soon as everything is hooked up they are working with the colors of the rainbow.

3.3 Running a Color Screen and a Monochrome Screen

Many IBM PC owners start out with a monochrome screen and then get a color monitor. At that point there are two options. You get rid of the monochrome screen

Fig. 3.2: Switch block 1 settings for color and monochrome monitors

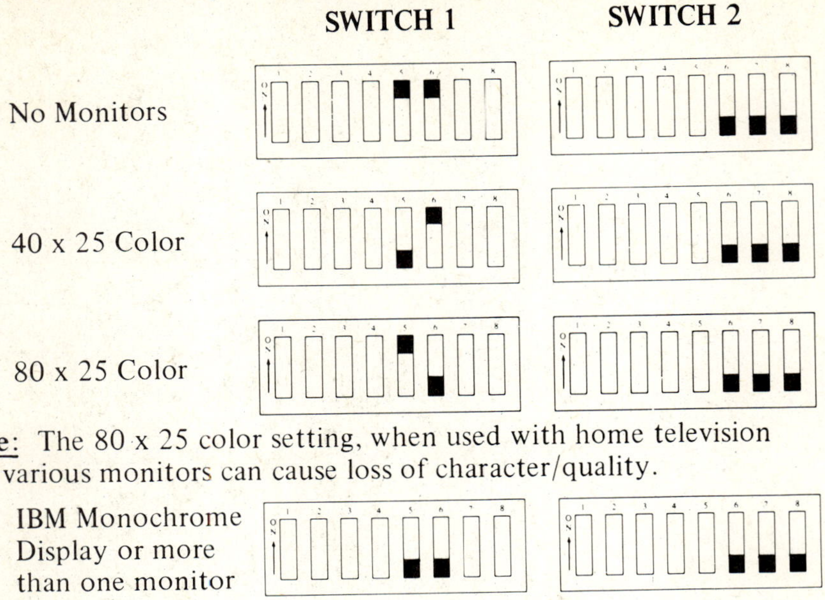

Courtesy of International Business Machines Corporation

or keep it running along with the color screen. A program like 1-2-3 from Lotus Software takes advantage of the two monitors by displaying the spreadsheet and text information on the monochrome screen, while displaying the graphs and charts on the color screen.

There are two ways to run both monitors. You can just add a color graphics adapter card to one of your PC's expansion slots and then just hook up your color monitor. The monochrome monitor will have already been hooked up through the monochrome display and printer adapter card (which is how the PC with a green screen comes standard). That adapter card also has a parallel port for a printer.

Whenever you want to switch back and forth between monitors you will need to do that through what is know as software control. All that means is that you must run a short program to tell the PC which monitor to use. Normally, when you turn on your PC it will default to the monochrome monitor. To switch from the monochrome monitor to the color monitor in BASIC you must run the following program, which is listed in Appendix I, page I-9 of the BASIC Manual (2nd Ed, Version 1.1, 1982):

```
10 ' switch to the color adapter
20 DEF SEG = 0
30 POKE &H410, (PEEK(&H410) AND &HCF) OR &H10
40 SCREEN 1,0,0,0
50 SCREEN 0
60 WIDTH 40 ' <NOTE: if you want 80 column width,
              replace the 40 with 80>
70 LOCATE ,,1,6,7
```

Fig. 3.3: The connection for the color monitor to the PC

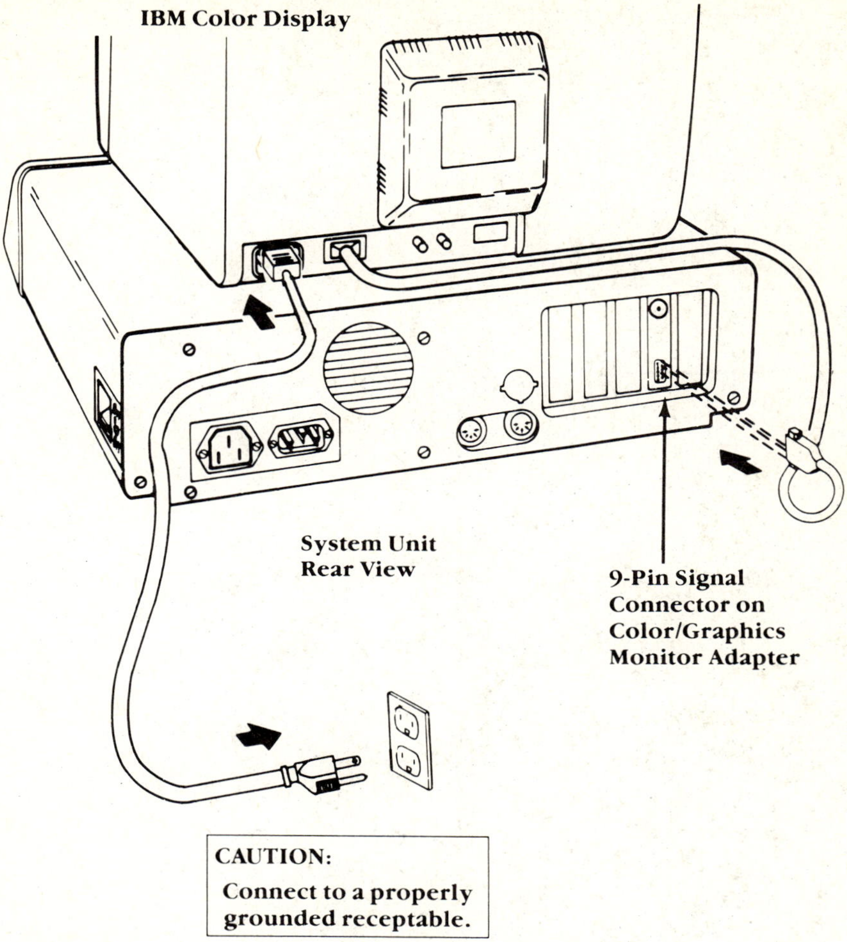

Courtesy of International Business Machines Corporation

To switch from the color to monochrome monitor while in BASIC, run the following program:

```
10 ' switch to monochrome adapter
20 DEF SEG = 0
30 POKE &H410, (PEEK(&H410) OR &H30)
40 SCREEN 0
50 WIDTH 40
60 WIDTH 80
70 LOCATE ,,1,12,13
```

Your local computer store (and some of the mail order houses) will have public domain software, which does the same thing, not only while you are in BASIC, but

Fig. 3.4: Power, brightness and contrast controls on the color monitor

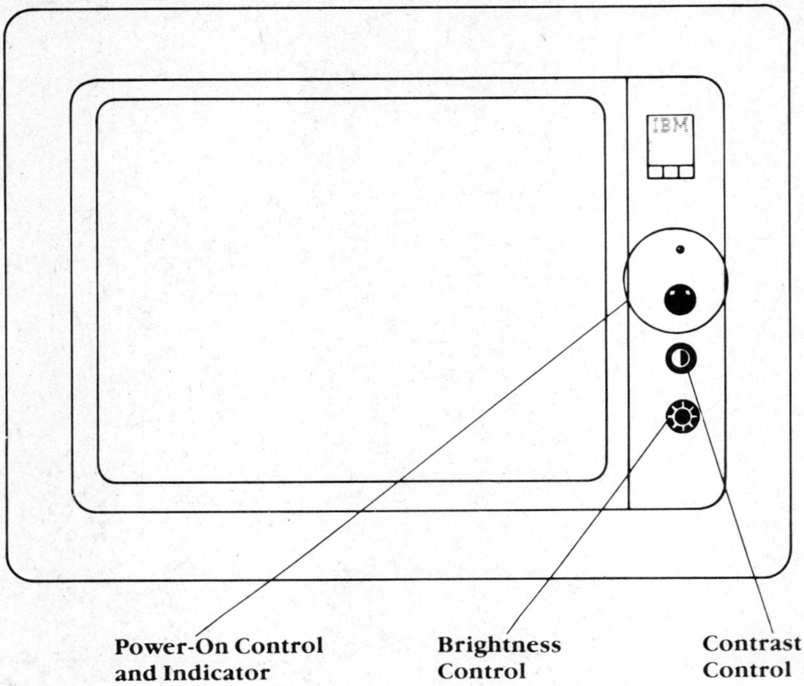

Courtesy of International Business Machines Corporation

also from the DOS A> prompt. Such information is also available from computer user groups and from bulletin boards. You can also check with someone you know who is already using both a color monitor and monochrome monitor to see how he or she is switching back and forth. In DOS 2.0 (and subsequent versions) the MODE command does this quite easily.

As you start doing more with your PC you will quickly find that five expansion slots (eight on the PC/XT) really get filled up quickly one way or another—making them precious. So consider this way of running both a color and monochrome monitor using only one expansion slot in the PC.

Some companies produce graphics adapter cards which can run a monochrome and a color monitor. All you need to do is flip a switch on the back of the adapter card to work between color and monochrome. The Paradise Multi-Display card (Figure 3.6) provides flicker-free scrolling in color word processing and also can be switched to accommodate a 40 column screen. There's even a parallel printer port, too.

There is one drawback to this adapter card, however. You can only use one monitor at a time. So in the case of 1-2-3, you won't have the luxury of both screens producing images at the same time. To get that from a Paradise card you would either need two such cards or have to use the Paradise card with another graphics card.

Many PC owners who like to experiment with color graphics enjoy having two monitors. Being able to go back and forth between color and monochrome provides great flexibility, too. If you're working on a program that you want to be sure runs on

Fig. 3.5: Vertical hold and vertical size knobs on the back of the color monitor

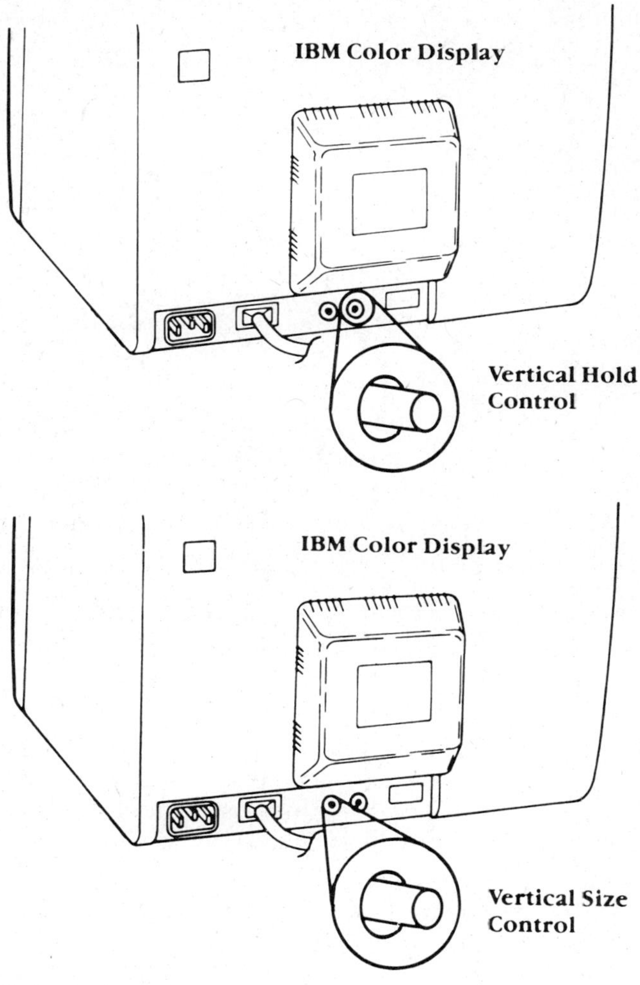

Courtesy of International Business Machines Corporation

both screens then you can try it out—experimenting with colors that still work on the green screen. Having color and monochrome isn't as much of a luxury as it seems. There are many practical, as well as purely entertaining, reasons for using both.

3.4 Working with a Color Monitor

You can even have word processing in color with programs like Microsoft WORD and Wordstar. If you get a high quality graphics adapter card, your color screen shouldn't flicker as the lines scroll up the screen. There are plenty of programs to help you specifically with graphics, too. Color graphics are impressive and use some of the PC's potential.

Fig. 3.6: Paradise Multi-Display card for running both color and monochrome monitors

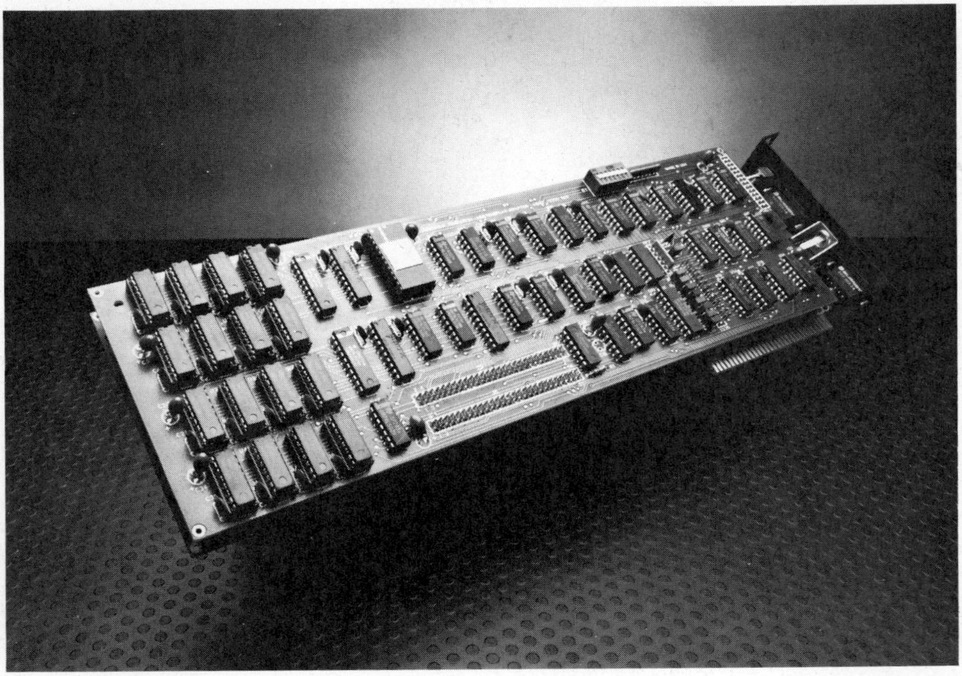

Courtesy of Paradise Systems, Inc.

Programs like Fast Graphs can produce bar charts, pie charts, point/line graphs, and other graphic displays in patterns and in colors. Some of the effects are even three dimensional. Many such programs can translate the screen graphics into printouts which can be done on everything from dot matrix printers to sophisticated plotters.

Besides all the programs available for graphics, there is plenty of information on graphics in the BASIC Manual, in all the computer magazines and, of course, in books. However, one area of graphics that needs a little attention is color. One of the first things you will notice working with a color monitor is that the colors seem to explode to life on the screen. It's quite a contrast from the monotony of the green screen.

To set colors on a color monitor you must first look at the screen from the standpoint of 1) Foreground, 2) Background, and 3) Border. For the foreground, which is the letters or image you look at, you have a choice of 16 colors. You have eight colors for the background (0 through 7) and 16 for the border. Figure that out mathematically and you'll discover that the combinations, though not limitless, are numerous—providing enough variety to please the most demanding artists.

You can also combine all of the colors with blinking, high-intensity, low-intensity, underlining, and reverse color combinations. That provides a broad spectrum of choices and options for just about any kind of imagination—from mild to wildly active.

Listed below are available colors, with their numbers:

Fig. 3.7: Fast Graphs charts and graphs, showing the variety of graphics capacity

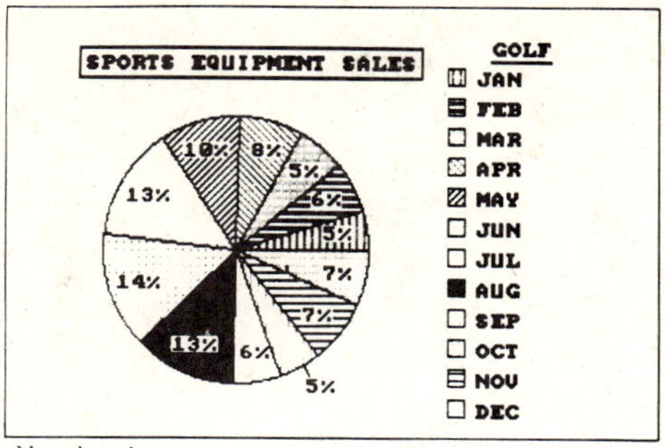

Normal pie chart

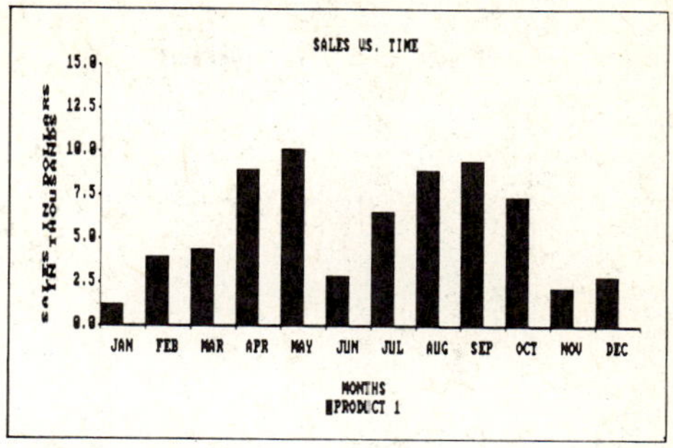

Vertical bar orientation

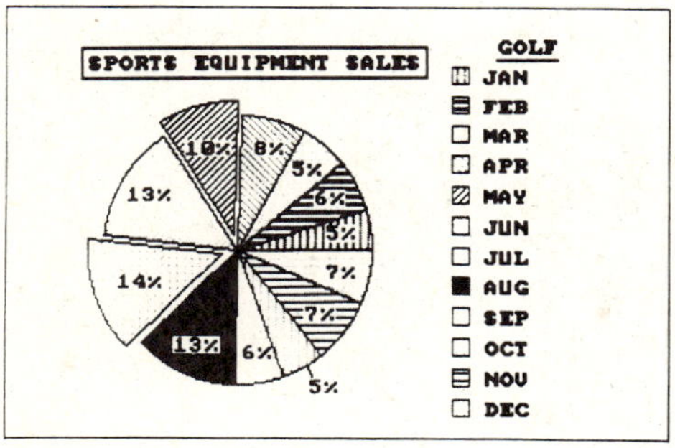

Pie chart with 2 slices pulled out

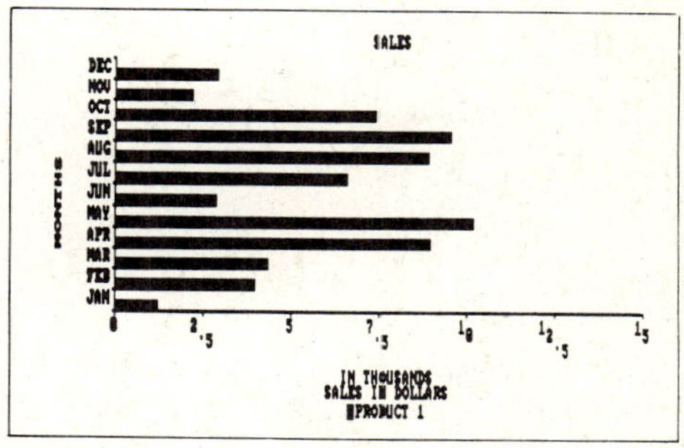

Horizontal bar orientation

Courtesy of Innovative Software

0	Black	**8**	Gray
1	Blue	**9**	Light Blue
2	Green	**10**	Light Green
3	Cyan	**11**	Light Cyan
4	Red	**12**	Light Red
5	Magenta	**13**	Light Magenta
6	Brown	**14**	Yellow
7	White	**15**	High-Intensity White

Here's how you get colors out of your color monitor:

STEP ONE: Go into BASIC or BASICA by typing either of those words at the DOS A> prompt.

STEP TWO: If you want black letters with a soft blue background (cyan) and a red border, all you need to do is type `COLOR 0,3,4` . You can see that 0 is for black, 3 is for cyan and 4 is for red. *The order of foreground, background and border will always be the same.*

If you want a color to blink, add 16 to its number. In other words, if you want red blinking letters you add 16 to the number 4 (for red), and type in 20 when you do your color statement. Remember that you are limited to 8 background colors—the numbers 0 through 7.

On the monochrome screen you are more limited. However, you can produce underlined text by using the number 1 for a white foreground color. Adding 16 to any of the numbers will still give you a blinking character. A background color of 7, with a 0 for foreground, will produce a reverse image on a monochrome monitor. The screen will be all green, the opposite of what you're used to, with black letters.

3.5 Graphics on the Monochrome Screen

There was a time when the monochrome screen meant strictly text and limited graphics. All of that changed when companies like Hercules Computer Technology released special adapter cards for the PC which brought the world of graphics to monochrome screens. You don't get color, but such an adapter card does mean impressive high resolution graphics. Be forewarned that you cannot connect your IBM monochrome monitor directly to a color graphics adapter card—doing so will cause serious damage to your monochrome monitor.

The Hercules Graphics Card replaces the IBM monochrome display card. It provides an 80 character by 25 line display and produces 720 by 348 point graphics. A parallel port is also provided for hooking up your printer (just like on the monochrome display adapter card). It's important to note that because of this card's design, you will be able to use a monochrome monitor, but not in conjunction with a color monitor.

The Lotus 1-2-3 specifically takes advantage of the Hercules Graphics Card for producing graphs and charts. To use a monochrome graphics card doesn't require too much work. You'll need to replace your present IBM monochrome display card with a graphics card like the Hercules Graphics Card. You should read the manual that comes with the graphics card *before* going through the steps listed here. The manual for the Hercules Graphics Card is clear, concise, helpful and informative.

Tools needed to replace monochrome display card:

- 1 medium flat head screwdriver (or nutdriver)

Here's all you need to do:

STEP ONE: Turn off your PC, unplug all the connections, and take off the PC's cover.

STEP TWO: Remove the monochrome display card which is presently in one of your expansion slots. This is the card to which your parallel printer is attached, as well as your monochrome monitor. For details on removing this card, please refer to Chapter 2, section 2.4.

STEP THREE: Now insert your monochrome graphics adapter card in the expansion slot you just removed the monochrome display card from. Section 2.6 in Chapter 2 tells you how to do this.

STEP FOUR: Put the cover back on the PC.

STEP FIVE: Reconnect all of the cables and cords to the back of your PC. Here's where you will need the small screwdriver. The monochrome monitor will be attached to the new graphics card you just installed. If you have a parallel printer you can also connect that to the new graphics card. Make all of the connections carefully and slowly. There is no need to be in a hurry at this point.

STEP SIX: You are now ready to begin experiencing graphics on your monochrome screen. The software package for the Hercules card includes commands called "primitives," which help you write impressive programs to produce graphics. You start producing graphics by using Hercules HBASIC, which loads BASICA into the user memory and modifies it to do monochrome graphics. What is especially clever about this is that BASICA is modified in memory (RAM) and not on your program disk. Your program is never altered.

There are other companies manufacturing similar graphics cards for the PC. The Hercules Graphics Card was used primarily for explanation and clarification purposes. As with everything else you get for your PC, you should buy the product that best suits your needs . . . after a thorough and careful examination of the options and costs.

3.6 Installing a Light Pen

A light pen adds a futuristic quality to your PC. Though not popular until recently, the light pen is now becoming a tool in education, business, design, and engineering. Figure 3.8 shows a typical light pen (from FTG Data Systems).

To use a light pen you will need a color graphics adapter card and a color monitor. Some light pens will work with a monochrome monitor equipped with a graphics adapter card. A light pen does nothing more than sense the beam of light from the screen (remember that what you are seeing on the screen is really a fast moving dot of light). A timing circuit lets the PC calculate where you are on the screen, as marks are made wherever the pen is touching the screen. The light pen will use the PC's main power supply, but the drain is minimal and certainly nothing to worry about.

A light pen can eliminate the need for many keyboard commands, because you use the light pen to point to the items you want—especially where you have a menu to choose from. Also, many tests have been designed for response directly on the screen with the light pen. In such cases you would pick your answer by using the light pen. Advocates of the light pen say it is even simpler to use than a mouse (see Chapter 9, section 9.1), because pointing is a basic human instinct. Also, the light pen requires no desk space.

Companies like FTG Data Systems also have software packages to go with their light pens. By using the games and other demonstrations in the software package, you quickly get a feel for what a light pen can do. You can then proceed to develop and write your own programs and applications. Many businesses and corporations are doing this.

Fig. 3.8: FTG light pen with cord

Courtesy of FTG Data Services

IBM has made provisions for a light pen through the BASIC statement PEN. Whenever you want to write a light pen function into one of your programs all you need to do is include the statement, PEN ON. The statement PEN OFF disables the PEN read function for BASIC, turning off the use of the light pen. The BASIC Manual explains it in more detail.

To use a light pen with your PC, you will need a screwdriver (medium, flat head) and, of course, a light pen. You must already have a graphics adapter card in one of the PC's expansion slots or be installing one as you install the light pen.

To install a light pen:

STEP ONE: Turn off your PC and remove all cords and connections. Take off the PC's cover. (See Appendix C.)

STEP TWO: If you are going to install a graphics adapter card you should do that now. (See Chapter 2, section 2.6.)

STEP THREE: Figure 3.9 shows where you will connect your light pen to the graphics adapter card (IBM Graphics adapter card shown here). If you are using a different graphics card, carefully and closely review its manual for the connector point location.

What you are connecting to the graphics card is the cable or wire attached to the light pen connector. The light pen connector is the device that attaches to the side of your PC, into which you plug the light pen's telephone cord-like cable. Some

Fig. 3.9: Light pen connector (P-2) on the IBM Color Graphics Adapter card

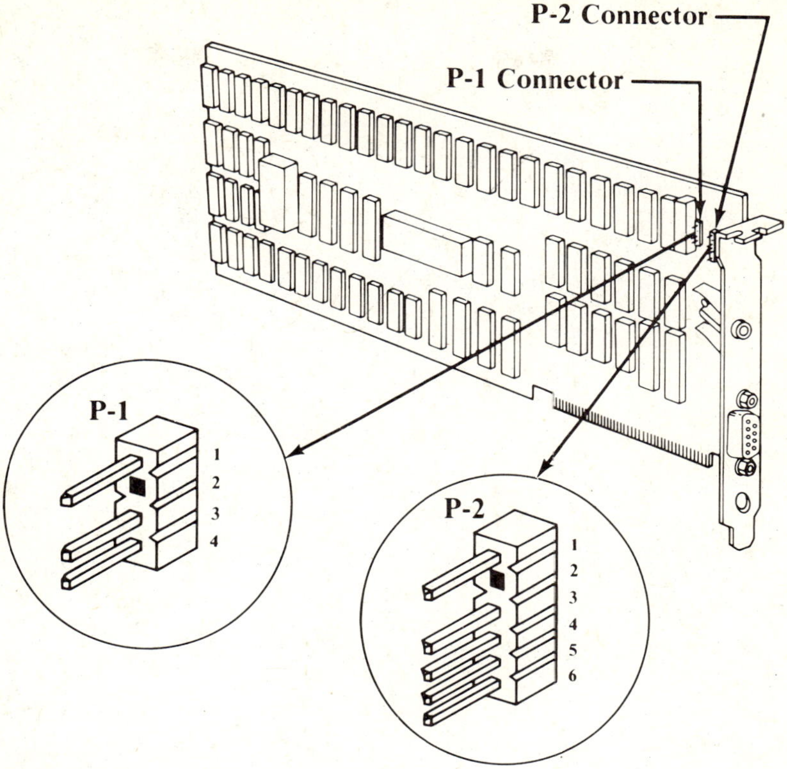

Courtesy of International Business Machines Corporation

light pens do not come with this type of connector so check the product manual for details.

On the IBM graphics card there are two connector points, known as P-1 Connector and P-2 Connector. You want to connect your light pen cable to the P-2 Connector, which is the one closest to the back of the PC, where all the other cable connections will be made.

Remember that other graphics adapter cards are different. Figure 3.10 shows the light pen connection on the Paradise Multi-Display Adapter card. Notice that there is only one connector point at the top (the RF modulator connector is toward the bottom).

STEP FOUR: Before connecting the light pen connector's cable to the graphics card you need to thread that light pen cable through an opening in the PC's chassis. The cable from the light pen connector then paases out of the PC chassis through a specific opening provided on the back of the PC, located just above the keyboard connector slot. See Figure 3.11.

You will need to remove the filler plug, easily done by pushing it outward from inside the PC chassis. After running the light pen cable through the opening, you can connect the light pen cable to the graphics card.

Fig. 3.10: Light pen connector point on Paradise Multi-Display Adapter card

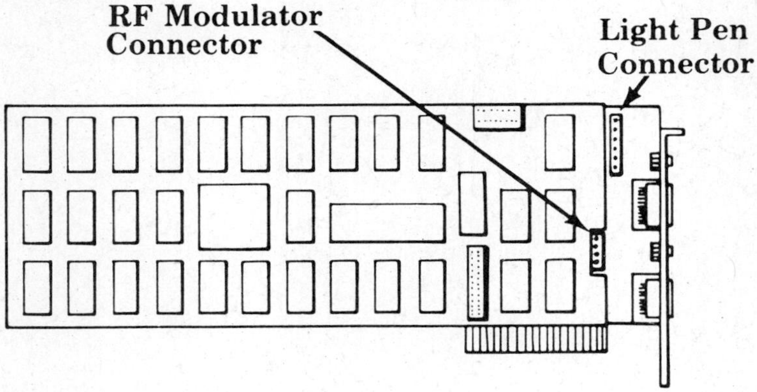

Courtesy of Paradise Systems, Inc.

STEP FIVE: A light pen cable like the one from FTG will have a black rubber ring on it. This ring is designed to fill the opening in the back panel of the PC (once the cable has been inserted through the opening). Move that ring up into position now.

STEP SIX: You are now through working inside the PC. Put the cover back over the chassis. Reconnect all cables to the back panel of your PC, and plug in the power cords.

STEP SEVEN: At this point you can remove the waxed paper covering from the bottom of the light pen connector. The surface will be quite sticky. You now attach the light pen connector to the side of your PC. Remember that you want that connector in a convenient position. Are you left or right handed? The best location for the light pen connector is close to the front of the PC (on whatever side is handy for you), about half way between the top and the bottom of the monitor.

STEP EIGHT: Connect the coiled cable from the light pen to the light pen connector, which should have a retaining clip on it. In some cases you will also need to attach the retaining clip by the adhesive surface to either the PC or the light pen connector.

At this point you are ready to try out your light pen, along with the pen's software demonstration disk. If you have any problems, re-trace your steps—those listed here and the ones in the manual which came with your light pen. If you still have problems, check with the store where you purchased your light pen.

3.7 Graphics Design Aids

You can do everything from art work on an electronic design tablet to just about any kind of drafting and design with graphics design aids for the PC. You can even create three-dimensional objects which rotate in any direction on your PC's screen.

Fig. 3.11: Opening in PC chassis, just above the keyboard connector slot, for light pen cable

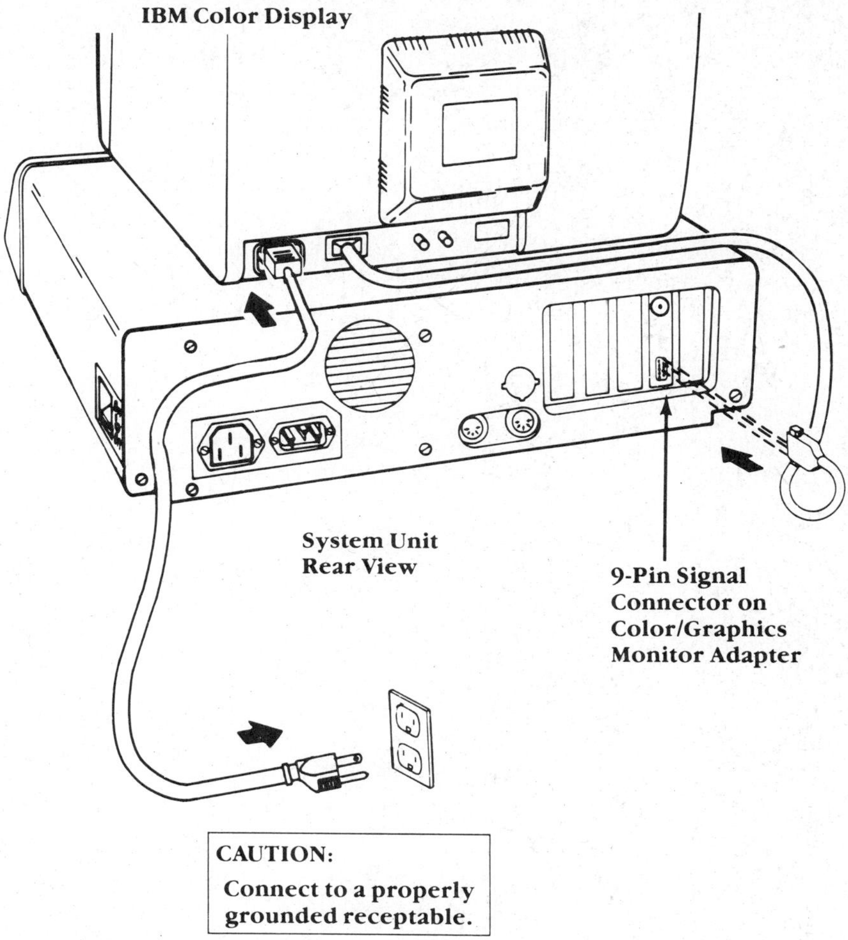

Courtesy of International Business Machines Corporation

All of this requires the proper programming (i.e., software) and, in some cases, additional equipment. But the point is that it can all be done on your PC. Much of this involves what plotters and digitizers can do (see Chapter 7, section 7.4).

The term Computer Aided Design (CAD) will become more common as the use of the PC's graphics design aids increases. Many people, including architects and engineers, are just now discovering the full potential of the IBM PC in relation to CAD's useful, practical, and timesaving applications.

It's one thing to design and draw on a computer screen: the crucial test is putting it all on paper. The dot matrix printers and, of course, the plotters, are where that kind of magic happens. When you are looking at graphics design aid programs for your PC, you want to be absolutely sure not only that the software works well, but that the final printed product is exactly what you want. See a demonstration of the product(s).

From drafting architectural plans for buildings to designing products in 3-D, you can really do just about anything graphically on your PC. However, this particular area of expanding the use of your IBM PC requires extreme caution. This is an emerging field of technology. There are many options and many products, making it far too easy for you to end up with the wrong one. By taking your time, doing your homework and trying out products and software, you will ultimately find what you need to do the job.

You can do a lot of experimenting with BASIC, if you have the time. That way you can begin to get a feel for the power of graphics on your PC. There are several books out on graphics programming, such as *Graphics Programming On The* IBM *Personal Computer* by J. Edward Volkstorf, Jr. (A Spectrum Book, Prentice-Hall, Inc. 1983), which explain how graphics work (in detail) and let you program everything from a map of the United States to shapes, movement, and games.

Monthly magazines are another excellent source for learning about graphics. The PC *Tech Journal*, for example, has feature articles about graphics on a regular basis, as well as programs for you to try out. If programming seems a bit too much, don't worry. More and more of the books and even the magazines are providing disks which already have the programs on them. That way you can see how they are written—and even modify them, if you want—but you don't have to go through the effort of programming line-by-line.

All it takes is a graphics adapter card to get started. You can do it in color or on your monochrome monitor. There's an exciting world, just on the other side of your monitor's screen, waiting to be discovered. It's a world that you, business associates, and members of your family will find fascinating.

4

This chapter and the next two chapters outline your options for data storage. All of your letters, reports, documents, spreadsheets, bookkeeping records, data bases and anything else you want to keep permanently have to be stored somewhere. In most cases, floppy disks are used. Hard disks are increasingly becoming an option, but the largest percentage of PCs sold to date function with floppy disk drives—usually two of them. Floppy disk drives and hard disks are permanent, meaning that even when you turn off the PC your information is still stored somewhere.

You do have one other option for temporarily storing information, but it can only be used while the PC is running. That is an emulated disk drive, which is actually created within the working memory (RAM) of the PC. Once the PC is turned off, however, the emulated disk drive, along with all of the information on it, is gone. The emulated disk drive must be reconstructed each time the PC is turned on.

Emulated disk drives have become popular in the past year and are definitely something to consider using—provided you know the risks involved. Emulated disk drives are much faster than floppy drives or even hard disks, because there are no mechanical or moving parts. The tradeoff for such speed, however, is impermanence. There are ways to work around the temporary nature of emulated disks, and those are outlined in Chapter 5. That chapter also explains how to use a combination of one floppy disk drive and an emulated disk drive to save money.

4.1 An Overview of this Chapter

This chapter will address many different needs. To begin with, there is a discussion of your options with floppy disk drives. Hard disks are briefly covered, because you do have an option to install a combination of floppy disk(s) with hard disks. The heart of this chapter is a three part guide for installing 5¼ inch floppy disk drives.

This three part guide can save you a lot of money. The computer stores won't tell you this, but it is possible to buy a "no drive" IBM PC. Such a PC, obviously, comes with no disk drives (and no disk drive controller). You can buy your own disk drives and install them, along with the disk drive controller, saving yourself as much as 60 percent of the retail cost.

Putting in your own disk drives might sound a little scary, but it really isn't too hard. This chapter will also show you how to upgrade your PC from single sided disk drives to double sided disk drives.

Installing the A drive is covered in section 4.3. If you are just going to have a one disk drive system, go to section 4.5 (on installing the disk drive controller). However, if you are installing a second disk drive—the B drive—proceed with section 4.4. That will then logically lead into the section on the installing the disk drive controller.

Section 4.5 will show you how to hook up the disk drive controller for either a one or two-drive system. Section 4.6 explains how to upgrade a PC from single sided to double sided disk drives. The last section (4.7) explains how to install half-height disk drives, and also covers combining half-height disk drives with a fixed disk.

You will need:

- 1 medium sized flat blade screwdriver.
- 1 3/16 inch nutdriver or wrench (this can be used in place of the screwdriver).

4.2 Floppy Disk Drive Options

Most people have an IBM PC with two disk drives—the one on the left (the A Drive) and the one on the right (the B drive). An IBM PC/XT comes with one floppy disk drive and a 10 megabyte fixed disk. There are IBM PC owners who have hooked up 8 inch floppy disk drives to their PCs, providing more storage space. The 8 inch drives, however, haven't really caught on.

In the past year the half-height 5¼ inch floppy disk drives have become popular. These are half as high as the regular disk drives most people are familiar with. IBM has made them even more popular by using them as standard equipment on the IBM PCjr and the portable IBM PC. Industry analysts say that the trends all point toward the half-height drive becoming an industry standard. It is feasible right now to install four half height floppy disk drives in your PC where the two regular disk drives now sit.

You can run your PC with several disk drives, if you need to, but most likely you will have two disks and maybe a hard disk. That's about all the average person (even in business) needs. This chapter focuses on the two disk drive concept and includes details on combining a hard disk with those disk drives. You can also install just one disk drive (the A drive). There are plenty of notations along the way for those who plan to work with only one disk drive.

This chapter also shows you how to do many things for yourself that are normally done by the local computer store. If you install your own disk drives (even the fixed disk) you can save a lot of money with about an hour's worth of work.

4.3 Installing the A Drive

You will need:

- The tools listed at the end of section 4.1.
- 1 5¼ inch disk drive (full height).

Such disk drives are manufactured by Tandon and Control Data Corporation. The typical 5¼ inch floppy disk drives made by Tandon for the PC are known as TM 100-2 (5¼″). You want to be sure that the drives you get are full height, unless you specifically want to install half-height disk drives (see section 4.7 if you do).

It should take you less than 30 minutes to install the A disk drive. Don't be in a hurry to beat the clock. Take your time and go slowly—without skipping any steps. Here's what you need to do to install the A drive on your PC:

STEP ONE: Unplug your PC. Remove the cover. (See Appendix C.)

STEP TWO: Remove the face plate which covers the front panel of the PC by unfastening the retaining clips. If your PC doesn't have this face plate, go on to the next step. Otherwise, refer to Figure 4.1.

STEP THREE: Figure 4.2 shows the power connectors coming from the power supply. This view is looking toward the back of the PC. You can use either connector for hooking up the A drive. You don't need to use the connector at this point—just be sure you know where it is.

STEP FOUR: Now slide your disk drive into the PC. With the front of the PC and the front of the disk drive facing you, carefully insert the disk drive. (See Figure 4.3.)

Fig. 4.1: Removing face plate retaining clips for A drive

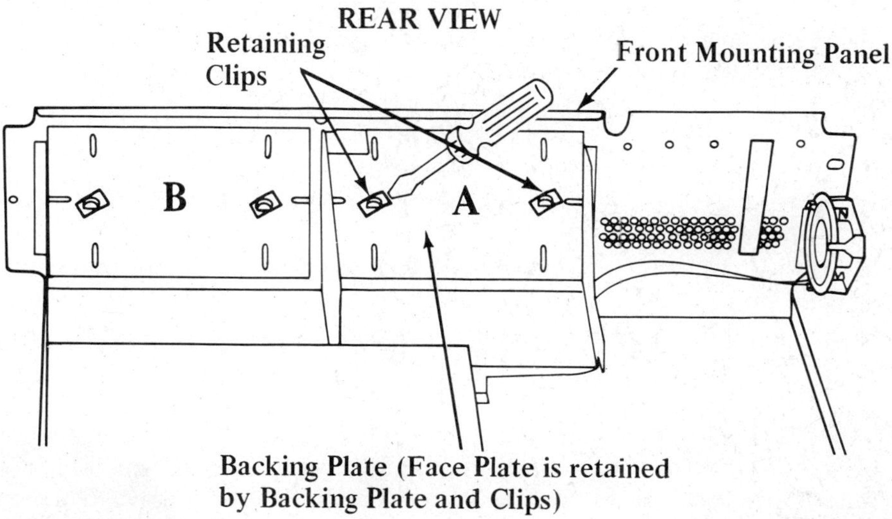

Courtesy of International Business Machines Corporation

Fig. 4.2: PC Chassis, showing the power connectors for the disk drives

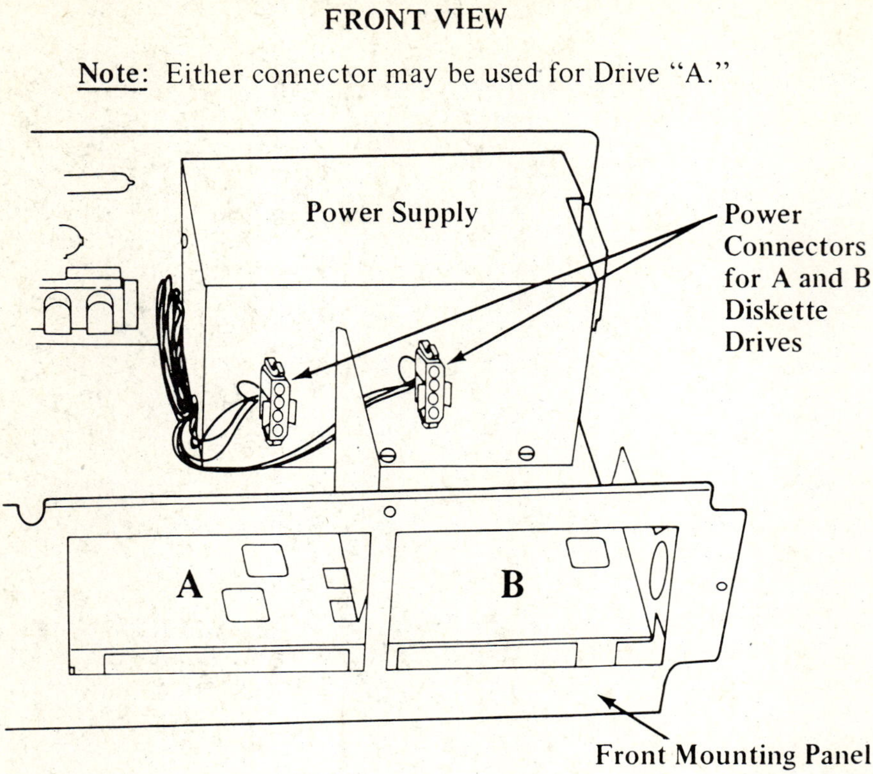

Courtesy of International Business Machines Corporation

Before pushing the disk drive all the way back into place, you need to insert the power connector which you located in the previous step.

The inset of Figure 4.3 shows how to attach the connector to the disk drive. Once that connector is plugged into place you can go ahead and push the disk drive all the way in. You will know it is in proper position when it rests flush with the front of the PC mounting.

STEP FIVE: Now that your A drive is connected and in place you need to secure it by using two mounting screws as shown in Figure 4.4.

STEP SIX: If you are going to install another disk drive (the B drive) next to this disk drive go to section 4.4.

If you are only going to have only one disk drive in your PC, proceed with the rest of the steps in this section.

STEP SEVEN: Now set the proper system switches for one disk drive in your PC, to tell your PC how many disk drives you will be using. There are two sets of switch blocks on the system board near the power supply. If you have a PC/XT there will only be one switch block. Refer to Figure 4.5. You will only be concerned with switch

Fig. 4.3: Front of PC chassis, with disk drive being inserted

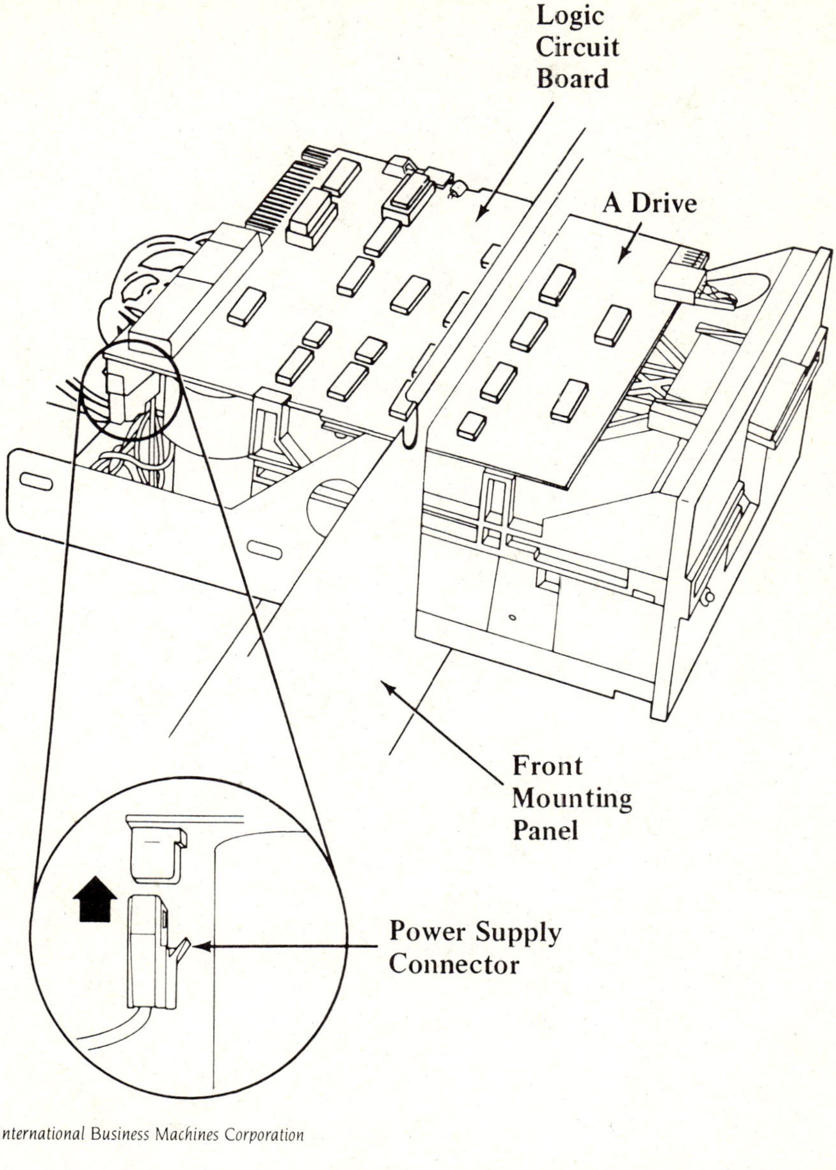

Courtesy of International Business Machines Corporation

block 1, located the farthest from the power supply. *Before you change anything, make notes* on the current switch settings.

Figure 4.6 shows you the different settings for switch block 1. With a ball point pen, set the switch block for one disk drive. That means setting #1 will be in the OFF position and settings #7 and #8 will be in the ON position. Check the settings of the other switches against your notes to be sure you did not accidentally move any.

STEP EIGHT: Once you have the proper settings on switch block 1, you are ready to install the Disk Drive Controller. (see section 4.5.)

Fig. 4.4: Disk drive A in place with mounting screws

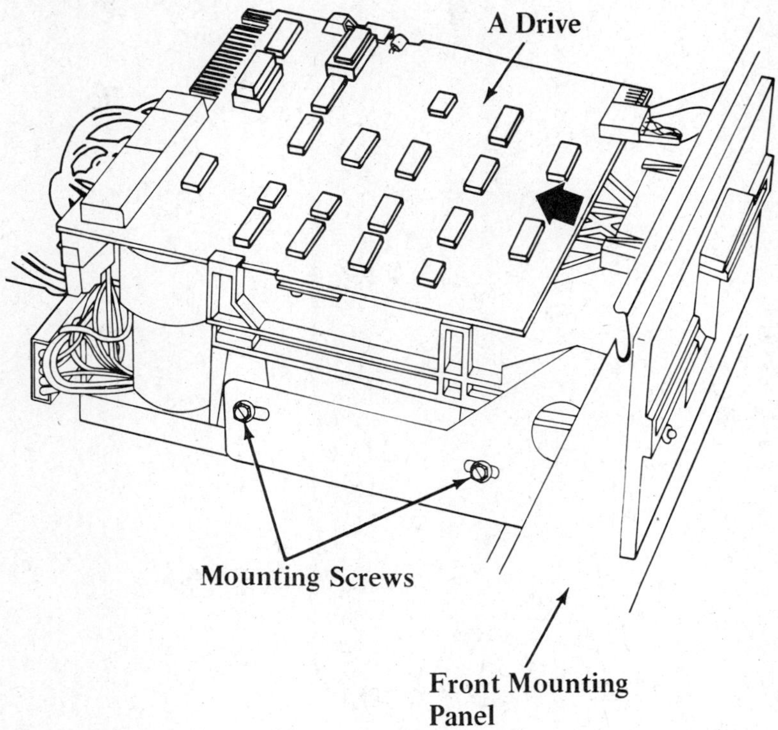

Courtesy of International Business Machines Corporation

4.4 Installing the B Drive

STEP ONE: If you are installing two disk drives at the same time you can skip this step. However, if your PC already has an A drive and you are now going to install the B drive, the first thing you need to do is remove the PC's cover. You will do that only after unplugging your PC. The procedure for removing the cover is outlined in Appendix C.

STEP TWO: Remove the face plate which covers the front panel of the PC by unfastening the retaining clips. Refer to Figure 4.7.

STEP THREE: Figure 4.8 shows the power connector coming from the power supply. This view is looking toward the back of the PC. You don't need to use the connector at this point—just be sure you know where it is.

STEP FOUR: You will now slide disk drive B into the PC. Facing the front of the PC, with the front of the disk drive facing you, you should carefully insert the disk drive. See Figure 4.9. Before pushing the disk drive all the way back into place, you need to connect the power connector which you located in the previous step.

The inset of Figure 4.9 shows how to attach the connector to the B disk drive.

Fig. 4.5: The PC system board, showing location of switch blocks

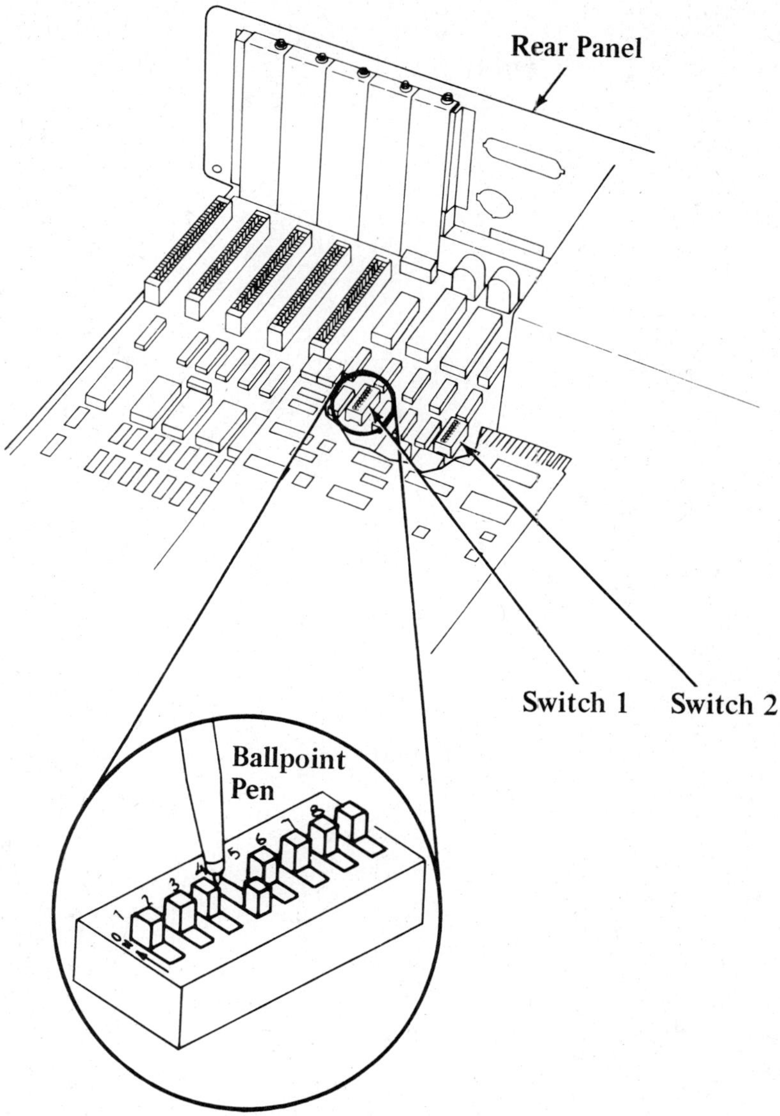

Courtesy of International Business Machines Corporation

Once that connector is plugged into place you can go ahead and push the disk drive all the way in. You will know it is in proper position when it rests flush with the front of the PC mounting panel.

STEP FIVE: Now that your B drive is connected and in place you need to secure it there. You will do this by using two mounting screws as shown in Figure 4.10.

STEP SIX: At this point you have completed installation of the B disk drive. You

Fig. 4.6: Chart showing switch block settings for disk drives

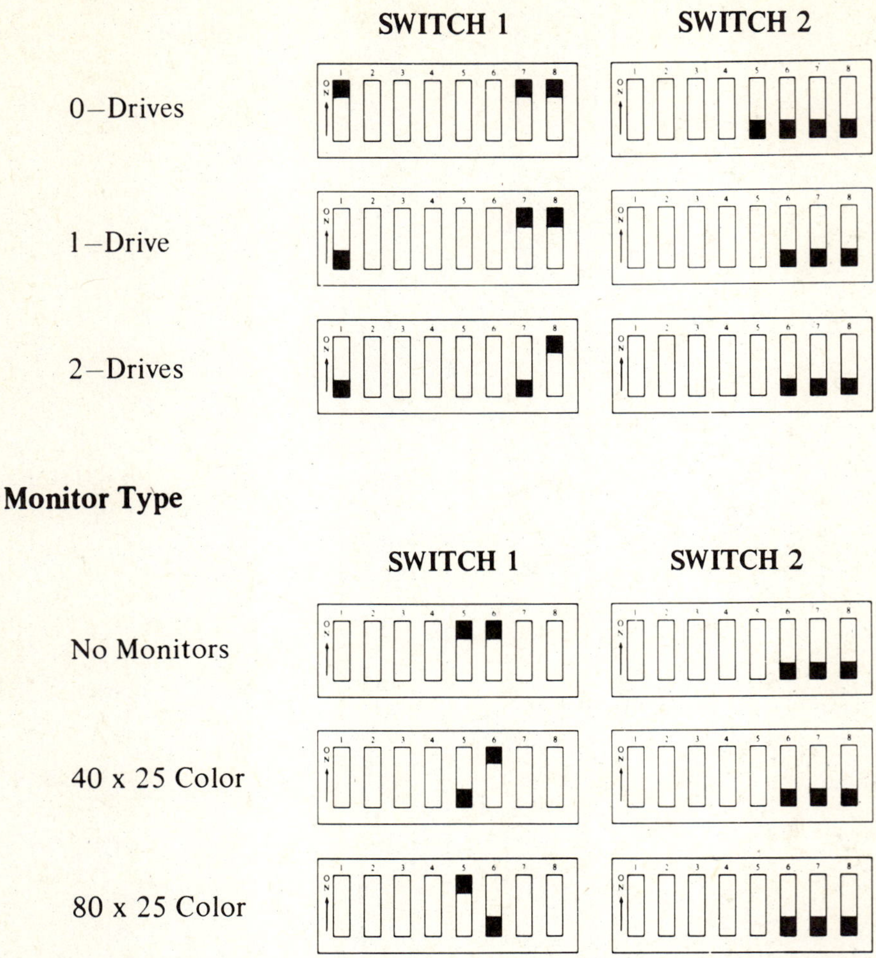

Note: The 80 x 25 color setting, when used with home television and various monitors can cause loss of character/quality.

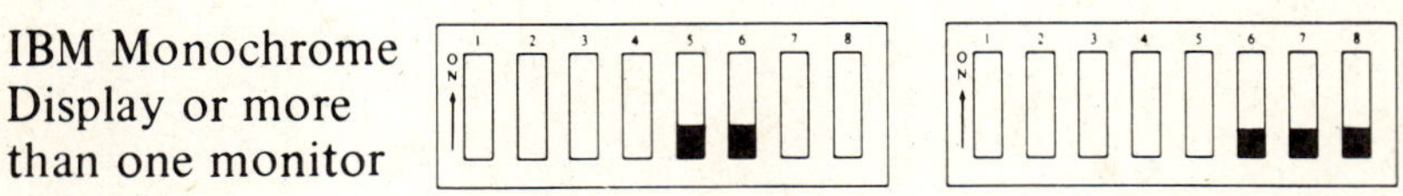

Courtesy of International Business Machines Corporation

will now set the proper system switches for having two disk drives operating in your PC, to tell it how many disk drives you will be using. There are two sets of switch blocks on the system board near the power supply. Refer to Figure 4.5, which shows you where these switch blocks are. You will only be concerned with switch block 1, the farthest from the power supply. *Make notes on the current settings switches before you do*

Fig. 4.7: Removing face plate retaining clips for B drive

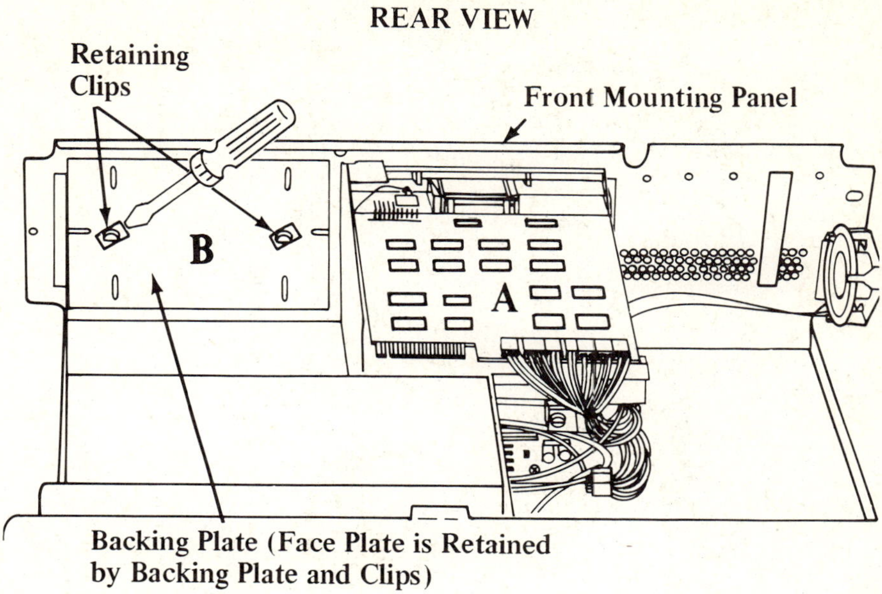

Courtesy of International Business Machines Corporation

anything. That way you will have something to refer back to if anything goes wrong.

Figure 4.6 shows you the different settings for switch block 1. With a ball point pen, set the switch block for two disk drives. That means setting #1 will be in the OFF position, setting #7 will be in the OFF position, and setting #8 will be in the ON position. *Then check the settings of the other switches against the notes you made earlier to be sure you did not accidentally move one of them.* They are all very close together. Once you have the proper settings on switch block 1 you are ready to install the diskette adapter.

4.5 Installing the Diskette Adapter

This is the third (second if you're only installing one disk drive) and final part of installing disk drives in your PC. The terms *disk drive controller* and *floppy drive controller* are used by some companies to refer to the diskette adapter.

The diskette adapter is an adapter card that fits into one of the PC's expansion slots. Those expansion slots are located in the left hand area of the system board. (See Figure 4.11.)

Your disk drives will function under the direction of the diskette adapter. It doesn't matter whether you have one or two disk drives, the diskette adapter will take care of things. You won't even know it is there. It will just do its job of letting you work back and forth between disk drives or, if you have a single drive system, it will allow you to work with that, including copying files between disks. Things will take a little longer with a single disk drive, but you will be able to accomplish just about all DOS functions.

Fig. 4.8: PC Chassis, showing the power connectors for the disk drives

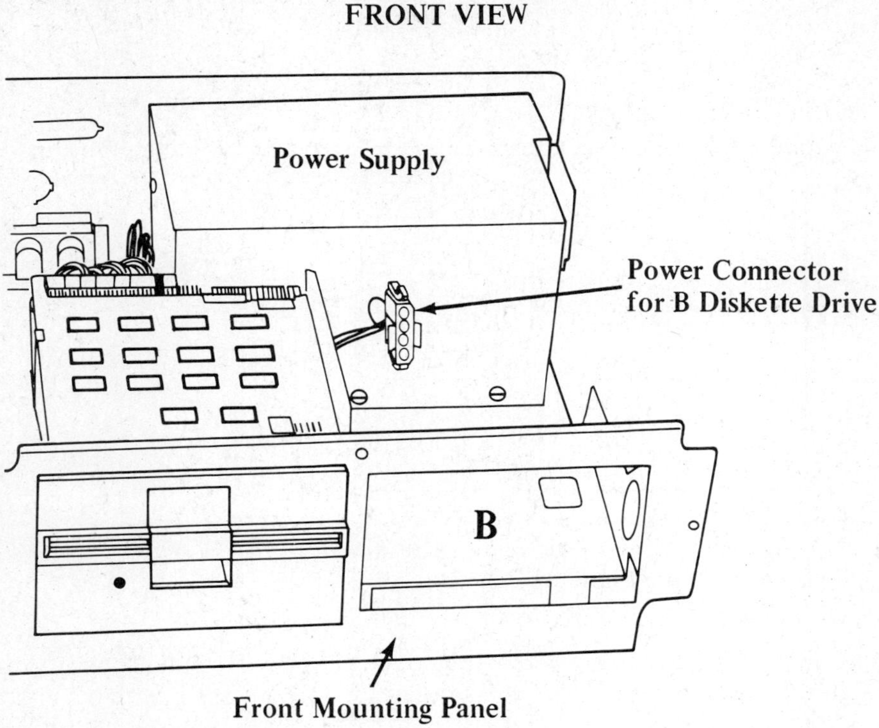

Courtesy of International Business Machines Corporation

There really isn't much to installing the diskette adapter. You insert the diskette adapter card in an expansion slot and then connect its cable (known as a signal cable) to the disk drive(s).

You will need only a medium sized, flat head screwdriver for removing a bracket at the back panel of the PC.

You will, of course, also need a diskette adapter card with a signal cable. Such adapter cards are made by several companies.

These are the steps for installing the diskette adapter card and cable, which complete the installation of your disk drive(s):

STEP ONE: Figure 4.11 shows a bird's eye view of your PC with the cover off. The diskette adapter card must be placed in the first expansion slot on the right as you face the PC, closest to the power supply. The cable from the diskette adapter will get in the way of other adapter cards if you don't place the adapter card in the expansion slot closest to the disk drives. The signal cable isn't that long, and you certainly don't want to crimp or pinch it.

The procedure for installing an adapter card is covered, step by step, in Chapter 2, section 2.6.

STEP TWO: Figure 4.12 shows how you will connect the diskette adapter signal cable to the disk drive(s). The connector at the end of the cable goes to the A drive

Fig. 4.9: Front of PC chassis, with disk drive being inserted

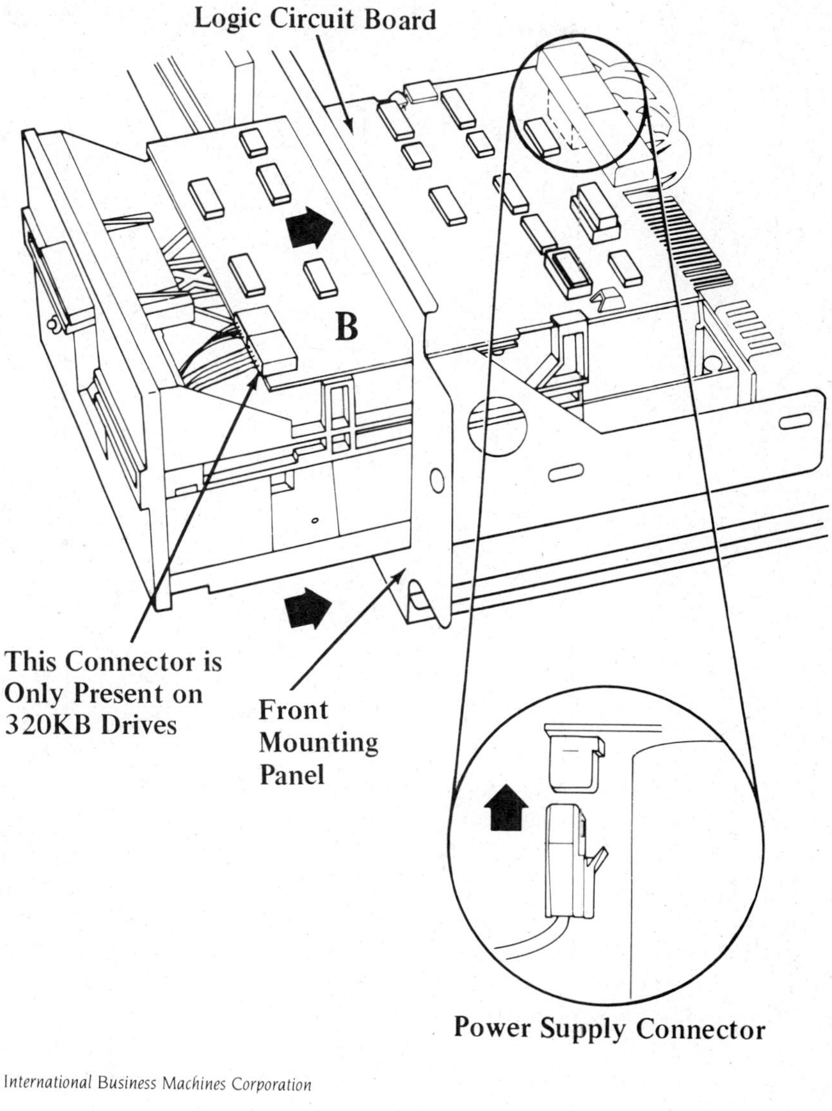

Courtesy of International Business Machines Corporation

Fig. 4.10: Disk drive B in place with mounting screws.

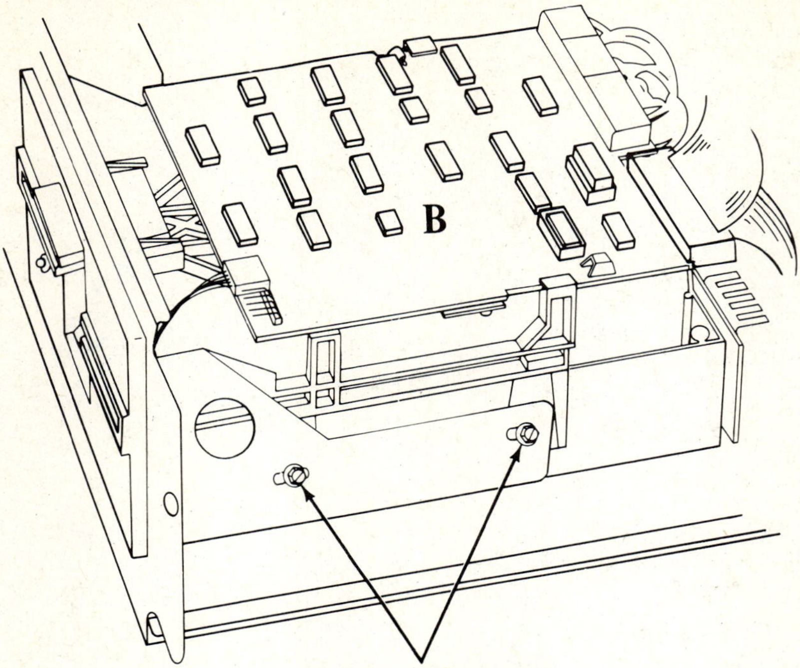

Courtesy of International Business Machines Corporation

(it doesn't matter here whether you have one or two disk drives—just be sure the end of the signal cable is connected to the A drive, as shown in Figure 4.12).

If you have two disk drives, connect the signal cable as shown in Figure 4.12. Be sure that the end of the cable is connected to the A drive. For a single drive system you will still connect one end of the cable to the A drive and let the connector normally used for the B drive remain unconnected.

The connectors on the signal cable should fit snugly into place on the disk drives. Referring to the inset of Figure 4.12 will show you how the connection should be made. To make the proper connection you must line up the signal cable's locating key with the disk drive's locating lug. This isn't as complicated as it sounds (especially after looking at Figure 4.12). The point here is to be sure you are connecting the Signal Cable properly. That's the sole purpose of the Locating Key and Locating Lug.

STEP THREE: You are just about done! The last piece of work you must do involves a pluggable terminator module. Don't let that term spook you (especially after all of the other terminology you've managed to make your way through). The terminator is nothing more than the place where all signals for controlling the disk drives stop. The terminator prevents the signal cable from becoming an RF (radio frequency) antenna.

Each disk drive has a terminator plug, which is located on the top near the back (see Figure 4.13). The B drive's terminator plug should be empty, because you don't

Fig. 4.11: View looking down on chassis of IBM PC, showing power supply, disk drives and expansion slots ·

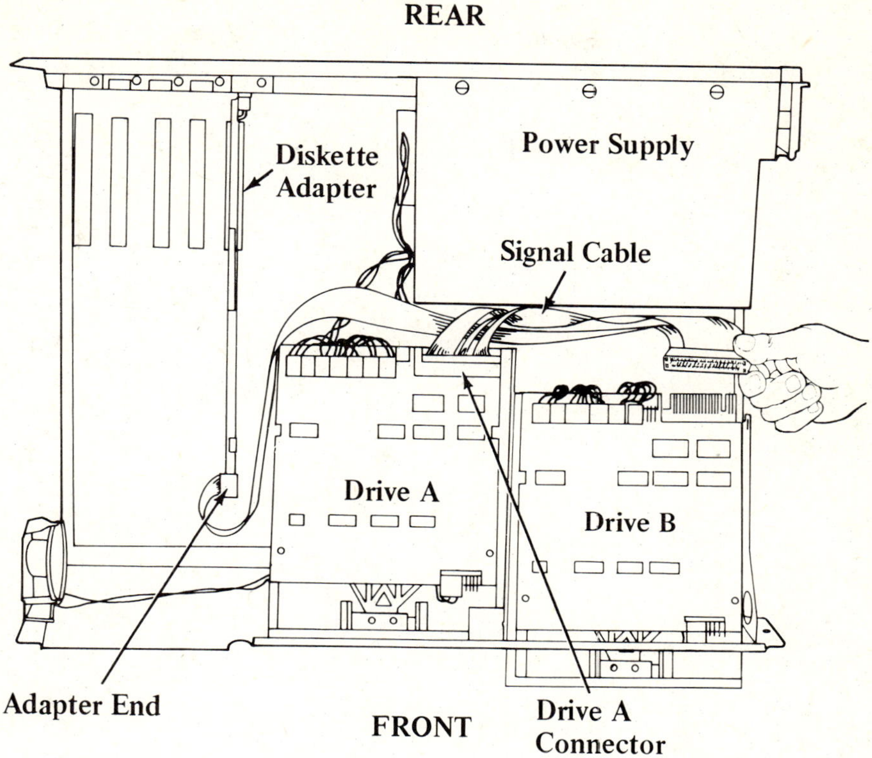

Courtesy of International Business Machines Corporation

want the signal to stop there. It will be the A drive's terminator plug that will have a chip or module in it. Go ahead and remove the terminator plug from the B drive (if it has one). Leave the one in place on the A drive.

The terminator plug must be placed in position facing a certain direction. The circular notch on the end of the terminator plug should be facing the same direction as all of the other chips' notches on the top of the disk drive. This is similar to the notches on the memory (and most other) chips in your PC.

Disk drives you buy from mail order houses usually will be marked A drive and B drive, so you won't need to worry about this step at all. The only difference between the two drives is the terminator plug. The A drive will have the terminator module in place and the B drive won't. *If you switch the two drives or get the signal cable connected incorrectly your disk drives will not function properly.*

This would be a good time to double-check all of your work. Don't forget to check the switch settings, too. Be sure you have set the switches on switch block 1 as outlined in section 4.6. (There are two switch blocks—the one you should have set is the one farthest from the power supply).

STEP FOUR: Your work is now complete. All you need to do is put the cover back on the PC. (See Appendix C.) When you turn on your PC everything should work

Fig. 4.12: View of PC chassis showing how to connect signal cable to disk drives

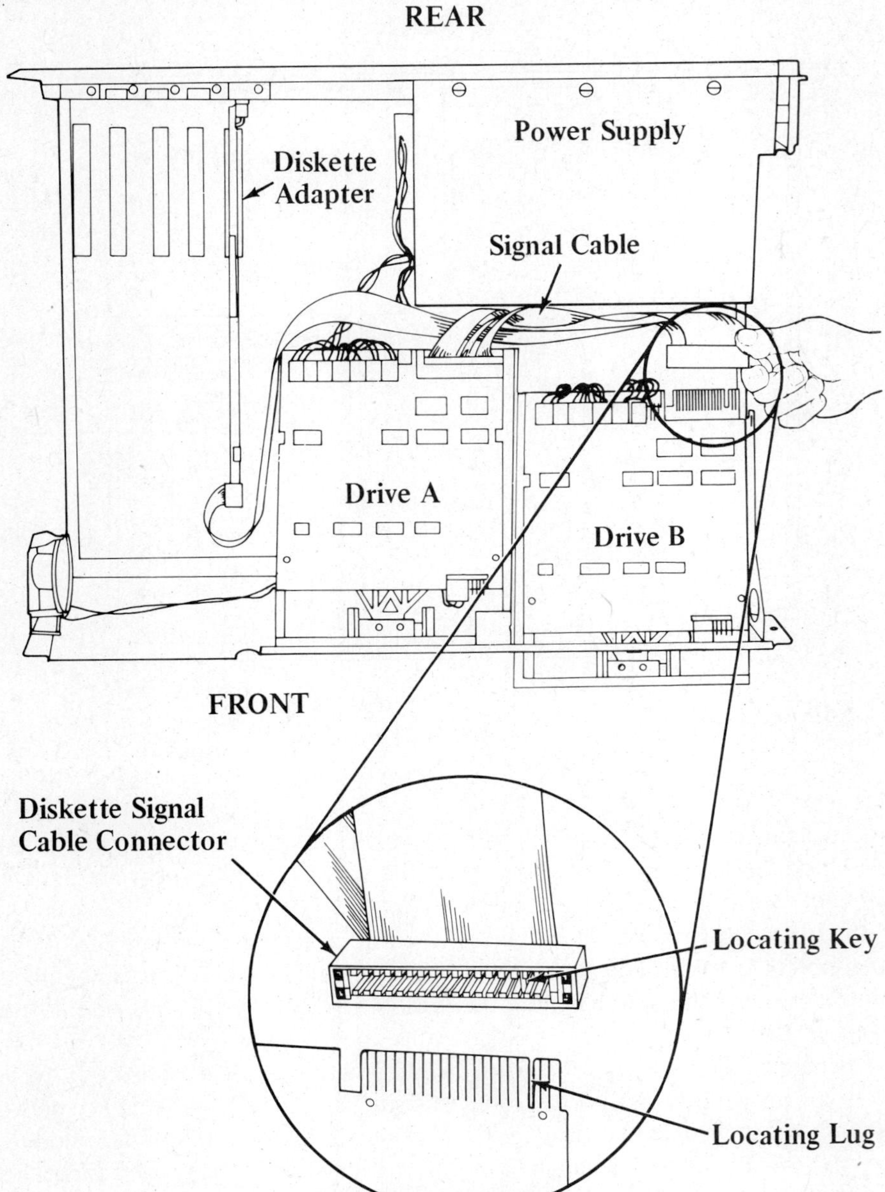

Note: Signal cables will only fit one way.

Courtesy of International Business Machines Corporation

properly. If it doesn't, re-trace all the steps listed here. That should help you track down the problem. However, if you find that you did everything correctly and you still have a problem, then it is almost certainly either the diskette adapter card or one of the disk drives.

Fig. 4.13: The PC's disk drives, showing the terminator plug

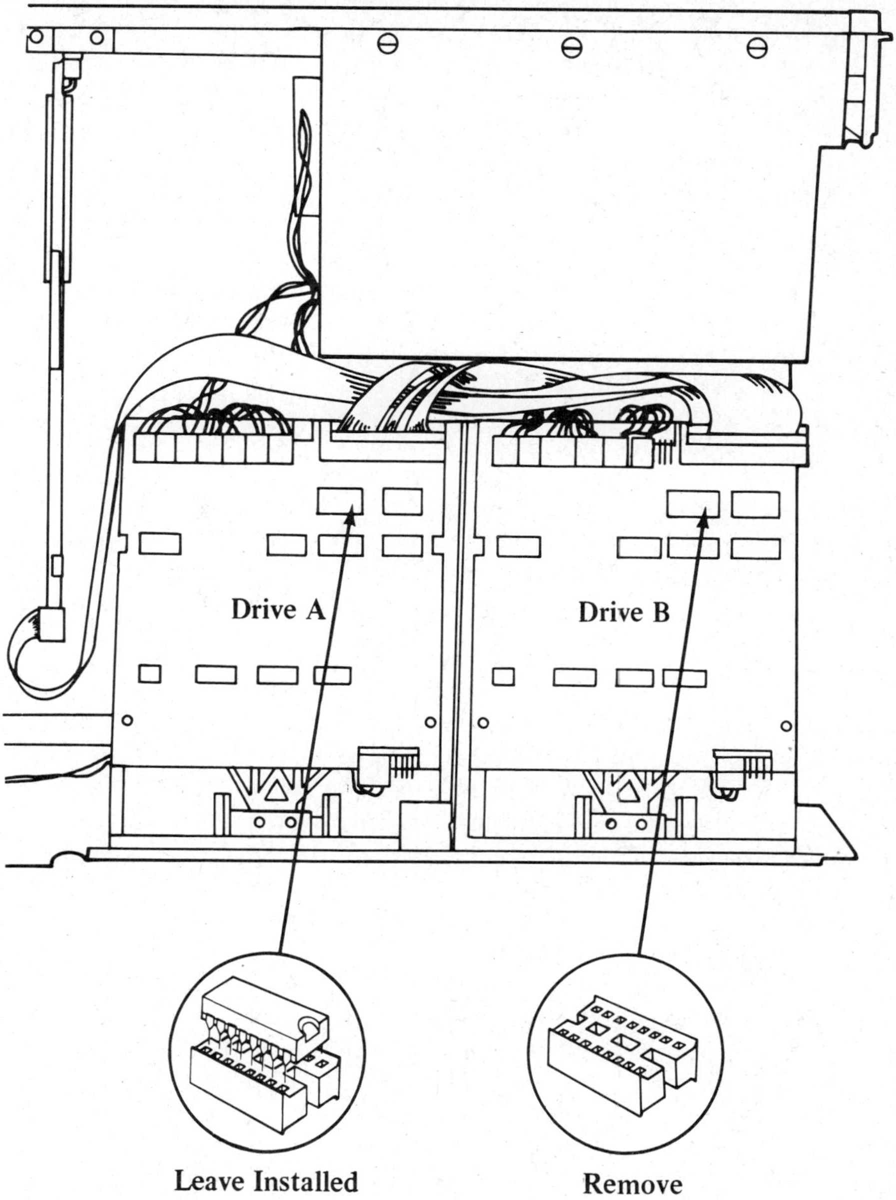

Courtesy of International Business Machines Corporation

4.6 Upgrading from Single Sided to Double Sided Disk Drives

In the early days of the IBM PC (the first half of 1982) the standard disk drives were single sided. For quite some time after that, even though double sided disk drives were then readily available, people continued to purchase PCs with single sided disk drives to save money on the purchase price. Today it's a different story, because just about all new PCs have double sided disk drives.

Single sided disk drives still serve a valid purpose. When PC owners upgrade to double sided disk drives, those single sided disk drives can provide real opportunities for many people to get started computing at significant savings. For people who otherwise couldn't have afforded an IBM PC, those older disk drives mean learning and benefiting in this age of the computer revolution.

At some point, most people with single sided disk drives will upgrade their systems. Those older disk drives might then get passed on to newcomers. Some people will get along just fine with single sided disk drives. That's one of the nicest features about the IBM PC—it is flexible enough to meet a variety of needs and uses.

Upgrading a PC from single sided to double sided disk drives isn't too hard and will take about an hour to complete. You will need the following:

- 1 medium sized, flat head screwdriver.
- 2 double sided disk drives (full height)

The steps below show you how to remove your single sided disk drives. After completing those steps you will be referred back to the three sections in this chapter which show you how to install disk drives and the diskette adapter.

STEP ONE: Unplug your PC and remove the cover. (See Appendix C.)

STEP TWO: Figure 4.11 shows what you will see inside your PC as you stand in front of it, facing the disk drives. Before you can do anything else you will need to remove the mounting screws on the side of each disk drive. To get to the mounting screws for the A drive (the one on the left) you will need to remove any adapter cards that are in the way. By doing that you will have plenty of working room not only for removing these disk drives, but also for installing the new double sided disk drives.

The adapter cards fill the expansion slots (located on the left portion of the PC's chassis—see Figure 4.11). To remove any adapter card you must first take out the screw holding it in place. That screw is located at the PC's top back panel.

Figure 4.4 shows the A drive and the location of the mounting screws. You should now remove those screws with your screwdriver. Place all screws you remove in a handy place so they will be easy to find when it comes time to install the double sided disk drives.

You should now remove the mounting screws from the B drive. (See Figure 4.10.)

STEP THREE: As you start to slide each disk drive out you will need to unhook the power connectors and the signal cable. Figures 4.2 and 4.8 show where the power connectors will be unhooked from the A and B drives. You should unhook those connectors first, and then unhook the signal cable.

The signal cable is attached to each disk drive at the back portion on the top (Figure 4.12). The signal cable connections should be unplugged completely from each disk drive. You can remove them by slightly rocking each cable connection back and forth as you pull outward.

Once both disk drives are free of the power and signal cable connections you can slide the disk drives outward. Do this slowly and carefully so you don't drop anything. Also, this can be the point where you might find that one of the power connectors or signal cable connections have not been unplugged. By going slowly here you won't hurt anything if something is still connected. Whatever might be connected should now be loosened and removed to allow for complete removal of the disk drives. Review this step if you are having any problems.

Now that you have the single sided disk drives out of your PC you are ready to proceed with installing your new double sided disk drives. At this point you don't need to worry about flipping system switches or anything else. All you need to do now is go to section 4.3. That section and the two following it will guide you through the entire process for installing the new disk drives.

It would probably be a good idea to put your single sided disk drives in the packing containers from your new disk drives. At some point you might want to sell or trade those disk drives so it is important to keep them as safe and protected as possible.

4.7 Installing Half-Height Disk Drives

Half-height disk drives are representative of the general trend in the computer industry—everything is getting smaller and smaller. The regular sized disk drives, known as full height drives, have a place for themselves in the world of computers. When you consider just how many PCs (not to mention the thousands of other personal computers) have been sold with those full height drives it is easy to understand why they will probably be in use for some time to come.

The used parts market and the on-going maintenance service for regular sized disk drives are impressive. However, now that IBM uses half-heights as standard equipment in both the portable PC and the PCjr, things are beginning to change. More and more people will be using half-height disk drives. Such drives can be easily installed in any model of the IBM PC.

Prospective PC owners, particularly of the PC portable, can now consider purchasing only one disk drive. They can install another disk drive later, at the same time they add extra memory chips, too. As with so many other things, there are pros and cons to half-height disk drives. Some tend to be noisier than the regular size disk drives. Initially, there were problems with the reading/writing heads on half-height disk drives, which increased the risk of errors. It is best to thoroughly check out the half-height drives you might be considering.

Installing a second disk drive on the IBM PC portable is as simple as purchasing the disk drive, slipping it into the empty disk drive slot, making a few connections and flipping a switch. It can all be done using the instructions in section 4.4 as a guide. While a few things will look different, the steps are all the same.

If you want to install half-height disk drives on your PC you will need the following:

- a medium, flat head screwdriver
- half-height disk drive(s)
- mounting brackets for half-height disk drives

Installing half-height disk drives on your PC should take less than an hour. However, don't rush. Take your time and be careful—following these steps and the those in the product installation manual.

STEP ONE: Unplug the PC and remove the cover. (See Appendix C.)

STEP TWO: It's important to remember that two half-heights will go where one full height disk drive goes. When buying the half-height drives, be sure that you get special mounting brackets. These are usually sold as part of the standard half-height package. The brackets (or clamps) allow you to fasten the half-height drives securely in place.

At this point you will either be removing full height disk drives or removing the front face plate on the no-drive PC (one which was ordered without disk drives). If you are removing the front face plate, see Figure 4.1. To replace full height disk drives with the half-heights, refer to STEP TWO and STEP THREE of the previous section.

Once you have an open spot to fill with your new half-height disk drives, you are ready to proceed with the next step.

STEP THREE: You should now place the half-height disk drives in the PC, one on top of the other. To do this, carefully follow the steps in section 4.3 thru 4.5. The only difference will be that the disk drives you are now installing rest in one spot, with one underneath the other (you will bolt them together before you install them). Once the connections are made you will need to secure the mounting brackets which will hold the two half height disk drives in place.

If you are installing more than two disk drives you will need the proper disk drive controller. To install two half heights along with a hard disk or to install more than two half height disk drives you will need a special disk drive controller adapter card. The place where you purchase your disk drives should have the controller card to meet your specific needs.

STEP FOUR: Once the half-height disk drives are connected and in place, you are ready to set the system switches on switch block 1. Refer to Figure 4.6 for the proper settings based on the number of disk drives you have. Figure 4.5 shows you the location of switch block 1 on the system board. There are two sets of switches. Switch block 1 (the one you want to set) is the farthest from the power supply, to the left of switch block 2 as you face the PC. *Before you do anything you should make a note of the current switch settings.*

If you will be using more than two floppy disk drives or two half-heights, combined with a fixed disk, the product manual for the drives you purchased will explain what to do. Before proceeding with the next step you should set the switches. Also double check the settings of all the switches on the block to be sure none were changed accidentally.

STEP FIVE: Close up your PC. (See Appendix C.)

STEP SIX: Test your system to be sure everything is working all right. If you have any problems, first review all of the steps listed here. At the same time you should carefully review the product manuals and instructions you received with your half-height disk drives and the disk drive controller adapter card. If you have done everything correctly, then there is a problem with one of the products you installed and you will need to work out the matter with the place where you made the purchase.

There is a lot of built-in flexibility with half-height disk drives. This is true primarily because of their size. You are now able to squeeze much more into the same amount of space. This section on half-height disk drives would not be complete without an overview of one of the most intriguing options provided by them.

Half-height floppy disk drives can make a regular PC more like a PC/XT, with two floppy disk drives and a fixed disk. It can be done without modifying the power supply, too, by using low power-consuming half-height floppy disk drives like the ones manufactured by TEAC. Those two floppys go into the left slot where the A drive normally goes. Then, in place of the B drive, you put a low power-consuming fixed disk. Maynard Electronics sells such a 10 megabyte fixed disk called the MicroScience 2, which works very well within the PC environment.

Maynard Electronics will provide you with everything you need to install two half-height floppies and the fixed disk. The complete package even comes with a Sandstar Disk Drive Controller and a "Hard Disk BIOS Module" which modifies the ROM of your PC. That modification to the ROM (Read Only Memory) is what allows your PC to function properly with the fixed disk. Many fixed disks require that you modify your DOS disk—sometimes to the point of making it do weird things when certain programs are run.

The Sandstar Disk Drive Controller adapter card takes not only the floppy disk drives, but the fixed disk, too. What is nice about all of this is that everything is inside your PC. There are no extra boxes like a fixed disk, no extra power supply or anything else, and, this comes pretty close to giving you an IBM PC/XT—only you did it yourself.

Installation of the complete setup mentioned here requires nothing more than a screwdriver and the instructions supplied by Maynard Electronics. The cost is a pleasant surprise, too. The fixed disk is in the $1,000 range. The prices for the half-height floppy disk drives are impressively reasonable, too ($160 range). The Sandstar Disk Drive Controller adapter card, (about $180) makes it well worth considering, if it meets your needs.

Be aware that there is a possibility of power supply and consumption problems when you start loading up your PC. Many people don't realize the PC's power unit does have limitations. When you stretch those limitations too far you run into problems. Maynard Electronics carefully designed their fixed disk around the limitations, but not every company is going to do that. Therefore the responsibility lies with YOU to be more cautious about what you are doing.

5

This chapter is all about the emulated disk drive. Terms such as speed disk, electronic disk drive, RAM disk, and memory disks are also used to describe the same concept. An emulated disk drive gives impressive speed to word processing, and is a real convenience in communications, where such speed is quite practical for a buffer.

An emulated disk drive is created from extra space in the RAM (Random Access Memory) of your PC and works just like a regular disk drive. In other words, a portion of the internal memory in your PC can also be used to electronically duplicate the function of a mechanical disk drive. However, since an emulated disk drive is created in memory, it exists only while the PC is on. That means you can lose your files on the emulated disk if the electrical power to the PC is turned off or interrupted. All files on the emulated disk need to be copied over to a floppy disk or fixed disk for safe, permanent storage.

Obviously, then, using an emulated disk is a little risky. This risk factor, however, is a trade off for quickness. Since an emulated disk isn't mechanical, it is impressively fast. It's even faster than a fixed disk.

If you have at least 256KB RAM (user memory) in your PC you should definitely consider using an emulated disk drive. If you are using DOS 2.0 or 2.1, and have 256KB RAM or more, then you already could have an emulated disk drive sitting right under your nose, just waiting to be used. You need to do a few things first to capture and use this disk drive, but once you do you will have the luxury of a extra disk drive that is lightning fast and so convenient to use that it quickly becomes habit-forming.

While you should consider using an emulated disk drive if you have the excess RAM, there is more you need to be aware of. The advantages of an emulated disk's speed are significant enough to convince you to use it forever, but don't forget that it isn't permanent. If you don't copy whatever is on your emulated disk over to a floppy disk or fixed disk, you'll lose everything when you turn off or reset your PC. It might sound like a simple matter to copy files over from the emulated disk, but even forgetting to do so just once means you've lost valuable files and probably hours of work.

5.1 A Word of Warning about the Phantom in Your PC

Think of an emulated disk drive as a phantom. The dictionary points out that a phantom is something that is apparent but with no substantial existence. An emulated disk drive is there and can be used, but its existence is not permanent and depends on electricity. So in the same way that a phantom can disappear in the blink of an eye, the emulated disk drive will instantly be gone when the electrical power is interrupted or turned off, as when the system is rebooted.

If you turn off your PC *(or the power goes out) everything on the emulated disk drive is lost.* Using the ALTERNATE, CONTROL and DELETE keys to reboot your system also kills everything in your emulated disk. You won't lose everything with all emulated disk drives, but is something to be concerned about.

So—A WORD OF WARNING! An emulated disk adds some risks along with the speed and overall convenience of using the PC's RAM. The odds are pretty much in your favor, but if the power happens to go out on a Sunday afternoon and you haven't yet saved the 25 page report on your emulated disk drive . . . well, the odds won't mean that much.

There is a lot you can do to work carefully with an emulated disk drive. However, be sure that you understand that no matter how careful you are, or how many precautions you take, an emulated disk drive has a dangerous phantom element to it.

5.2 Setting Up an Emulated Disk Drive with DOS 2.0

Many PC owners have yet to switch over to DOS 2.0. With the built-in electronic disk drive (not to mention an extra 40KB of storage on each double sided disk) the cost of DOS 2.0 or 2.1 really pays for itself. The DOS 2.0 or higher series has many more features, including the capacity to work within fixed disks, which make it an important consideration as an upgrade for any PC. If you currently have DOS 1.1, this would be the ideal time to switch over to DOS 2.0 or DOS 2.1. If you want to stick with DOS 1.1, you can still use an emulated disk. The steps to do that are outlined in the next section.

With DOS 2.0 you can create your own 180KB disk drive, and the DOS manual even shows you how to do it. Before you read the DOS manual you should finish this section. This will help you interpret the DOS manual. Remember that you need DOS 2.0. This won't work with DOS 1.1.

Chapter 14 of the DOS manual is titled "Installable Device Drivers." Don't let that term or the word install cause your heart to flutter, because a device driver isn't really that complex or hard to work with (unless you want to wade through the DOS manual on your own).

Creating an emulated disk drive within the RAM (internal memory) of your PC will be done by the PC through a specific set of instructions, which is really a program. That program is then driven by a device driver, which DOS knows how to handle. It will all be done automatically with no effort, sweat, or work on your part, once things are set up. As with so many other aspects of expanding the use of your PC or PC/XT you really don't need to know the intricacies of how it works. All you need to do is set things up and the PC, along with DOS, will take care of the rest.

To set up an emulated disk drive with DOS 2.0 or 2.1:

STEP ONE: Through DOS your PC will be able to configure part of its RAM into an electronic disk drive. This will be done each time you boot up (i.e., turn on your system), provided you set up a special file to tell DOS what you want it to do. This file is called an AUTOEXEC.BAT file and will be explained in detail as you work your way through these steps.

Before you can get started, you must be sure that you have at least 256KB RAM. That means the internal memory in your PC must be capable of holding 262,144 bytes of information. Each KB represents 1,024 bytes, and 256 × 1024 = 262,144. If you aren't sure how much internal memory your PC has, you can easily check by putting your DOS diskette in the A drive of your PC.

Turn on the PC and then enter the time and date. At the cursor prompt of `A>`, type `CHKDSK` and press the enter key (carriage return). Your screen will display:

```
   362996 bytes total disk space
   102400 bytes in 31 user files
   260596 bytes available on disk

-> 262144 bytes in memory
   229744 bytes free
```

The arrow above points to the line which tells you how much RAM (Random Access Memory) your PC has. This is the amount of internal memory you have to work with and is what you will be using to construct your emulated disk drive. If you have less than 256KB, you will find things a bit cramped when you try to run programs and still allow enough room for 180KB worth of disk drive in the RAM. Take whatever figure you see next to where it says "bytes in memory" and divide it by 1,024. That will give you your "KB figure"—256KB, 320KB, 192KB or usually some other multiple of 64 (memory is usually added in multiples of 64KB).

It is really recommended that you have 320KB or more of RAM to use an emulated disk drive. You can get by with 256KB, but if you plan to use programs like Wordstar, Lotus 1-2-3, dBASE II, and Prokey (which enhances the use of all three) the internal memory of your PC should be 320KB or more. You can get by fairly well with 256KB, but you won't be able to use a program like PROKEY in conjunction with other programs. It will take 320KB to do that.

STEP TWO: If you have 256KB RAM or more, you are now ready to set up your emulated disk drive. Turn to pages 14-27 through 14-34 of the DOS manual, which give you the program that is actually the device driver DOS needs to construct your emulated disk.

The beginning of the program says, "This is an installable device driver for an in storage diskette (virtual) with 180KB capacity." That wording is how the DOS manual tells you this is a device driver which allows you to have an emulated disk drive in the RAM of your PC. This program is actually the magic way DOS creates an extra disk drive out of the RAM.

You can't go any further now until you physically put this program on disk, under the file name RAM180.COM, and assemble it. That means typing it line by line and then running it through an assembler (which does not come with DOS and is another expense). If that seems a bit much for you to do, all hope is not lost. Check with a local computer user group to see if someone has already done it for you. They might not only have it on disk for you, but someone might have altered it so you have the options of an emulated disk drive of 180KB or 360KB. Remember that you will need to have enough extra RAM to handle larger amounts.

If this all makes you feel like you're out of your league, you might want to look at your options for an emulated disk drive under section 5.4. You get the software to set up an emulated disk drive with most multifunction adapter cards. You won't need to bother typing the program onto disk with the adapter card. This device driver in the DOS manual really shouldn't be an obstacle for you; but if it is, you do have the multifunction adapter card option.

STEP THREE: Once you have the DOS device driver program from the DOS manual on disk, you need to be sure it is named RAM180.COM. This program will have to be put on whatever disk you use when you turn on your PC or reboot the system (using the ALTERNATE, CONTROL, and DELETE keys). Actually, it can be on several disks, because it doesn't take up much room.

STEP FOUR: DOS can't do anything with a device driver (that's the RAM180.COM program on your disk) until you tell it what to do, with another file on the same disk. This file is called CONFIG.SYS, and it does nothing more than configure your system so that your device driver is properly installed (i.e., ready to use). During startup of your PC, DOS loads this CONFIG.SYS file into memory as an extension of itself. From that point on, the device driver (i.e., emulated disk drive) is installed and working.

The CONFIG.SYS file is very small and can be set up with just about any word processor in the non-document mode. The EDLIN text editor on the DOS program disk can even be used if you so choose. Using Wordstar you would set up the CONFIG.SYS file as follows:

- From the Opening Menu (or No-File Menu on older versions of Wordstar) press N to open a non-document file
- Type `CONFIG.SYS` for the name of the file and press the enter key
- Once the file is opened, type the following exactly as you see it here: `DEVICE=RAM180.COM`
- Close the file by holding the CONTROL key down and pressing K D

You can also set up a CONFIG.SYS file without Wordstar, or just about any other word processing program, by doing the following:

- From the DOS prompt `A>`, type: `COPY CON: CONFIG.SYS` and then press the enter key
- Now type `DEVICE=RAM180.COM`
- Press FUNCTION KEY 6 (F6) on the left hand side of the keyboard (you will see `^Z`, which is DOS's symbol for end-of-file) and then press the enter key

Any text editor or word processor with a non-document mode can build the same CONFIG.SYS file.

You now have your CONFIG.SYS file all set up. Each time your PC is turned on, DOS will read this CONFIG.SYS file first—even before an AUTOEXEC.BAT file. When DOS reads the CONFIG.SYS file it will install your emulated disk drive with your device driver (that's the RAM180.COM file).

From the `A>` of DOS on your computer screen you can now reach your emulated disk drive in the same way that you would normally go back and forth between disk drives. If you have one floppy disk drive you should type `B:` and press the enter key. You will now be on the emulated B drive. If you have two floppy disk drives, type `C:` and you will then be on the C drive, which is your emulated disk drive, constructed within the RAM (Random Access Memory) of your PC. You can now use this emulated disk drive in the same way you use your floppy disk drive(s). The only difference is that the emulated disk drive will be much faster and quieter.

If you have a fixed disk or more than two floppy disk drives, the emulated disk drive will be automatically labeled the next letter in line—in other words if you have three floppy disk drives and one fixed disk, your emulated disk drive will become the E: drive. The RAM180.COM program from the DOS manual will take care of setting that up for you.

5.3 Setting Up an Emulated Disk Drive with DOS 1.1

The modifications to DOS 2.0 (and higher numbered versions) make it much easier to set up emulated disk drives. However, if you have DOS 1.1 you can use the software that comes with most multifunction adapter cards to create an emulated disk drive in the RAM of your PC. The emulated disk drive created with DOS 1.1 doesn't work in quite the same way as the one with DOS 2.0, but the result is the same.

A good example of how an emulated disk drive is installed with DOS 1.1 is the TECMAR PC-Mate Captain multifunction adapter card. It allows you to set up an emulated disk drive, called a SPEED DISK, with either DOS 2.0 or 1.1. While there will be variations in the way different multifunction adapter cards accomplish the creation of a disk drive in the RAM of your PC, the steps outlined here for the TECMAR board will provide a general blueprint for you to follow. TECMAR refers to the emulated disk drive as a Speed Disk.

You will:

- Install the Speed Disk onto DOS. You will just do this once.
- Load the Speed Disk into memory (RAM). You will do this each time you turn on the PC or reboot the system.
- This is all done through two files: INSTALL.EXE (installs the Speed Disk) and GTBIOS (loads the Speed Disk).

To set up a Speed Disk for the Tecmar PC-Mate Captain:

STEP ONE: When you install the Speed Disk you are actually tricking DOS 1.1 into thinking the Speed Disk is just another disk drive. You will do this through a program labeled INSTALL.EXE . This program will ask you a series of questions, as will most other multifunction adapter card programs when setting up the Speed Disk.

To run the INSTALL.EXE program you need to be at the DOS prompt `A>`, with the INSTALL.EXE file on the disk in the A drive. Running the program is accomplished by typing in the word `INSTALL` .

STEP TWO: When the program asks for the `User ID`, respond by typing in the number `0` . To the question `Will this system support an 8 inch floppy disk subsystem with a Tecmar PC-BRIDGE disk adapter (Y/N)?` respond by typing `N` for no.

STEP THREE: The next series of questions will be asked for each disk drive. The purpose of this portion of the install program is to allow you to define your disk drives. After you have defined (i.e., told the program) what the A drive and B drive (if you have one) are, you will do the same for the Speed Disk. If there is no fixed disk, your Speed Disk will become the C drive.

STEP FOUR: You will define the C drive with the same specifications you used for the regular disk drive(s) in your PC. However, when the PC asks `Will the Speed Disk occupy low (L) or high (H) memory (H/L)?`, you should respond by typing in the letter `L`.

STEP FIVE: This is where you will actually determine the size of your Speed Disk. If you hit the enter key (carriage return) at this point, your Speed Disk will become 160KB in size. You can set up your Speed Disk in 1KB blocks from 64 to 512. Remember that you must have enough RAM (internal memory in your PC) to support not only the RAM drive, but to handle ROM (the Read Only Memory, which has programs necessary for the PC to function) and still leave enough room for DOS and other programs.

If you try to use up more RAM than you have, you won't find out until later that you have problems (i.e., error messages), so be sure at this point that you are not overdoing the size of your Speed Disk.

STEP SIX: The final part of the INSTALL.EXE program summarizes the information you have typed in. If you see something wrong, you can re-do the installation. Assuming everything is correct, you will respond with a `Y` to the question, `Is this configuration satisfactory (y/n)?` At some point in the future you can add other disk drives, reconfigure your Speed Disk or remove some options by running this program again.

STEP SEVEN: To complete this installation you need to press the ALTERNATE, CONTROL and DELETE keys *all at once*. You are now done with the INSTALL.EXE program. Now whenever you want your Speed Disk, all you do is type `GTBIOS` at the DOS prompt. But first you must copy the GTBIOS file onto your program disk.

Ideally, you should have the GTBIOS as part of your AUTOEXEC.BAT file. That will automatically configure your Speed Disk each time you load your program or turn on the PC.

5.4 An Emulated Disk Drive on a Multifunction Adapter Card (DOS 2.0)

Setting up a emulated disk on a multifunction adapter card with DOS 2.0 is almost effortless. That is because of the new features of DOS 2.0 (and higher number versions), which were not part of DOS 1.1. Again we will use the TECMAR PC-Mate Captain as an example to follow. This will also allow an interesting comparison as to the ease of setting up the same Speed Disk, which took several steps with DOS 1.1.

You will need two files. One is called SPEEDISK.SYS and is copied from the Tecmar program diskette. The other file, called CONFIG.SYS, is something you will have to create. The CONFIG.SYS file is going to be used to set up your device driver. That means that the device you want to use (i.e., the Speed Disk) will be driven (i.e., configured and operated) through the SPEEDISK.SYS file. The only way that will work is if you tell DOS what to do with it—which the CONFIG.SYS file accomplishes.

The steps below will not apply to all emulated or RAM disks. In some cases, you will need to set internal switches to reflect the new disk drive. Also, some RAM disks do not use or need a CONFIG.SYS file. Again we come back to how important it is for you to read the product documentation. The steps outlined here will give you a general idea of what is involved in setting up an emulated disk drive in user memory.

Here's what you need to do to set up the Speed Disk with DOS 2.0:

STEP ONE: The SPEEDISK.SYS file must be on your program disk (i.e., the one you will be using). Do that now if you have not already done so. Once that is on your program disk you only need one more file to set up your Speed Disk.

STEP TWO: This other file is called CONFIG.SYS, and it does nothing more than configure your system so you have your device driver properly installed (i.e., ready to use). During startup of your PC, DOS loads this CONFIG.SYS file into memory as an extension of itself. From that point on the device driver (i.e., emulated disk drive) is installed and working through the SPEEDISK.SYS file.

The CONFIG.SYS file is very small and can be set up with just about any word processor in the non-document mode. The EDLIN text editor on the DOS program disk can even be used if you so choose. Using Wordstar, you would set up the CONFIG.SYS file as follows:

- From the Opening Menu (or No-File Menu on older versions of WORDSTAR) press the letter N to open a non-document file
- Type `CONFIG.SYS` for the name of the file and press the enter key
- Once the file is opened, type the following exactly as you see it here: `DEVICE = SPEEDISK.SYS---K#`
  Note: The # symbol after the K in the line above is where you plug in the amount of memory you want to set aside for the Speed Disk. In other words, the number you put there in place of the # will determine the size of your Speed Disk. If you put 256, then the Speed Disk will be 256KB in size. The

number must be greater than 7 and not higher than what you can afford to set aside in terms of extra space in the RAM.

- Close the file by holding the CONTROL key down and pressing K D.

You can also set up a CONFIG.SYS file without Wordstar, or any other word processing program, by doing the following:

- From the DOS prompt `A>` type: `COPY CON: CONFIG.SYS` and then press the enter key.
- Now type: `DEVICE = SPEEDISK.SYS---K#`.
- Press FUNCTION KEY 6 (F6) on the left hand side of the keyboard and then press the enter key.

Any text editor or word processor with a non-document mode can build the same CONFIG.SYS file.

You now have your CONFIG.SYS file. Each time your PC is turned on, DOS will read this CONFIG.SYS file first—even before an AUTOEXEC.BAT file. When DOS reads the CONFIG.SYS file, it installs your Speed Disk with your device driver (the SPEEDISK.SYS file).

5.5 Emulated Disk Drives and AUTOEXEC.BAT Files

It is important to remember that you won't have your emulated disk unless you have copied the proper files on to your program disk. In the case of DOS 2.0, you will need the CONFIG.SYS file and the RAM180.COM file on the disk. For multifunction adapter cards, you need files like GTBIOS and INSTALL.EXE in DOS 1.1 and SPEEDISK.SYS and CONFIG.SYS in DOS 2.0 with the Tecmar PC-Mate Captain. You might want to have the necessary files on several of your working disks, so you are sure the emulated disk drive will always be there when you want it.

Instead of typing C: (or whatever the emulated disk drive designation is) each time you want to work on the emulated disk you can use an AUTOEXEC.BAT file to do that for you. An AUTOEXEC.BAT file does things automatically for you. After DOS reads for the CONFIG.SYS file, it then reads for an AUTOEXEC.BAT file. That's just the way DOS is structured to work. The term AUTOEXEC.BAT stands for *automatic execution of a batch file*. A batch file is nothing more than a series of DOS commands you want the PC to take care of automatically.

More and more programs are now coming with AUTOEXEC.BAT files on them, so that as soon as you turn on your PC you are in the program and ready to work. By setting up your own AUTOEXEC.BAT file, you can have DOS not only switch over to the emulated disk drive for you, but also copy any number of programs you want to use to the emulated disk drive.

Let's say you want to set up your emulated disk drive (the C drive) with Wordstar and you want to go to the C drive automatically when the PC is turned on or rebooted. You can do all of that with the following AUTOEXEC.BAT file (which is set up similarly to the CONFIG.SYS file):

```
Copy a:ws.com c:
```

```
Copy a:wsmsgs.ovr c:
Copy a:wsovly1.ovr c:
Copy a:mailmrge.ovr c:
c:
ws.com
```

To understand all of this you need to remember that DOS first read the CONFIG.SYS file. Because of that, the C drive was constructed before the AUTOEXEC.BAT file was read. When DOS came to the AUTOEXEC.BAT file it executed each command in that file in order, starting at the top. With the C drive already in place in the RAM, DOS proceeded to copy the four Wordstar files over to the C drive. Then, just as you would have done by hand, DOS switched over to the C drive. That done, it then called up Wordstar, in the same way you would by typing `ws.com` from the DOS prompt.

Think about how much time can be saved by having DOS automatically do things for you. The entire process is much, much faster than doing things line by line, because of the speed with which DOS can work, combined with the quickness of the emulated disk drive.

Setting up an AUTOEXEC.BAT file is as simple as setting up the CONFIG.SYS file discussed in the sections above. Here is the procedure for setting up an AUTOEXEC.BAT file using Wordstar:

- From the Opening Menu (or No-File Menu on older versions of Wordstar) press N to open a non-document file.
- Type `AUTOEXEC.BAT` for the name of the file and press the enter key.
- Once the file is opened, type what was listed above for the AUTOEXEC.BAT file.
- Close the file by holding the CONTROL key down and pressing K D .

Your AUTOEXEC.BAT file is now set up. This must be on the same disk as your programs, CONFIG.SYS file, and device driver file. Now, whenever you turn on your PC or reboot the system, you will not only have your emulated disk drive, you will also have your Wordstar program all set up and ready to go.

There are other ways to set up AUTOEXEC.BAT files. Those are outlined in Chapter 12, under section 12.5.

5.6 Tips and Pointers for Working with Emulated Disk Drives

While there is some risk in using an emulated disk drive, you can use it at different levels of risk. This section will explain the options you have, which range from playing it very safe to boldly playing against the odds.

It isn't just loss of electrical power that causes problems with emulated disk drives. You can create your own problems by forgetting to copy files from your emulated disk over to a floppy disk or a fixed disk when you turn the machine off. Or if you hit the ALTERNATE, CONTROL, and DELETE keys to re-boot the system, you may instantly wipe out your emulated disk (and all of the information on it).

The key to working around such problems is to develop good working habits. If you want the benefits of working with a RAM disk drive, you need to be sure that files created there are moved to permanent storage before you stop working. It sounds easy, but you must remember that you have already established habits in working with your PC. Now that you will have an emulated disk drive you must modify your habits each time you turn off your PC.

The safest way to work with an emulated disk drive is to have only your program files there. In other words, if you are using Wordstar you can copy all of your Wordstar program files over to the C drive. Then you will work with your data disk in the B drive (if you have a dual disk drive system). By doing this your file can be easily be saved to disk regularly (using CONTROL K S). If the power is interrupted or goes out, you won't have any problems, other than the loss of a page or two, because you have been regularly storing your working file on the disk.

If you use Wordstar in the emulated disk drive, you should be aware of one of Wordstar's little quirks. Wordstar comes defaulted for the A drive. That means that when you are moving back and forth between disk drives (i.e., changing logged disk drives) Wordstar will always look to the A drive for program files. This creates problems when you change from the C drive to the B drive to work with your data disk (i.e., the disk that has your working files, like letters, reports and documents). The minute you change to the B drive Wordstar—even though it started out on your emulated disk drive C—will try to work off the A drive.

To get around this problem, never leave the C drive, but still pull files from the B drive. You can easily do that by using a B: to preface the name of the file you want to open. When you tap the letter D to open a document file in Wordstar, it then asks for the name of the file. At that point if you want file LTR-10, which is on the B drive, all you need to do is type in B:LTR-10.

From that point on you will still be working in the C drive. Wordstar will then pick up information from the B drive and it will even store the information back on that drive. Using this technique with a fixed disk, you can access data files on the A drive, or any other drive for that matter. Other programs might have quirks like Wordstar; when you find such problems you need to exercise a little ingenuity and creativity.

What has been outlined above is by far the safest way to work with an emulated disk drive. However, with longer data files you still find yourself waiting at many points as the disk drive whirls and clicks away. All of that can be eliminated if your emulated disk drive is large enough to hold program files and data files. Remember, though, that this means more risk, because everything will be in the RAM, which is dependent on electricity.

To use Wordstar again as an example: you have the program files copied over to your C drive with an AUTOEXEC.BAT file. Then you create your working files on the emulated disk drive or copy them over from one of your data disks on another drive. You're going to need at least 200KB of user memory, to do this. If you have a huge amount of user memory (400KB or more) you might want to create two emulated disk drives—one for the program files and one for data files.

You will notice impressive speed when you do all of your work in the emulated disk drive. Commands are almost instantaneous and working this way becomes addictive. Everything is not only much quicker; it all seems effortless.

It is still possible to save your working file to a permanent disk by saving the file and exiting Wordstar (tapping X from the Opening Menu). This will put you at the **C>** prompt. At that point you can use the COPY command to transfer your working file to permanent disk storage. Copying this way is much faster than using the copy command built into Wordstar.

When using an emulated disk drive, it is always best to save your data to disk (permanent disk) on a regular basis. You need to determine what is best for you: but in making your decision, remember that if the power goes out you want to lose as little data as possible. Saving to disk every page or two might seem like an irritation, but it really doesn't take that long (even if you have to exit from Wordstar to do so).

If you so choose you don't ever have to save to a permanent disk until you're finished working on your file. There are many people who do this. However, remember that you work in an emulated disk drive at your own risk, because if the power is interrupted or goes out, EVERYTHING is lost. One way around this is to buy an *uninterruptible power source*. With such a device you have 20 minutes of battery power once the electrical power goes out. The price starts at $300.

Having an extra disk drive is a luxury that allows you to do your work more effectively with less disk swapping. With your word processing program files on the C drive and your data files on the B drive you can use the A drive for the spelling checker program. That means you can do all of your work in the emulated disk drive. When it comes time to proof what you have written, you can use a program like the Word Plus.

The Word Plus's 45,000 word dictionary on your A drive not only allows you to proof what you have written; it also counts the number of words and even tells you how many times you have used each one. While you're working on a file you can also use the Word Plus as a dictionary to find the correct spelling of a word by just typing in an approximate spelling.

You can even combine another program like Punctuation + Style, with your spelling checker on the A drive. Punctuation + Style does what the name implies, looking for problems with writing style and punctuation. It also checks for 700 overused words and phrases. If all of that isn't enough, it also checks for passive verbs.

All of this means that by using an emulated disk drive you can be more effective in what you are doing—with less effort. Once you set things up you won't need to be switching floppy disks around anymore. You will also develop a regular working routine around which you can work with many more programs beyond word processing, which was used as an example here because just about everyone has experience with it.

An emulated disk drive also comes in handy as a buffer area in communications. Its speed can prove quite useful when receiving information over telephone lines. This is explained in detail in Chapter 8.

5.7 The Case for One Floppy Disk Drive Combined with an Emulated Disk Drive

An emulated disk drive gives you another option which offers speed and savings. It is feasible to have your PC running with one floppy disk drive and a large emulated disk drive (at least 360KB). It's not the best way to go and does require getting used to, but there are specific reasons why you might want to consider it.

For the person who really wants to save money, the one floppy combined with a RAM disk is quite attractive—especially if you install your own disk drive and purchase memory chips through a mail order house. Remember that there is a risk here (the emulated disk drive in the RAM disappears when the electrical power is turned off).

By having one floppy (which will be the A drive) you will need to load your working program into the emulated disk drive each time you turn on your PC. Then, once the program is copied over into the RAM, you will put your data disk (the one with your working files, like letters, reports, and documents) in the A drive. It will all work just as if you had two disk drives, but it is a little awkward to get used to. Also, going back and forth between different PCs (those at work and at home) can be problematic when your PC is configured with one floppy disk drive and an emulated disk drive.

However, by having only one floppy, combined with an emulated disk drive, it will probably be feasible for many more people to afford an IBM PC (assuming they buy the memory chips at discount prices). The PC can always be upgraded to two disk drives at some point in the future, too.

This idea of one floppy and one disk created out of RAM becomes an attractive option for someone getting a second PC. It means that now, with the IBM PC portable or even another PC (or PC compatible) in the same household, you can effectively cut your costs, still do the job, and have the luxury of two or more IBM PCs. IBM's portable PC comes with one half-height floppy disk drive and 256KB RAM on the system board, which is expandable to 512KB. Once you expand that memory you are all set to create the emulated disk drive and use it as outlined above.

It is important for you to remember that an emulated disk drive is not permanent. Also, working with one disk drive and an emulated disk drive requires an altogether different routine. Your programs will be on the B drive and you will save information to the A drive, which is exactly the opposite of how you normally work with a two-drive PC. That could result in some confusion, constantly readjusting to using two different setups on the PCs you own. This isn't a major point, but worth mentioning since you will definitely notice differences.

It isn't impossible to make the adjustment to an emulated disk with one floppy disk. If it means the difference between having and not having an IBM PC, the decision seems obvious. If it means that you can afford a second PC, then the decision is also obvious. The emulated disk drive, despite the risks, is a significant option, which will allow more people to benefit from the convenience of the IBM PC.

6

There was a time when the term "fixed disk" sounded so exotic that mere mortals never expected to use such a contraption. Well, things have certainly changed. Most people who own PCs at least have an idea of what a fixed disk is, if not a fair amount of knowledge about such technology.

A fixed disk definitely expands your PC's potential. Using a fixed disk requires some getting used to, in terms of the new fixed disk features of DOS (2.0 and higher versions), but it all makes sense after a while. Of course it will take some effort and practical working experience to really grasp it all.

This chapter should give you an understanding of:

- background and general information on fixed disks
- your options with fixed disks
- what is needed to hook up a fixed disk
- the steps for installing a fixed disk
- tips and pointers in using a fixed disk.

The previous two chapters focused on floppy disk drives and emulated disk drives. You can certainly get by with those two options and never need to graduate to a fixed disk. However, before deciding that you won't ever need a fixed disk, you should have an understanding of what's involved with fixed disks—the good and bad.

The starting point for learning more about fixed disks might be looking more closely at floppy disks. Someone once observed that working with floppy disks is like driving in rush hour traffic—you eventually get where you're going, after a lot of starting and stopping.

Anyone who uses floppy disks knows the routine of putting disks in the A or B drive and then taking them out—over and over again. Swapping disks back and forth, in and out, does wear on the nerves at times. Also, there are those moments when the floppy disk you need with all the important files on it just can't be found. These points—and many more—can be used to build a case for making fixed disks standard equipment for all PCs.

This chapter will be somewhat general because of the variations in fixed disks and the multitude of configurations. With dozens of fixed disks on the market it would be next to impossible to put together an all-purpose, specific guide. However, this chapter will prove a good point of reference. A step by step instruction on fixed disk installation is included, but use this only as a general guide . . . it will be critical for you to read the manual supplied with your fixed disk.

6.1 Background and General Information on Fixed Disks

A fixed disk, also known as a hard disk or Winchester disk, is a mass storage device. The disk is usually made of aluminum or a ceramic material which is coated with a thin film of ferrous material. This Winchester technology was developed by IBM in the late 1960s and is much different than fixed disks prior to then. What set Winchesters apart from previous fixed disks was the air-sealing of the internal working parts from the outside world's dirt and dust.

Fixed disks come in a variety of shapes and sizes, some even fitting into one of the floppy disk drive slots (see section 6.2). Use of the fixed disk has become most popular in business, but now it is used in the home, too.

Fixed disk developments have even led to the removable fixed disks (see section 6.5). The development of fixed disk technology is continuing. There is much work being done on Stretched Surface Recording (SSR), which would make removable fixed disks almost as durable as floppy disks. The remarkable part about SSR is that it would allow recording capacities of up to 100 megabytes on a 5¼ inch surface. It is expected that initially SSR removable fixed disks will offer from 5 to 10 megabytes of storage on each disk—impressive enough, to say the least.

A fixed disk eliminates the need for handling floppy disks. Storage capacity is typically 10 megabytes on a fixed disk. That's roughly the capacity of 27 floppy disks (figuring 360KB per disk). The advantage of fixed disks is that all of your working programs and data files can be permanently stored on the fixed disk. Never again will you have to boot up your system with a program disk in the A drive (except for copy-protected programs).

The convenience of having programs on the fixed disk is just the beginning. A fixed disk functions about 20 times faster than a floppy disk. Storing all of your data files (letters, forms, reports, documents, spreadsheets, data bases and EVERYTHING else) on a fixed disk is also extremely convenient. You will need floppy disks only to make backup copies and to load new programs. However, you can purchase a fixed disk with tape back-up (see Figure 6.1) to avoid making back-up copies on floppy disks.

The price of fixed disks has gradually come down, and they are now considered quite affordable. High prices were originally the major drawback, and now the one remaining negative point about fixed disks is that they are susceptible to crashes. A crash simply means a damaged sector, track, or disk. Sometimes you can recover

Fig. 6.1: Sysgen fixed disk, with tape back-up next to IBM PC

Courtesy of Sysgen Incorporated

from a crash. Other times it requires repair. A fixed disk crash can be caused by software commands, which leave the disk physically unharmed, though the data stored on the fixed disk is lost.

The read/write head of the fixed disk is usually the central point of a crash. That read/write head normally hovers about 15 to 20 millionths of an inch above the surface of the disk. If it moves from that position, you can end up with a crash, and physical damage from the head pounding into the disk surface.

Maybe a crash won't ever happen to you. If it does, though, you'd better have back-up copies of all your files. Most of the time a crash means reformatting the fixed disk—and that means the information stored on the fixed disk is erased.

This discussion about crashes and reformatting wouldn't be complete without a brief mention of a little problem with the DOS 2.0. This will seem like an innocent, small point, but if you overlook it just once you'll regret it. While crashes are not the major concern here, reformatting is. DOS 2.0 allows you to reformat your fixed disk very easily.

If you forget to put the `A:` after the word `format` (assuming you are formatting a floppy disk in the A drive) you will reformat your entire fixed disk. That means everything on your fixed disk will be lost! *This is true for all fixed disks using* DOS 2.0.

To avoid this problem you can rename the FORMAT.COM file (i.e., the file which does the formatting) to DOFORMAT.COM . Create a batch file called FORMAT.BAT that contains:

```
DOFORMAT A:/S/V
```

That will format the disk in the A drive, with the DOS system (i.e., /S) and a volume label (i.e., V), and should eliminate the problem. If you ever want to format differently, you can just type this:

```
DOFORMAT+<parameters>
```

The statement `<parameters>` would be where you change the `/S/V` to something else.

All things considered, a fixed disk is an important option for your PC—if you need one. The following points highlight the reasons for getting a fixed disk.

Storing large amounts of data If you have a lot of floppy disks all over your desk and in disk trays, you are probably a likely candidate for a fixed disk. Most businesses have enough paper flow to consider getting a fixed disk at the start. Home uses of PCs are turning more and more to fixed disks, too. If you have a large number of files for general correspondence, forms, reports, documents, articles, and a book or two, a fixed disk helps you better organize your data.

For anyone using a large data base program or spreadsheet programs, a fixed disk is a dream, because there is never a worry about floppy disk storage limitations. With the subdirectories of DOS 2.0 (see section 6.6) you can easily put your data files into separate areas for quick retrieval.

One other point to consider about fixed disks is that new software is being written specifically to take advantage of fixed disks. This trend is expected to continue.

Convenience Even for those who don't have large amounts of data files to keep track of, a fixed disk means organization and convenience. If everything is on your fixed disk, you can't misplace disks. Also, you won't need to shuffle floppy disks in and out of the disk drives too often. The elimination of the need to constantly handle floppy disks has probably been the strongest selling point for fixed disks—no matter what your PC workload is.

Networking Means you can link two or more PCs together. For this a fixed disk is recommended. Chapter 8 covers communications as well as networking in detail. Several companies offer networking capabilities with their fixed disks. The significant point here is that with those options, and especially now with IBM's cluster program (basically a very, very primitive networking package), you can link several PCjrs to one IBM PC with a fixed disk. You can also link several PCs together, but the PCjr presents an option with considerable cost savings—as do PC terminals and PC compatibles.

In such a network the PCs or PCjrs linked to the fixed disk really won't need disk drives. Since they work off the fixed disk, the programs and data files are all stored to and accessed from that fixed disk.

Remember that you must review your specific needs and, of course, the costs involved. "Don't get caught up in the I really need a fixed disk" syndrome. Be sure that you have a valid need for a fixed disk. Floppy disks, though they might be inconvenient and slow, still get the job done. They can be filed in an orderly manner and can hold up to 360KB (formatted under DOS 2.0).

6.2 Internal Versus External Fixed Disks

It was more than a year before IBM introduced a fixed disk for the PC. In March of 1983, IBM released the 10 megabyte XT version of the PC. Up to that point companies like Davong, Corvus, Tecmar, and Genie provided fixed disks for the PC. DOS 1.1 was not the best operating system for managing fixed disks, but through software modifications PC owners were able to use them.

Most fixed disks for the PC have been external—housed in a unit separate from the PC. However, there have been fixed disks, known as add-ins which could be installed in place of the B drive. Since the regular PC wasn't built to handle the extra power strain, those add-in fixed disks required an additional power supply and fan. The work involved for the complete installation wasn't minor either.

There hasn't been much discussion on the merits of external versus internal fixed disks. It is really a matter of preference. If you buy a PC/XT you get a fixed disk within the unit. If you buy an external fixed disk you will have one more piece of computer equipment to arrange on your desk. Should you choose to have an add in fixed disk you will be faced with removing the B drive, unless you purchase a one-drive or no-drive PC (i.e., one without disk drives), and then install the fixed disk.

The Add-In Fixed Disk: Maynard Electronics has simplified things quite a bit for anyone who wants to install a fixed disk in place of the B drive. With Maynard's low power 10 megabyte fixed disk, combined with half-height disk drives (see Chapter 4, section 4.7), you can come pretty close to having a PC/XT. See Figure 6.2.

Fig. 6.2: Maynard Electronic's add-in fixed disk

Courtesy of Maynard Electronics

You can easily install two floppy disk drives and a fixed disk in any PC without modifying the power supply, by using low power-consuming half-height floppy disk drives like the ones manufactured by TEAC. Those two floppy disk drives go into the left slot where the A drive normally goes. Then, in place of the B drive (the one on the right), you put a low power-consuming fixed disk. Maynard Electronics' 10 megabyte fixed disk, called the MicroScience 2, works very well within the PC environment and puts no real drain on the PC's power supply either.

Maynard Electronics will provide you with everything you need to install two half-height floppies and the fixed disk. The complete package even comes with a Sandstar Disk Drive Controller (see Figure 6.3) and a "Fixed Disk BIOS Module" which modifies the ROM of your PC. That modification to the ROM (Read Only Memory) is what allows your PC to function properly with the fixed disk. Many fixed disks require that you modify your DOS disk—sometimes to the point of making it do weird things when certain programs are run.

The Sandstar Disk Drive Controller adapter card manages the floppy disk drives and the fixed disk. Best of all, everything is internal. There are no extra boxes like a fixed disk, extra power supply, or anything else to clutter up your desk. This comes pretty close to giving you the approximation of an IBM PC/XT, only you did it yourself, with impressive cost savings!

Installation of the complete setup requires nothing more than a screwdriver and the instructions supplied by Maynard Electronics. The cost is a pleasant surprise, too. The fixed disk costs approximately $1,000. The prices for the disk drives are as impressively reasonable—as much as 60 percent off the retail price. The Sandstar Disk Drive Controller adapter card (at about $180) makes the package price worth considering if it meets your needs.

Fig. 6.3: Maynard's Sandstar Disk Drive Controller card

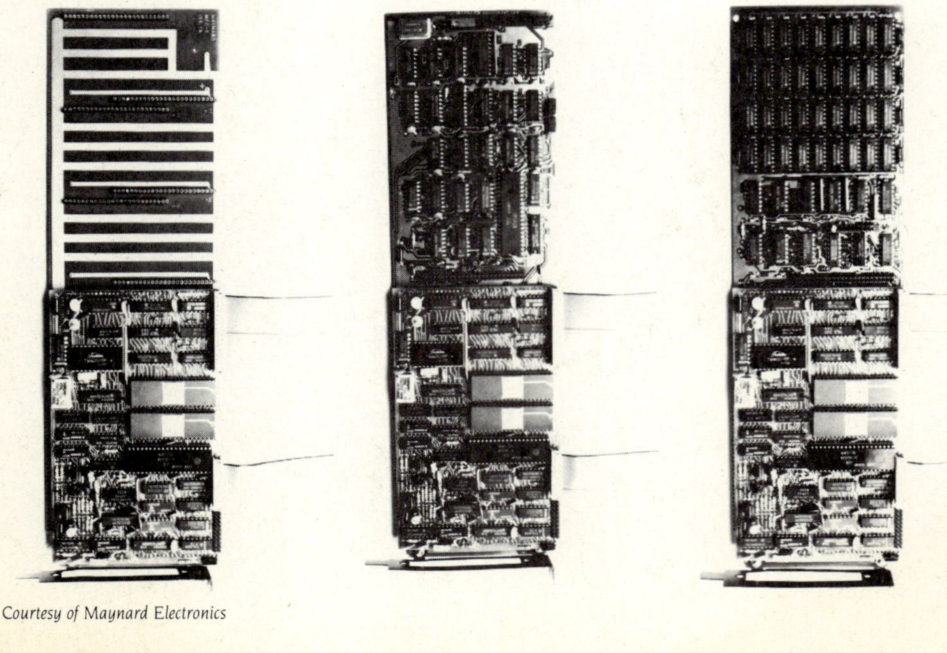

Courtesy of Maynard Electronics

The Expansion Unit A unit such as this provides you the opportunity to not only get a fixed disk but to obtain several expansion slots in the bargain. Turn to Chapter 2, sections 2.8 and 2.9, for a detailed discussion of the expansion unit.

An expansion unit is separate from your PC and sometimes almost as big as the PC itself. That means more room taken up on your desk. However, it is well worth re-arranging your work area to get a fixed disk (even beyond 10 megabytes) and up to eight extra expansion slots.

External Fixed Disks In all of the talk about external versus internal fixed disks, it is easy to forget that PC owners just want to hook up a fixed disk with the least amount of hassle or bother. External fixed disks like the Sysgen fixed disk in Figure 6.1 are the answer. With a minimum amount of work (see section 6.4), you can leave your PC as it is and hook up a fixed disk. Your two floppy disk drives will remain exactly as they are. All that you will need to do is install a fixed disk interface adapter card in one of your PC's expansion slots. After that all you need to do is connect your PC to the fixed disk with the cable that comes with your fixed disk.

6.3 What Is Needed To Hook Up a Fixed Disk?

You really won't need very much to hook up a fixed disk. However, before you purchase your fixed disk you should take a close look at the documentation for the fixed disk you plan to buy. Review the instructions for the installation procedures. Are they clearly written? Do you understand them? Can the salesperson explain and clarify the points you don't understand? Remember that the better written the installation manual, the less heartache and headache you will experience when it comes time to hook up your fixed disk.

Review the fixed disk's power requirements. If it is an add-in fixed disk, will you need an additional power supply and an extra fan? Even if it is an external unit, you need to check into the power requirements.

The software is an important consideration. How much do you have to modify DOS to get this fixed disk to work? Is the documentation for the software understandable? Remember that this software is what will make your fixed disk work with your PC and, of course, with DOS.

Check with people who are already using the fixed disk you want to buy, ask the store for references, or check with a PC user group. It is important to get an accurate, true representation of the product. A testimonial means you should seriously consider buying the fixed disk. Complaints mean you should at least look into other products.

While there are many variations, with most fixed disks you will need:

- 1 small flat head screwdriver
- 1 medium flat head screwdriver
- 1 fixed disk unit
- 1 fixed disk controller (interface adapter card)
- 1 connector cable (between fixed disk and PC)
- 1 software utility disk (for controlling the fixed disk functions)

6.4 General Steps for Installing a Fixed Disk

This section does not distinguish between add-on (external) or add-in (internal) fixed disks. Instead it shows you the basic procedures for installing the adapter card, hooking up the fixed disk, and working with the fixed disk software.

The details, especially for installing an internal fixed disk in the B drive, will be found in the installation manual which accompanies the fixed disk. An internal fixed disk installed in a regular PC might require an extra power supply and fan. You should check into all of that before buying the fixed disk.

To install an external fixed disk in your PC system:

STEP ONE: Read the manual and all instructions which came with your fixed disk. Before doing anything you need to be totally familiar with every aspect of the particular fixed disk you will be installing in your PC system. While the steps in this book will provide a guide for you to follow, *you must thoroughly understand the specifics for the fixed disk you have purchased.*

STEP TWO: Turn off your PC and remove the cover. (See Appendix C.) Be absolutely sure you have unplugged all connections to your PC, including the electrical power cord.

STEP THREE: Place all of the items you will be installing and using (don't forget about the screwdrivers) within easy reach on your work area. You should have the installation manual right in front of you for reference. Remember that it is extremely important for you already to have read the manual to be familiar with the specific installation procedures for your fixed disk.

STEP FOUR: Place the fixed disk interface adapter card in an open expansion slot—preferably the slot closest to the disk drives. This procedure is covered in Chapter 2, section 2.6. When you have completed the installation of the adapter card, there will be a fixed disk cable connection point either at the back panel of the PC, or, for an internal fixed disk, on a ribbon cable. If the drive is internal, install it according to its manual now. Then go to STEP SIX before putting the cover back on the PC.

STEP FIVE: You may now put the cover back on the PC. Hook up everything else to the PC.

STEP SIX: Using the fixed disk connector cable, connect the fixed disk to the PC. Here the small screwdriver will come in handy. You now are ready to begin using your fixed disk.

STEP SEVEN: Plug in both the PC and the fixed disk to the AC power outlet. Once you have done that, turn on both the PC and the fixed disk. Be sure that your DOS disk is in the A drive of your PC. *It's important to note that some manufacturers recommend not turning both off at once or using a multi-outlet strip.*

STEP EIGHT: At this point you are ready to go through the software installation routine. Before you do anything else, make a copy of the software utility diskette which came with your fixed disk. Put the original disk away for safe keeping. You will now format and configure your fixed disk. The fixed disk's software utility disk will have a program to walk you through the necessary steps.

The entire process usually doesn't take long, and there are procedures for checking that you have to do to be sure everything is being done properly. Once installed, the fixed disk will be the C drive (this might be another letter on different makes of fixed disks) and can easily be accessed by typing `C:` at the `A>` prompt.

If you have any problems or something goes wrong, you should first check all of your work. You will usually find where you overlooked something or misinterpreted a step. However, if you find that you have done everything correctly, then you have a problem somewhere within the fixed disk setup. Ask the store where you purchased the fixed disk package to resolve the problem.

6.5 Removable Fixed Disks

A removable fixed disk does exactly what a fixed disk does. It looks very much like the back-up tape for fixed disks. See Figure 6.4. The fixed disk is still sealed in an air tight container, only it pulls out for convenient transportability, so you could send it to another department in the company or across the country to another firm.

Fig. 6.4: Genie fixed disk with removable fixed disk

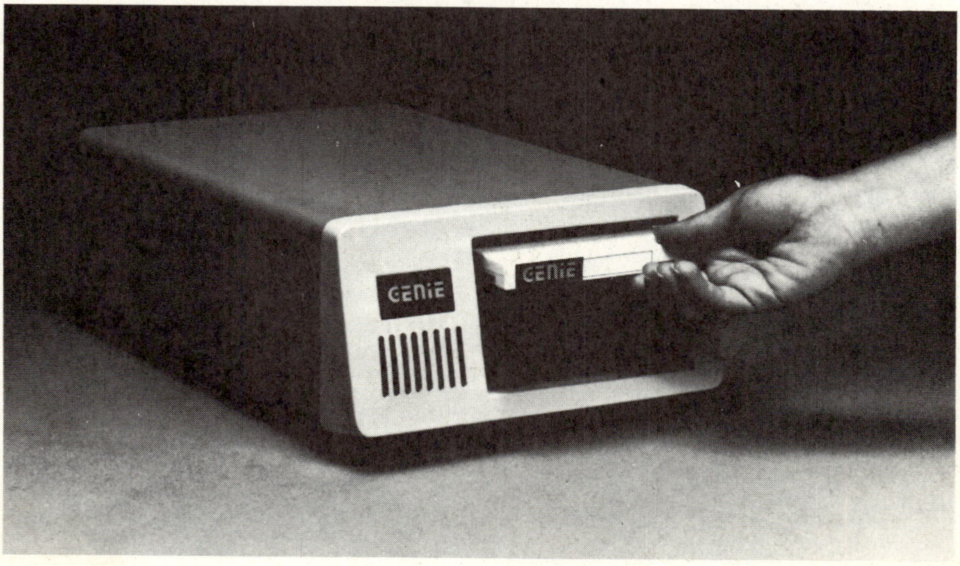

Courtesy of Genie Computer Corporation

The internal working mechanism of a removable fixed disk is modified to handle fixed disk cartridges which can be inserted and removed. The sturdiness of the cartridge tends to make them even safer than floppy disks for carrying or mailing.

Removable fixed disks, like the one made by Genie Computer Corporation, come in separate units which sit next to your PC once they have been connected. Tecmar makes a removable fixed disk designed to fit right into the B drive of the PC. The Genie removable fixed disk doesn't take any time to install—other than putting the adapter card in one of the expansion slots.

The Tecmar removable fixed disk, because it replaces the B disk drive, takes more time. These two removable disks also show the differences in the amount of storage space available—the Genie disk (with a maximum of 5 megabytes) holds about three times as much as the Tecmar.

Despite the advantages of removable fixed disks, the regular fixed disks are still less expensive. Prices are expected to get lower and more competitive over a period of time, as everything else has in the computer industry. Also, the fact that non-removable fixed disks can hold such large amounts of data—50 megabytes and beyond—will keep them important as tools in business and industrial computing. Critics of removable fixed disks also claim regular fixed disks are more reliable.

6.6 Tips on Using Fixed Disks

It's most important when working with a fixed disk that you *religiously make back-up copies of your files*. Back-up copies can be made to floppy disk or tape—if the fixed disk is set up for that. See Figure 6.5. In large businesses, back-up copies are even made from fixed disk to fixed disk.

While it is easy to get in the habit of not making back-up copies (especially when nothing bad ever happens), it is very wise to have at least one extra copy of each file on the fixed disk. It only takes one mistake, like reformatting your fixed disk by accident (which can easily happen with DOS 2.0), and you have lost everything. Even though most people learn the hard way about making back-up copies (i.e., they lose a file or two), you should develop a regular routine of backing up your files.

Before you can back up files you need to create them. With older versions of DOS that wasn't too difficult. However, now that DOS supports fixed disks which keep large amounts of information and a nearly unlimited number of files, things are a little more complex. DOS 2.0 works in what is called a *tree structure*.

Through that tree structure you can create sub-directories in which you can separate word processing files from all of the bookkeeping records. Sub-directories allow the user to see and use only those files of immediate concern, rather than to have all files displayed on a single directory. Different employees can keep their own data files in sub-directories and always get to them with path commands. A path is the route you will use to work your way from one sub-directory to another.

It would take pages to explain the tree structure of DOS, but one way to learn more about using DOS is through a tutorial program. Not only are tutorials great ways to learn how to use the popular programs on the market, they also explain the ins and outs of DOS—especially DOS 2.0. Companies like CDEX and ATI have

Fig. 6.5: Sysgen Image fixed disk, with tape back-up displayed

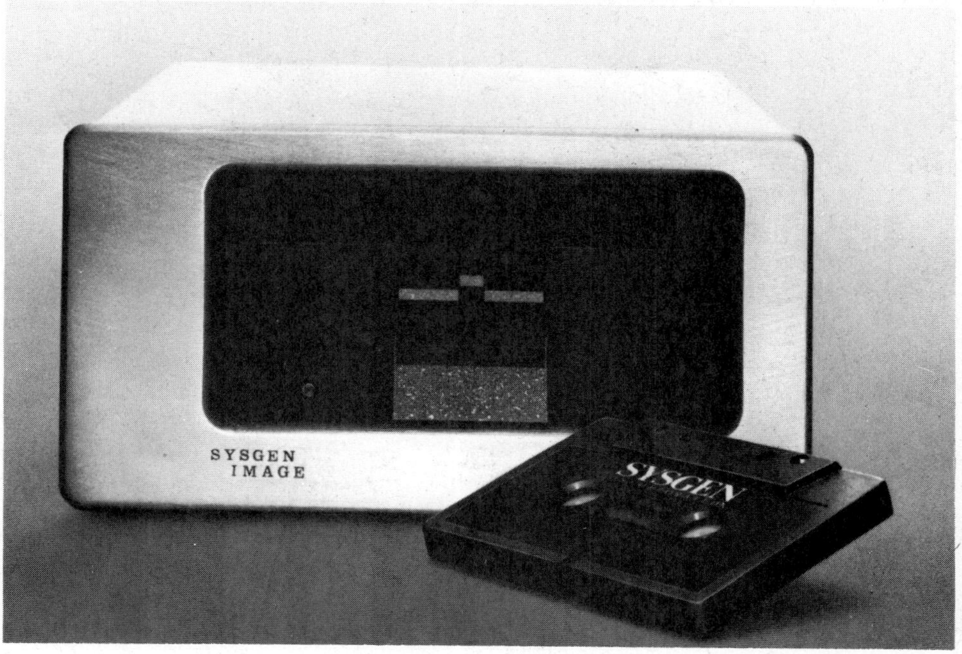

Courtesy of Sysgen Incorporated

programs which make it much easier to learn the complexities of DOS. And tutorial programs let you work at your own pace.

If tree structures, sub-directories, and paths are too much for you to handle, there are other ways to use DOS within a fixed disk and still be able to keep track of information easily. Since a fixed disk can hold millions of bytes of data (i.e., letters, numbers, spaces, carriage returns, and so on) you can quickly have trouble finding specific files.

One simple way to create your own sub-directories is to use coding symbols in front of file names. Anyone who has gone through the DOS manual knows that the following symbols can be used in file names:

```
! @ # $ % ^ & ( )_ - { } ' `~
```

In Chapter 12, section 12.4, these symbols are reviewed as a way of sorting different kinds of files. For example, you could assign one symbol to word processing and one to bookkeeping. Individual users could also have their own symbols. Here's how the symbols would look with the file names:

```
^refltr
$budget.84
```

The symbols can be used in any part of the file name and even more than once, so you could have a file read `^ltr-#12`. This isn't the world's most sophisticated system of keeping track of files, but it does get the job done in a simple and effective way.

Once you begin using such symbols you can always list your specific files by typing the following command:

```
DIR ^*.*
```

That will list all the files under that symbol and no others, keeping the directory screen fairly uncluttered. Using the `DIR/w` command you can have the files listed out all the way across the screen. For listing files that way you would type `DIR ^*.*/w`.

You might find that the tree structure of DOS is no problem at all to master. Maybe you'll develop your own unique system for working within a fixed disk or modify the one presented here. And some people will just load up the fixed disk like they would a floppy disk and somehow manage to sort things out. Once again we come to the point that whatever works for you is what you should use.

One way to get a good in-depth understanding of DOS and how it works is Peter Norton's book, MS-DOS *and* PC-DOS *User's Guide* (Robert J. Brady Company, 1984). This book is written in readable, understandable language, with illustrations that not only make specific points about working with computers and operating systems, but make you laugh aloud.

7

One of the nicest things about working with computers is that you do everything on the screen. You don't print something until you want a draft or final copy. When it does come to the point of putting it all down on paper you will need either a printer or a plotter.

Everyone knows that a printer is much like a typewriter and that you have certain options when it comes to choosing a printer. Those options are outlined in this chapter, along with the step by step details of hooking up whichever kind of printer you do buy. Or, if you have more than one printer, this chapter will show you how to handle that, too.

Plotters are specifically for graphics printing and probably not something most PC owners will rush out to buy. But if you do get a plotter this chapter shows you how to install it.

7.1 Printer Options

Before we take a look at your options with printers, we will briefly review the different types of printers available.

Dot Matrix Printer This type of printer produces letters, numbers and characters (including graphics) on paper, using a series of pins in a matrix pattern which strike the page through a ribbon at high speed. Dot matrix printers can print graphics (including pictures) quite well, with the proper programming or software. Figure 7.1 shows the popular Epson Printer's matrix patterns for the alphabet. Though it has been considered by many to be a secondary or draft quality printer, the dot matrix printer today has become commonplace and accepted. In fact, many people use dot matrix printers because they want their clients and customers to know a computer is being used.

Letter Quality Printer This printer produces a fully formed character much like that of a typewriter. In business, the letter quality printer is usually preferred because of the

Fig. 7.1: Character fonts from a dot matrix printer—the alphabet

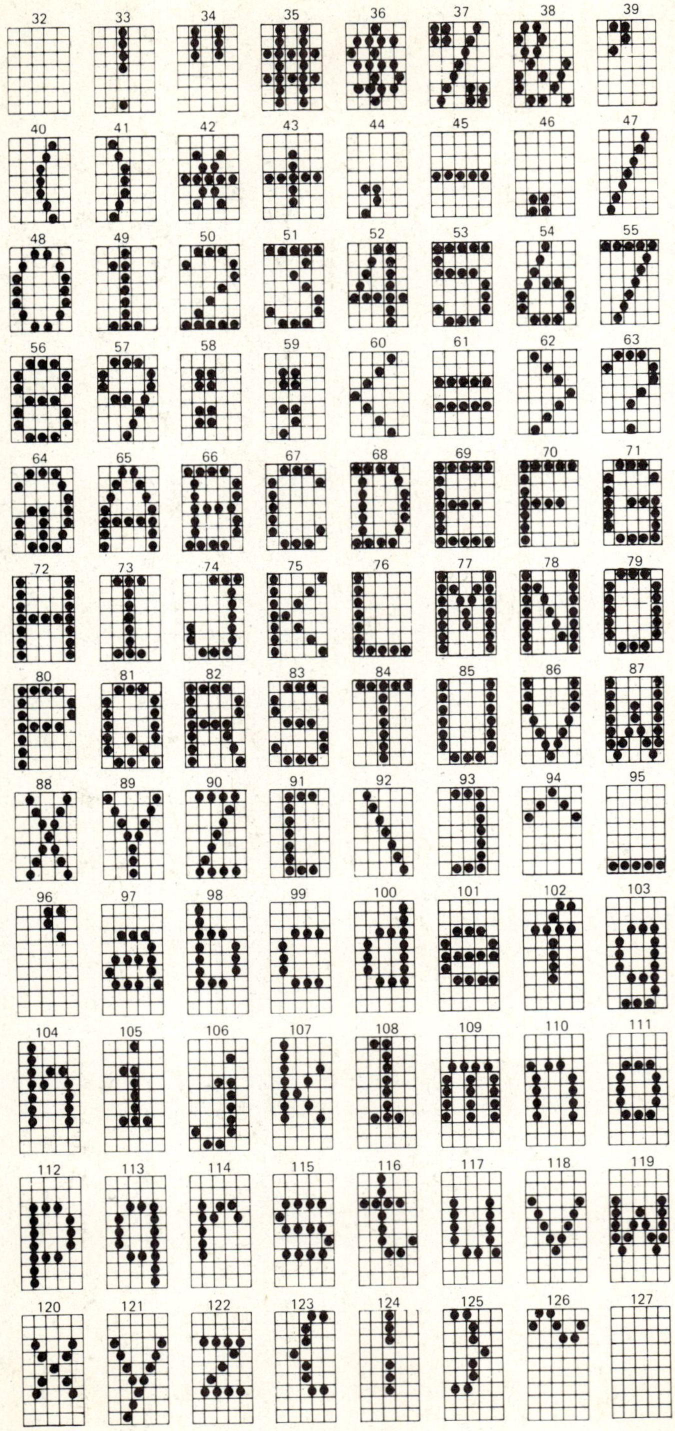

Fig. 7.2: Diablo 630 ECS printer

Courtesy of Diablo Systems Incorporated

professional look of documents. Figure 7.2 shows a Diablo letter quality printer. This printer works on the daisy wheel concept (see Figure 7.3).

All of the letters, numbers, characters, and symbols are located on the spokes of a plastic or metal wheel which spins vertically as characters strike the page. Other letter quality printers function through the use of thimble shaped print elements, which spin horizontally as they strike the page (see Figure 7.4).

Two In One Printer Texas Instruments, as well as other companies, has combined letter quality printing with dot matrix printing, using a more tightly packed matrix pattern. In other words, for dot matrix printing, it uses a 9 × 9 matrix (instead of the usual 6 × 9 matrix); for letter quality printing, it uses a 32 × 18 matrix pattern, combined with printing the same line twice. See Figure 7.5.

Use this technique in the TI 855 makes the quality of the letters, numbers, and symbols so close to that of a typewriter's fully formed characters that, even with a magnifying glass, it's hard to tell the printing was done with matrix technology. This technology also improves the graphics printing capabilities.

Texas Instruments has combined one other advanced feature, called font modules, in this printer. If you want to change the type style you just change font modules. The font modules offer a variety of type faces, and they simply plug into the front of the printer (see Figure 7.6).

Ink Jet Printer This type of printer has been primarily a sophisticated design experiment until recently, when the technology was perfected. Ink jet printers are commercially available right now and the prices are competitive. Many industry analysts view

Fig. 7.3: Daisy wheel print element for Diablo printer

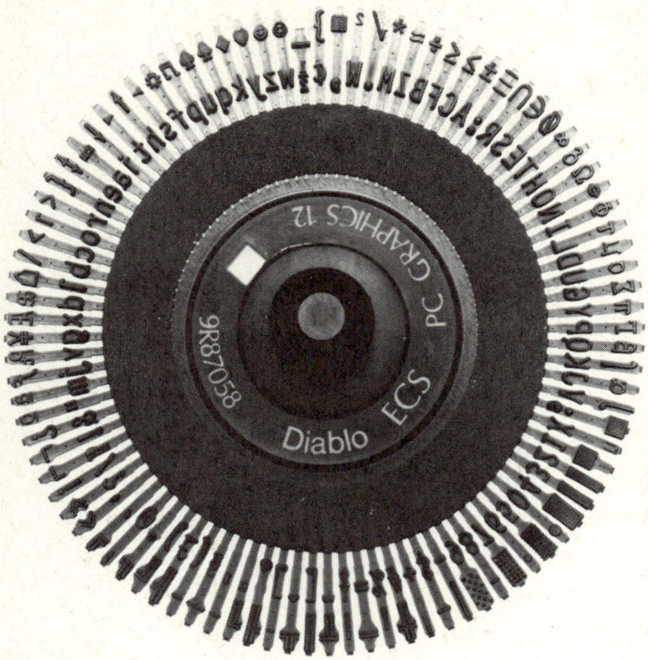

Courtesy of Diablo Systems Incorporated

Fig. 7.4: Thimble printer wheel for NEC printer

Courtesy of NEC Information Systems, Inc.

Fig. 7.5: Print sample from a letter done by TI 855

WHY IT MAKES GOOD SENSE TO USE DICTATION EQUIPMENT

Paperwork--written communications, documentation...just about everything that gets put on paper--is the lifeline of every business organization. No matter how hard we try to avoid the issue, our business world still revolves around paperwork.

Every executive **must** communicate. However, not all communications can remain verbal. Many must be transferred into hard copy form for a good reason.

Hard copy is the most convenient vehicle for the dissemination of information. It serves as a basis for follow-up...a clear statement of objectives...and acceptable evidence in many legal matters. Let's face it, written communications and documehtation will continue indefinitely!

One of the most difficult tasks, though, is originating a communication. Have you ever sat at a desk, pen and pencil in hand, and attempted to write fast enough to capture the brilliant ideas going on inside your head? Those who have quickly realize that the brain works so much faster than the hand...in the neighborhood of 20 times faster. The mind thinks at about three hundred words per minute and a person writes at a rate of only about 15 words per minute.

Obviously then, longhand is a major block to effective communication. Too many ideas are lost because your hand can't keep up with your brain.

Punctuation Can Inhibit Your Thoughts

Aside from spelling, we are also conditioned by your instructors to feel guilty if we don't punctuate properly. Do you have to stop and think about the difference between a colon and a semicolon, or whether an exclamation point goes inside or outside quotation marks?

That, of course, becomes another block to your communications capabilities. And quite frankly, it also has nothing to do with actual communication skills. Punctuation is merely a technical skill that can be applied by any reasonably intelligent secretary during the transcription process. So, another great advantage of using a dictation machine is that you **don't have to concern yourself with punctuation**.

Courtesy of Texas Instruments Incorporated

Fig. 7.6: TI 855 Printer, showing font modules on the front

Courtesy of Texas Instruments Incorporated

these printers as up and comers. Several companies currently offer ink jet printers at a price range from under $500 to well beyond $10,000 (which includes color options).

An ink jet printer sprays the ink on a page. It is fast and quiet as it zips across the page spreading the ink (which can easily be in colors) in the form of letters, numbers and symbols. Graphics take a whole new dimension with an ink jet printer because of limitless variety in tones and shades of colors.

The technology behind an ink jet printer is actually quite simple, creating characters similarly to the way dot matrix printers do.

The ink flows out of a cartridge just behind the print head, through a channel, into nine jet channels that are closed off by nozzles. From there everything is controlled by pulses of voltage which create pressure for ejecting ink out toward the paper. The nine nozzles are arranged in the same order as the print head of a dot matrix printer. It is from the patterns created by those nozzles that everything is created on the page—from letters and numbers to impressive graphics.

Not to be overlooked is the ink jet printer's *quiet*. The mechanical pounding on the page of typewriters, letter quality printers, and dentist drill-sounding dot matrix printers are all eliminated with the ink jet printers. One drawback here is that ink jet printers cannot use multi-part forms. Since there is no impact the printing won't go through carbons. Ink jet printers, like most modern printers, can be hooked up to a PC with either a parallel or serial connection.

If you take the technology of ink jet printers one step further, as is already being done, you can have outstanding color graphics. Using the combination of three basic colors (yellow, magenta, and cyan) a printer like Printacolor Corporation's TC1040 (see Figure 7.8) can produce a graphic image in up to 4913 different shades.

Fig. 7.7: Siemens PT 88 Print Head diagram, showing how the ink jet system works

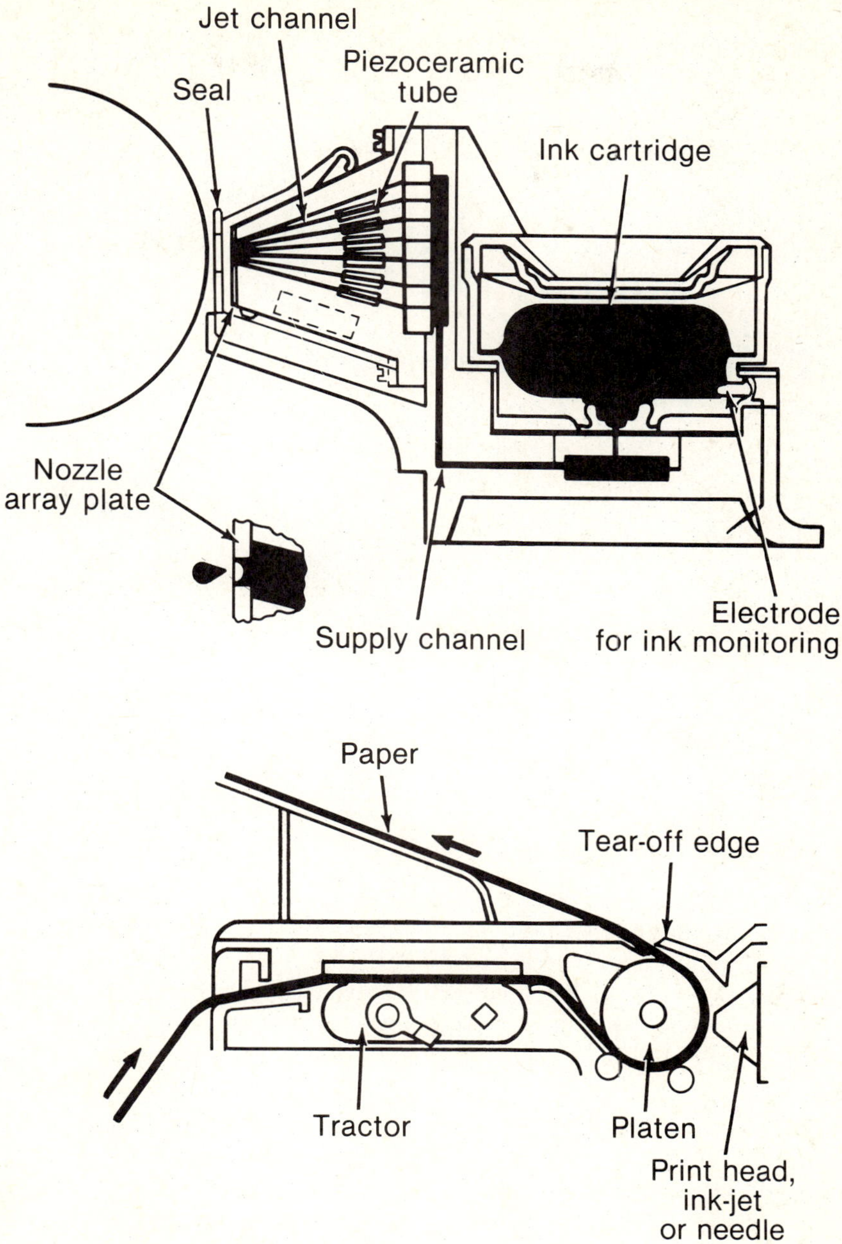

Courtesy of Siemens Communications Systems, Inc.

Full Page Printing Through laser printers and copier printers full page printing is now possible. Companies are already marketing such products. As technology develops, this type of printing will become more popular. Large corporations are currently using full page printers which can print from 100 to 200 pages per minute. The price is impressive—up in the hundreds of thousands of dollars.

Fig. 7.8: Printacolor Corporation's TC1040 color ink jet printer, with some of the graphics it prints

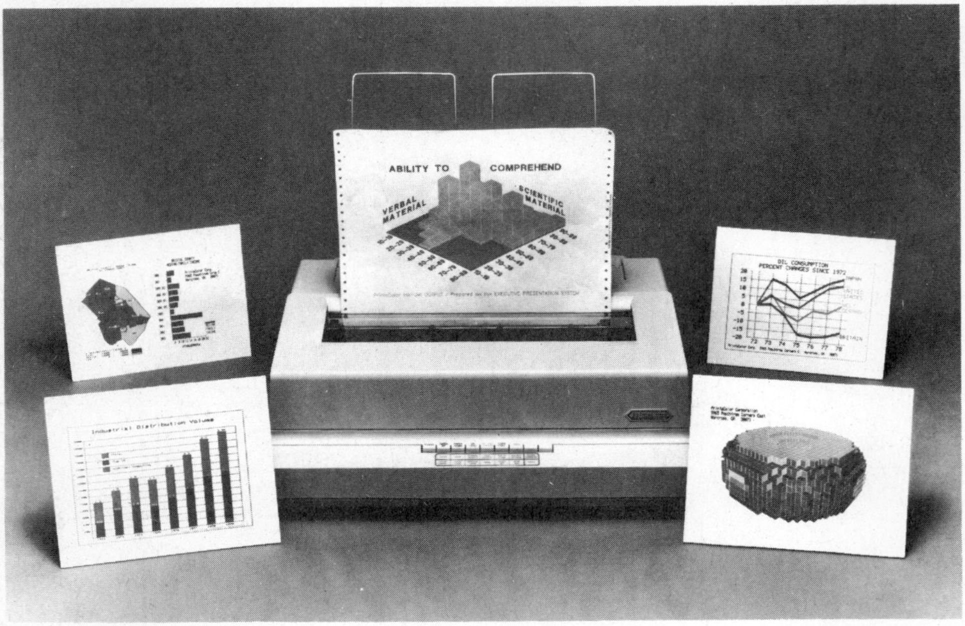

Courtesy of Printacolor Corporation

Laser printers work in the same way as dot matrix printers, only the matrix pattern is packed together, so whatever ends up on the page is letter quality. Graphics as well are extremely clear and sharp with laser printers. The companies manufacturing copy machines have recently developed, and are now marketing, more reasonably priced laser printers.

Typewriters This might be an option you want to look into. There are several limitations, but you can turn a typewriter, like an IBM Selectric, into a printer for your PC. Section 7.4 explains how to do this.

For quite some time now the discussion on which printer to buy has focused on dot matrix printers and letter quality printers. The dot matrix printers have been the most popular, primarily because of lower prices and graphics capabilities. However, the prices of letter quality printers have decreased significantly, providing a real challenge to the supremacy of the dot matrix printers. Recent developments in dot matrix printers have led to print quality close to letter quality. This chapter will discuss installing and using printers (dot matrix or letter quality), and take a look at what is coming in the new technology.

Ink jet printers will be hooked up to the IBM PC in pretty much the same way as the dot matrix and letter quality printers, so even if you have an ink jet printer, much of this chapter will apply.

This chapter will also cover other aspects of printing, like installing re-inked ribbons in both letter quality and dot matrix printers to save money. You'll get a little bit of ink on your fingers when you re-fill a dot matrix ribbon cartridge, but to save close to 75 percent of the retail price "What's a little ink going to hurt?"

It is important to remember that the thing most likely to go wrong with your PC setup is the printer. Printers are becoming more and more reliable, but they are still mostly mechanical (especially the letter quality printers). Mechanical parts do break or wear out in time. This points to the importance of buying a quality printer, so check around with friends and business associates to see what they are using. Most important of all, ask them what the maintenance and reliability have been like on their printers.

Many PC owners get service contracts on their printers. You need to look at the costs involved, because many times a lot of the items you're getting a service contract on are covered under the warranty. Find out how long the guarantee is on the printer you're considering. More than likely there will be a problem or two—at some point in your computing experience—with a printer.

You also need to deal with the noise. A printer is not very quiet. Many people take their PCs home or into the office without much thought of the noise that the printer will be producing. For whatever reason, this is something that tends to get handled after everything is already set up; and that, many times, means moving and reorganizing things. Your options range from putting the printer out of the way (if you can) to getting a sound cover, also referred to as an acoustical enclosure (see Chapter 11, section 11.6).

Save yourself a lot of trouble, heartache, and frustration by considering the noise problem before you set up your PC system. The sound covers do deaden a lot of the printing noise, but not all of it. Many people work out schedules for printing, which creates harmony for everyone involved—both in the office and at home.

Once you have a printer you will, obviously, be running paper through it. You need to consider how you will be doing that. This is something else many PC owners usually don't think about until they discover the implications. There are basically two ways to run paper through your printer. One is sheet by sheet, much the way you put one piece of paper at a time in a typewriter. This can quickly get to be a very boring task if you print many long documents.

Your other option, which is now fairly common, is to set your printer up with a tractor feed mechanism (see Figure 7.9) to handle continuous feed paper—the paper with the holes along both sides. Such paper comes fan-folded in quantities of 1,000 to 5,000 sheets. You can even get bond paper that has been laser perforated to tear apart cleanly and which looks much like regular bond paper. No one would ever know it was continuous feed paper from a computer. You can also get many types of forms—even custom designed forms—on continuous feed paper.

Continuous feed paper does cost more than single sheets, but when you consider the amount of time saved, it really is a bargain. The nicest part of all is that while a long document is printing, you can do something else. The continuous feed paper unfolds as it goes into the printer and then folds back up again as it comes out. When the document is printed all you need to do is remove the tractor feed edges and separate the pages.

Some dot matrix printers come with both friction and pin feed options built in. However, letter quality printers usually don't. You need to specify your needs when you purchase the printer. Then you receive exactly what you ordered. If you decide you want a pin feed (tractor feed) on the day you set up your PC, you might wait a while for it. Because the tractor feed mechanisms for the letter quality printers are

Fig. 7.9: Tractor feed mechanism for the Diablo printer

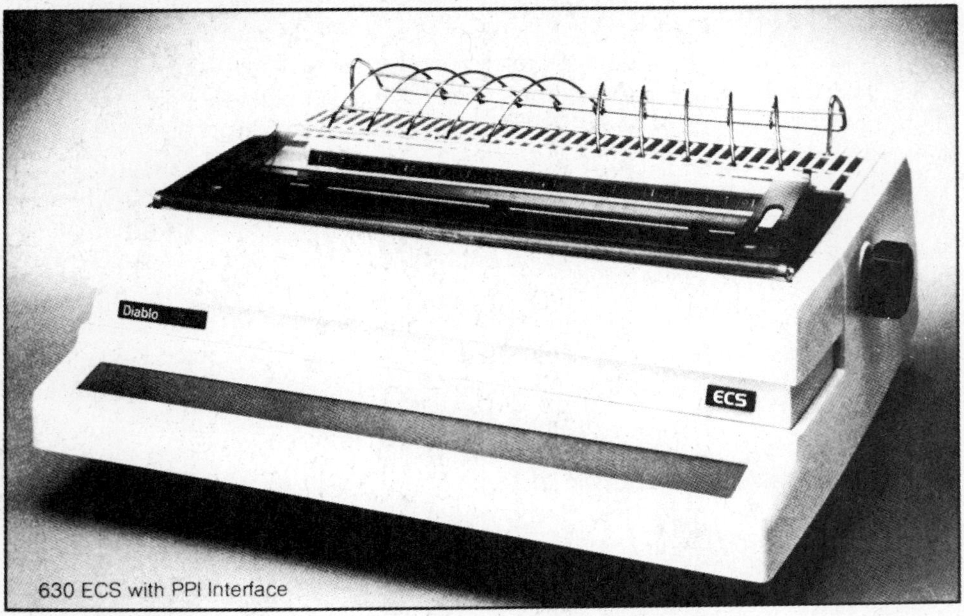

Courtesy of Diablo Systems Incorporated

much more complex than they are for the dot matrix printers, they are still considered a specialty item, which needs to be ordered specifically when you order the printer.

A tractor feed mechanism for a letter quality printer can easily cost more than $200. If you want to get fancy, you can get a single sheet feeder (see Figure 7.10), which not only feeds in your letter head but also the second page of your stationery. Be prepared to pay much, much more for such devices.

Two other options to consider are doing without a printer at all, or sharing one. This isn't as strange as it sounds, but does apply more to PCs in the home than in the office. Because most of what you do with your PC is on the screen, you can get by without owning a printer. Computer stores and print/copy shops are beginning to provide printer services. You just bring in your floppy disks and print out your documents on their printers, paying for time usage and paper.

If you have one or more PCs and printers at the office, you might consider working out a printing arrangement with your employer—thereby eliminating your need for a printer. And groups of PC owners have gone in together to purchase a printer and then shared it.

There are a few drawbacks with this no printer option, like not being able to print out a document, especially a letter, when you need it. Also, there are many times when you spot mistakes after something has been printed. That can cause delays and return trips.

7.2 Hooking Up Your Printer

Hooking up a printer is the easy part—getting it to work with your software (interface) is another story. The problem stems from trying to create software that works with

Fig. 7.10: Single sheet paper feeder for Diablo printer

Courtesy of Diablo Systems Incorporated

just about any kind of printer. Things are getting better, however. There was a time when it would take hours and hours of work, not to mention trying several cable configurations, to get a printer to work properly. This was even true with popular programs like Wordstar and many others. MicroPro pretty much solved this problem with Wordstar by making provisions for just about every printer on the market.

You will be connecting a printer to your PC by either a serial or parallel connection. The serial connection (known by the RS-232 connector you use to attach its cable to the PC) means bits are transmitted one at a time. Through the parallel connection 8 bits (1 byte) are transmitted at once.

Your only concern with parallel versus serial connections is having the proper adapter card in your PC and having the right cable to connect the printer to your PC. If you have the IBM monochrome adapter card on your PC (for the IBM green screen), then you have the parallel connection already built in. However, for a serial printer you will need an adapter card with a serial port (i.e., connection) on it. A serial port is standard on the PC/XT.

Most multifunction adapter cards have serial ports on them. If you don't have a serial port, you'll need to either get one or buy a printer with a parallel interface. Most letter quality printers have serial interfaces. However, some letter quality printers, like the Diablo 630 API, come set up for parallel interface.

The easiest way to purchase a printer and be sure you can connect it to your PC is to *make sure it all works before you leave the computer store.* If you're buying your printer through the mail, check first to see what other people have gotten and how their printers perform.

You want to be absolutely sure that the printer you are considering works with the software you have or want to use Don't be afraid to take your time on this, because printers can be expensive items. You certainly don't want to end up with a printer collecting dust week after week while you attempt to get everything worked out for a connection that works.

To hook up a printer you need:

- 1 small, flat head screwdriver
- 1 Printer
- 1 Printer Cable

STEP ONE: Read printer manual completely—especially the section on installation. Be sure that your PC has the proper port for connecting your printer. If you have a serial printer you will need a serial port for connecting the printer cable to your PC. If you find that you don't have a serial port, then you will have to install a serial adapter card or a multifunction adapter card that has a serial port. The IBM PC/XT comes with a serial port.

STEP TWO: Carefully unpack your printer. There will probably be mounting screws, packing material, and tie wraps holding many of the moving parts in place, to protect the printer during shipment. Save all of these items and the box your printer comes in. It will all come in handy to protect your printer when and if you happen to move.

STEP THREE: Turn off the power on your PC and be sure the power switch on the printer is turned off. Move your PC to a position that will make it easy to connect the printer to the port (i.e., connection) at the back of your PC. Don't try to do this from an awkward position. If necessary, turn your PC all the way around so the back of it faces you.

STEP FOUR: If there are specific printer switches to set on your printer, set those now. Refer to your printer manual for the details on this. If there is no such procedure on your particular printer, go to STEP FIVE.

STEP FIVE: Connect one end of the printer cable to the printer and the other end to the PC. A small screwdriver will allow you to tighten the tiny screws properly. Follow the printer installation manual closely here to be sure you are making the proper connections.

STEP SIX: Check to be sure the print ribbon is in place. If your printer requires a print wheel you should check to be sure that is in place. With many printers you will need to install this at the same time as you install your printer (which means NOW).

STEP SEVEN: Turn on the printer, but **not** the PC. Most printers have a self-test you can run to be sure everything is working properly. A good example of a self-test for a printer is the one done by a Diablo printer. Before turning on the Diablo printer you set the slide switch to position #8. Once that is done you turn on the power.

The self-test begins by printing a few short lines of text and then repeatedly printing its entire extended character set. Each time it begins printing a new row it starts with the next character in sequence. (See Figure 7.11.) If you notice a problem with the self-test, you should re-check the installation procedure in your printer's manual, along with the steps listed here. After running the self-test you are ready to try your printer with your PC.

STEP EIGHT: Place your DOS disk in the A drive of your PC and turn on the power. Once you reach the `A>` prompt, hold the CONTROL key down and tap `P`. Then type something (anything) on the screen. When you press the enter key the printer should print out everything you just typed.

Don't forget to hold the CONTROL key down and tap the letter P again to stop this process. That CONTROL key combined with the letter P works like a toggle switch turning the printing on and off—so don't forget to turn it off after checking it out.

You can also hold the shift key down and tap the `PrtSc` key (next to the shift bar on the right hand side of the keyboard) to be sure your printer is receiving the proper messages from your PC. Your next step will be to try your printer with all your programs.

If you experience problems in getting your printer to work with your programs (like word processing and data bases) you should first read the printer and installation sections of those program manuals. That way you can usually figure out how to solve any problems.

If you find yourself doing things over and over again to no avail, there just might be a serious problem somewhere. At that point you should contact the store where you bought the printer. Many of the companies manufacturing printers have toll-free numbers to call for assistance (this is true of many software companies, too).

Do your homework before you buy your printer. By doing that little bit of extra work you can almost guarantee yourself the joy of hooking up your printer without any hitches or frustrations.

Fig. 7.11: Self-test for Diablo 630 ECS printer

```
630-API.SELFTEST
ROM1.OK
ROM2.OK
INT.RAM.OK
EXT.RAM.OK
ɸ!"#$%&'()*+,-./0123456789:;<=>?@ɦ  rstuvwxyz{|}~=0123456789ℓ ° ñ å ⁰fΦr456789 è é ¦ ä ü ö ¡¢£
!"#$%&'()*+,-./0123456789:;<=>?@AB  ʒtuvwxyz{|}~=0123456789ℓ ° ñ å ⁰fΦr456789 è é ¦ ä ü ö ¡¢£$
"#$%&'()*+,-./0123456789:;<=>?@ABC  ɩuvwxyz{|}~=0123456789ℓ ° ñ å ⁰fΦr456789 è é ¦ ä ü ö ¡¢£$¥
#$%&'()*+,-./0123456789:;<=>?@ABCΓ  uvwxyz{|}~=0123456789ℓ ° ñ å ⁰fΦr456789 è é ¦ ä ü ö ¡¢£$¥#
```

96 Lines

Courtesy of Diablo Systems Incorporated

7.3 Two or More Printers with One PC—Just How To Do It!

Many PC owners find themselves suddenly faced with the prospect of hooking up a second printer. Some people start out with dot matrix printers and then purchase letter quality printers. There are even PC owners using more than two printers. There are three ways to use two (or more) printers. The tedious way is to hook up and unhook the printer cables each time you want to use a specific printer. The easier ways are to use DOS commands to change printers or to invest in a switching box.

Advanced Systems Concepts, Inc. (ASCI) produces the ASCI Switch (see Figure 7.12), which allows you to switch back and forth between two or more printers almost effortlessly. All you need to do is set the connection for whichever printer you want to use. With such a device you can also switch back and forth between your printers, a plotter, and a modem—all without taking up any extra expansion slots in your PC. You can also use this kind of switch to connect more than one PC to a printer (as shown in Figure 7.13).

Several companies make such switches. While the cost of these switches ranges from $80 to more than $600, the convenience and simplicity they provide make them worth considering. All you need to do whenever you want to change back and forth between printers (and other devices) is set a switch. It's that simple, and you won't be using up any of your PC's precious expansion slots in the process. Your printers must both have the same type of interface to the PC. The parallel interface is much simpler to use.

Fig. 7.12: ASCI Switch for switching back and forth between printers

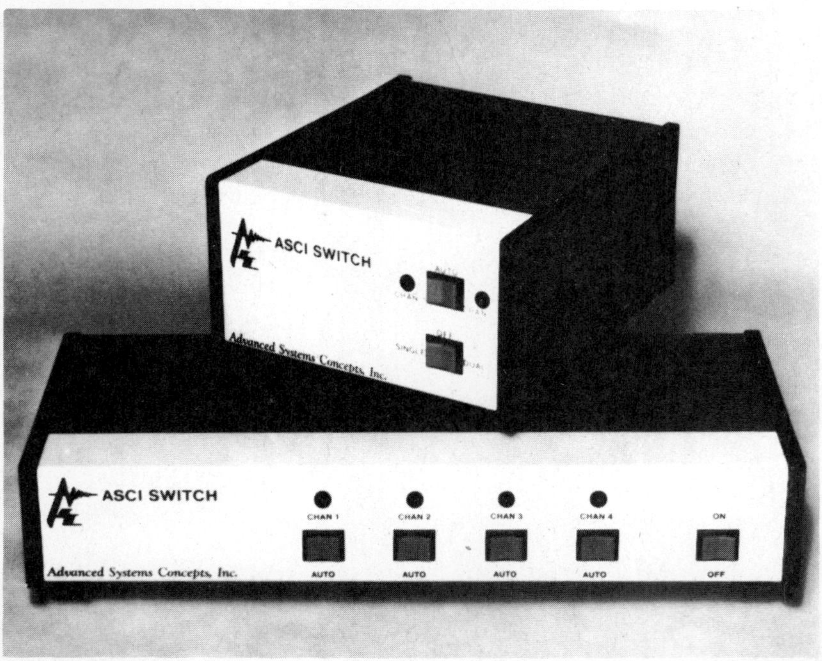

Courtesy of Advanced Systems Concepts, Inc.

Fig. 7.13: Typical configurations for printer switch

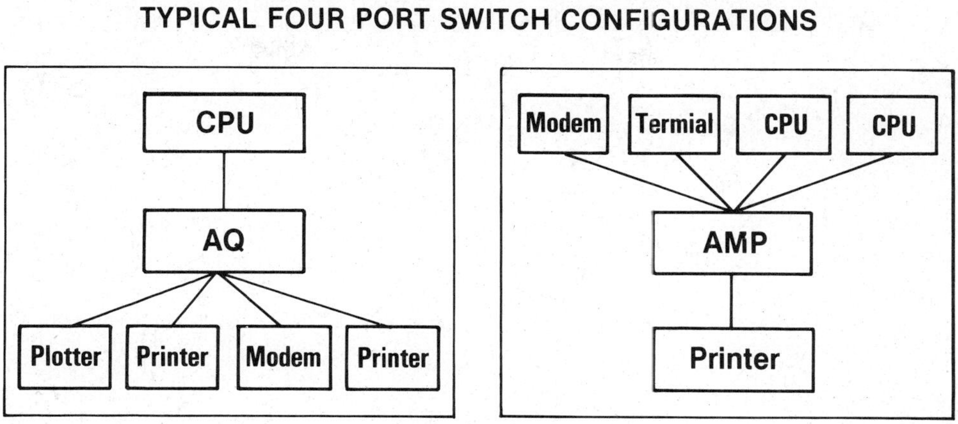

Courtesy of Advanced Systems Concepts, Inc.

7.4 Using a Typewriter as a Printer

If the price of letter quality printers seems too high, and you happen to own an IBM Selectric typewriter, you might want to consider using that typewriter as a printer. This won't be the ideal way to print, but it will allow you to use an already existing office resource for letter quality printing (i.e., fully formed characters).

California Micro Computer Company makes a device, called the CMC 5060, which allows you to connect your PC to Selectric typewriters. The older the Selectric the more difficult it will be to make the connection—but it will work. Making the connection requires opening up your Selectric and making modifications as you hook things up. The connection can be made through either a serial or parallel port on your PC.

However, you should be aware of the following points:

- Using a typewriter as a printer is painfully slow.
- You will need to modify your service contract on your Selectric. Since the Selectric wasn't designed to be a printer (running continuously at its maximum speed of 16.5 characters per second) you can plan on mechanical problems from the extra strain of mimicking a printer. The increased cost for a service contract on a Selectric used as a printer will range from $100 to $200 per year.
- Many of the characters on the Selectric's typing element will not match up with symbols and characters on the IBM PC keyboard. You will need to experiment with this—for each type of Selectric element you will be using.
- The Selectric typewriter is noisy.
- Underlining, boldfacing, and setting tabs will all require special control codes. These are awkward, but do work. You should be prepared to go through certain gymnastics to do what a printer normally does without much effort.

- Proportional spacing elements will create unique problems when you try to line up columns or underline something. It's much less trouble to use 10 or 12 pitch typing elements.

It will cost more than $300 to modify your Selectric typewriter. When you compare that cost to prices that range beyond $2,000 for letter quality printers, your typewriter just might be the printer for you. It would be best for you to actually see (and hear) a Selectric typewriter modified to work as a printer before you purchase a device such as the CMC 5060.

IBM now sells an Attachment Device which connects IBM's Electronic 65 and 86 typewriters to the PC. The Attachment Device, installed inside the typewriter, acts as an interface to the PC through a standard parallel port. The cost for this connection is under $250. IBM service technicians will install the Attachment Device on site (i.e., in your office or home). There is no extra charge for this service.

While this provides excellent letter quality printing for a very reasonable price, there is one point worth considering. The IBM typewriters are not designed for continuous feed paper. That means when you are printing a document you must insert the paper a page at a time. Most word processing programs allow you to pause between pages, but this is a slow, cumbersome process, which doesn't take advantage of one of the PC's most important aspects—saving you time. However, if changing paper individually doesn't present any problems for you, then this just might be the option you're looking for.

7.5 Just What Are Plotters?

Dot matrix printers are known for producing graphs and bar charts. However, when it comes to producing really professional quality graphics, a plotter is the answer.

Plotters are actually special printers which are dedicated to doing graphics—in black and white and in color. Figure 7.14 shows two plotters made by Hewlett Packard, along with two graphic charts. One is a bar chart and the other one is a point line graph.

What sets plotters apart from any kind of printer is that plotters actually draw with pens (see Figure 7.15). Some plotters use as many as eight different colored pens. The plotters are designed to mechanically use special pens, changing colors as needed. The colors are what really make graphics done by plotters spectacular. The lettering done by plotters is superb too.

Plotters cost as much, or more than, printers, depending on what kind you buy. If a plotter is beyond your means, you might want to look at software packages for your dot matrix printer. Programs such as Fast Graphs do give you impressive plotter-type graphics in black and white—all from different brands of dot matrix printers (set up to do graphics). This particular software package also works with plotters for a highly refined printed image.

Then there is the very specialized graphics instrument known as a digitizer. Figure 7.16 shows a digitizer being used in a design application. This will not be a common item for the IBM PC, but in fields of design work, science, and engineering, it is a useful tool.

Fig. 7.14: Hewlett Packard 7470 (2 pen) and 7475 (6 pen) plotters, along with printed graphs

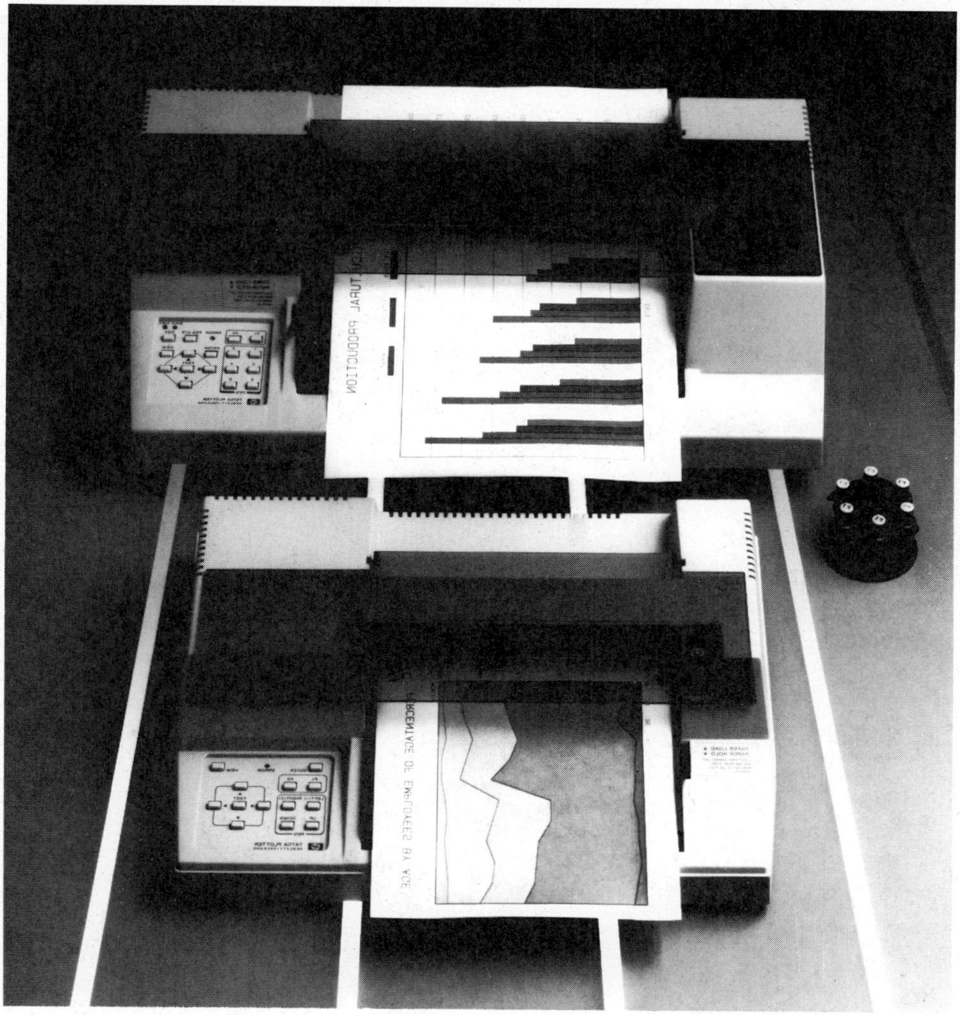

Courtesy of Hewlett Packard Company

7.6 Hooking Up a Plotter

Making the connection between a plotter and your PC is the same as hooking up a printer. Using the Hewlett Packard plotter as an example, you would follow the procedures outlined in section 7.2 of this chapter. Make certain you read the plotter manual, along with the Interconnection Guide (that's what tells you how to hook up the plotter and how to build a cable).

The Hewlett Packard plotter has specific switches that need to be set according to the Interconnection Guide. One switch can easily be changed for different sizes of paper (up to 210 × 297 mm). You will need to adjust other settings for parity and baud rate—all of which is explained in detail in the product/installation manual. The

Fig. 7.15: Houston Instrument DMP-40 Plotter, showing chart being drawn with special pen

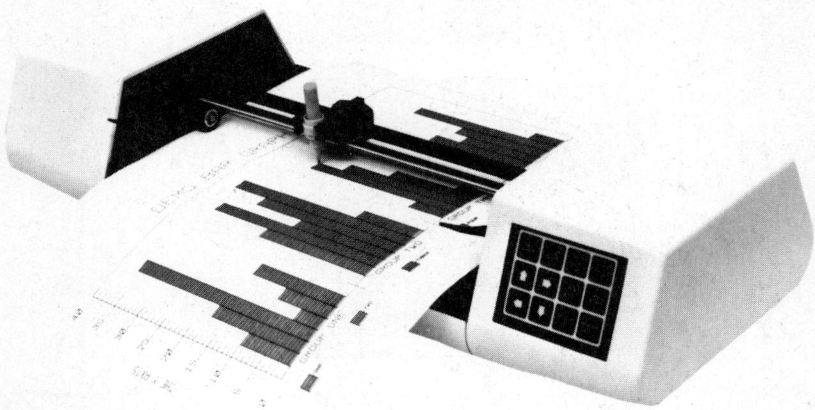

Courtesy of Houston Instrument

instructions even list a short BASIC program for you to run, which uses the plotter to print out "COMMUNICATION OK" to let you know everything is connected properly.

7.7 Save Money By Refilling Printer Ribbons

All PC owners quickly discover that:

- printers go through ribbons quickly; and
- ribbons are not cheap.

When you consider the time saved (and other factors), printer ribbons aren't really that expensive. However, it is possible to save up to 75 percent on ribbons for printers. Just about any IBM PC owner should be interested in that. (If you aren't interested you can skip to the next chapter).

American Ink Products Company provides interesting, unique, and money saving options for printer ribbons:

OPTION #1 You can send in your old ribbon cartridges and have them refilled with fresh, new ribbons. This service is provided for just about every make of printer on the market today. You can save as much as 50 percent by doing this. Most people don't realize how much money is wrapped up in those throw-away plastic ribbon cartridges.

OPTION #2 PC owners with dot matrix printers now have the option of do-it-yourself when it comes to replacing ribbons. Some dot matrix printer ribbons cost

Fig. 7.16: Houston Instrument Hipad Digitizer

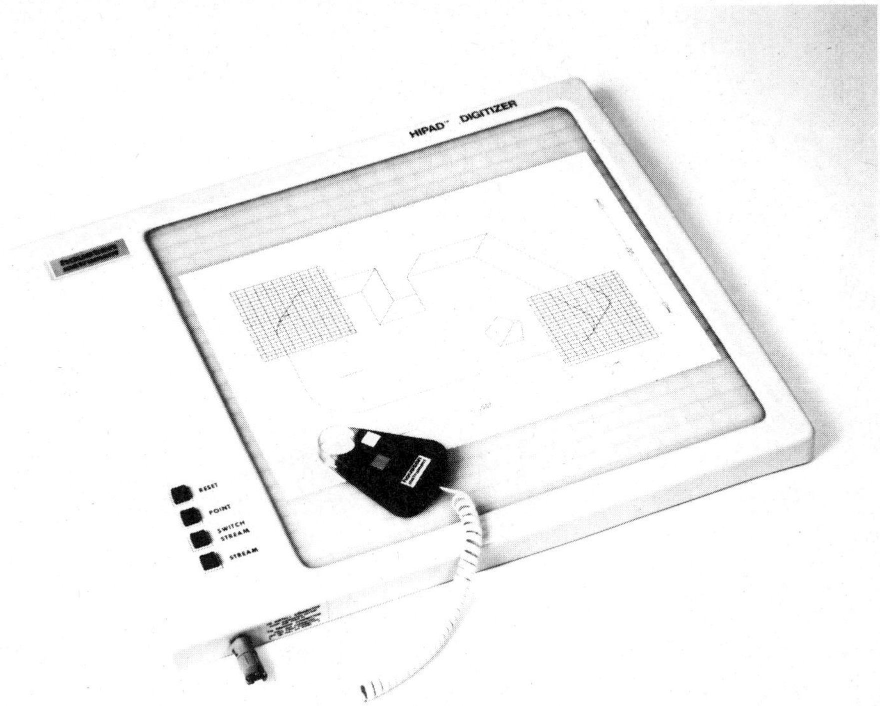

Courtesy of Houston Instrument

$16.00 or more in retail stores. By purchasing just the inked ribbons from American Ink Products Company you can save approximately 75 percent of that cost. What's more important is that these ribbons are well inked, providing dark printing.

When you replace the ribbons yourself you will get some ink on your fingers, even though plastic gloves are provided. However, for such significant cost savings, what's a little ink among friends?

Here's how to refill your own dot matrix printer ribbon cartridges (using an Epson ribbon as an example):

STEP ONE: Pry open the top of the ribbon cartridge with a small screwdriver. You will need to do this carefully around the edges. After you work the top a little bit, it will pop right off.

STEP TWO: Remove the old ribbon from the cartridge. Be sure you don't lose any plastic pieces of the cartridge (like the two little wheels on the end where the ribbon enters the cartridge) See Figure 7.17 which shows the new ribbon in place.

STEP THREE: Place the roll of new inked ribbon outside the cartridge as shown in Figure 7.17. Thread the new ribbon through the two wheels on the far end of the

Fig. 7.17: Epson ribbon cartridge opened up with new ribbon in place

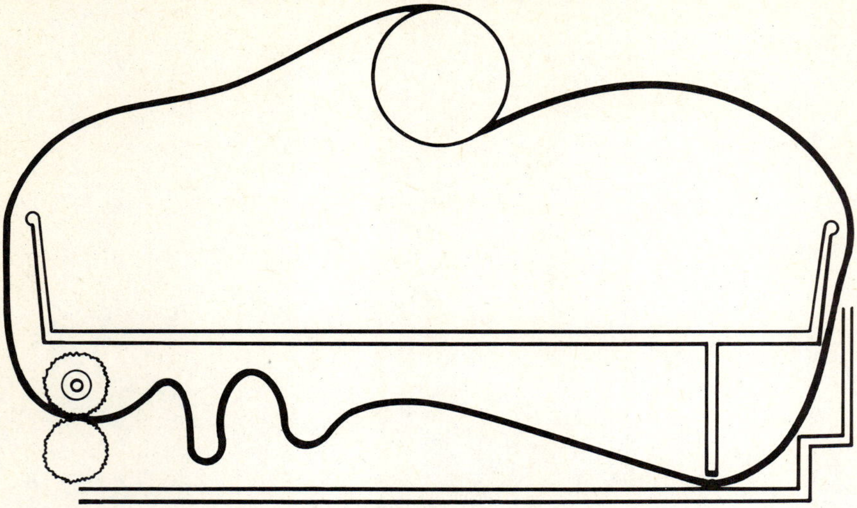

cartridge. Make sure that you have the ribbon straight and upright as it goes out the other side of the cartridge.

STEP FOUR: Replace the top of the cartridge. This entire process will never work unless you replace the cover. Before replacing the cover make sure everything looks exactly as it does in Figure 7.17.

STEP FIVE: Turn the spindle (which is attached to one of the little gears inside the cartridge). Do this slowly by hand as the ribbon is pulled into the cartridge. As you do this the ribbon will begin to unfold. Keep the part that is unfolding as orderly as possible, letting it pile up on itself. It will unravel perfectly as the entire ribbon is pulled into the cartridge. Your fingers might ache a little bit, but just go slowly and carefully (thinking of the money your fingers are saving you).

STEP SIX: Once all of the ribbon is inside the cartridge you can use it just as you would any other ribbon. It takes just a few times to get good at it.

If you have any problems with ribbons you refill on your own or the ones you buy already refilled, American Ink Products is only a phone call away—and they are very helpful.

There are specific re-inking machines, which operate both by hand crank and electric motor. The costs are fairly reasonable (under $100) and just might be an option you want to look into further.

8

The world of communications via your PC presents you with a bold leap into the future. Hooking up a modem and using your PC to venture off to the exciting experiences of bulletin boards, information utilities, and electronic mail might seem a bit overwhelming. But as with so many other aspects of your PC, if you take it all a step at a time you quickly discover you can do it all yourself. In no time at all you'll find yourself traveling all over the United States (and possibly the world)—without ever leaving the comfort of that chair in front of your PC.

The secret of your success will be in looking closely at the pieces of the puzzle before you put it all together. You don't need to be a programming genius or communications wizard to use a modem with your PC. By following the steps in this chapter you and your PC will be zooming off through the telephone lines before too long. The only real problem you will face is the telephone bills.

This chapter is a little different from the rest of this book. It presents information beyond the step-by-step procedures for hooking up devices. You will learn not just what a modem is and how to hook up one, but how to use a communications program (i.e., the software) in conjunction with the modem. This chapter will also explain how to access and use an information utility like Compuserve. Electronic mail will be explained and explored using MCI Mail as an example.

Finally, bulletin boards are covered to give you a good feel for as many areas of communications as possible. Even if you think you aren't interested in some of these subject areas, take a little closer look at them. You'll be surprised at what you're missing. Bulletin boards are tied very closely to Special Interest Groups (SIGs) and provide a vast resource in information and assistance with computer related problems.

Electronic mail, while somewhat new, will become increasingly significant. With companies like MCI now providing regular electronic mail service, you can use a PC to send letters, files, reports, and documents almost instantaneously—throughout the United States and to some other countries.

Networking is only briefly covered in this book, because of rapid changes, development, and complexities. To get in-depth information on communications and networking, look at books like *Communications and Networking For The* IBM PC by Larry E. Jordan and Bruce Churchill (Robert J. Brady Company, 1983). This not only explains just about everything, but also gives you guidelines and checklists useful for both purchasing equipment and using it.

8.1 Communications as a Magic Carpet

Communications make you feel like you're on a magic carpet, riding your PC wherever you want to go. Through the world of communications you can access distant computers for information ranging from electronic letters to hundreds of different kinds of data bases. You can even use your PC now for electronic banking.

Any time of the day or night you can be whisked off across town or across the country through communications. All it takes is a basic understanding of what you're doing and the proper equipment. The costs involved aren't too bad. A modem and the software to go with it range from $100 up to $900 (depending on what you get). The only costs (which can add up quickly) after that are for the telephone bills and any time charges you might have to pay for accessing data bases.

To get started with communications you will need two things—a modem and a software package to use the modem. This chapter is designed to help you work your way through the communications maze of technical language and complexities. It isn't really as bad as it sounds. With just a little bit of hand holding you will quickly find yourself off on a world tour with your PC.

8.2 It All Starts with a Modem

A modem is a device which permits the transmission and reception of information for your PC over telephone lines. Figure 8.1 shows what an external modem looks like.

The modem shown in Figure 8.1 sits outside your PC and is connected to it by an RS-232 serial port. If you don't have a serial port you will need to buy either an adapter card with a serial port or a multifunction adapter card, which would also have a serial port. If your printer also requires a serial port, you will need two serial ports.

This problem is eliminated when you install an internal modem (see Figure 8.2). With such a modem no port is required, because everything is built-in.

Once you hook up a modem, your PC is ready to communicate with the outside world. But let's first look at three basic questions and a checklist of things you want to be aware of when shopping for a modem.

Acoustic Versus Direct Connect In the old days of communications for personal computers, the computer user inserted the telephone receiver into the modem's two black rubber connectors. You dialed the telephone, and when you heard the high-pitched noise the connection was made. That is an example of an acoustic modem. About all an acoustic modem does is hold the phone.

Fig. 8.1: Hayes Smartmodem 1200 (external)

Courtesy of Hayes Microcomputer Products, Inc.

Fig. 8.2: Hayes Smartmodem 1200B (internal) and Smartcom II software

Courtesy of Hayes Microcomputer Products, Inc.

Things have changed a little bit. With direct connect modems, you don't even dial the number any more. You certainly don't need the telephone receiver—in fact, you don't even need a telephone. All you do is connect the modem into the telephone wall outlet.

Direct connect modems are pretty much the name of the game today. They offer convenience and advantages that certainly make life easier for the person who works with communications. Acoustic modems are still available and are certainly cheaper. In some cases, the portable and lap size personal computers will still use acoustic modems. These are also more convenient for transmitting data and files from airport telephones and when you're out of the office. However, for normal use in communications you'll find direct connect modems are the only way to go.

External Versus Internal Modems While an external modem is one more piece of computer equipment to sit outside your PC (or even on top of it) there are a few significant reasons why you might want to use one. First of all, by hooking an external modem into the serial port of a multifunction adapter card you are saving a precious expansion slot in your PC. An internal modem will use up one of those expansion slots.

An internal modem will also use power from the PC's main power supply. This isn't a problem until you start installing an internal fixed disk, which will also draw on the PC's power supply. This might never cause problems, but you should be aware that you are taking power away from the PC with an internal modem. An external modem has its own power supply and doesn't use any of the PC's power.

An internal modem requires removing the PC's cover. However, after that the set up is nothing more than plugging in the telephone modular cable connection. The external modem has one other real advantage in that you can see what is going on. There may be red lights on the external modem which can signal that the terminal is ready, the phone is off the hook, or the modem is receiving and sending data. Another advantage to an external modem is that it can work with just about any computer (that has a serial port).

The best way to decide which modem is best for you is to make a list of what you are presently doing, and also what you plan to do, with your PC. Place an X next to each item on your list which will require the use of an expansion slot. When you review how many expansion slots you will need versus how many you have (five in a PC and eight in a PC/XT, three of which are short slots) it will be obvious whether or not you can afford to install an internal modem.

300 Baud Versus 1200 Baud The term *baud* has to do with how much information, in the form of bits, is transferred per second through a modem and over telephone lines. The higher the number, the faster things go. At 1200 baud you are communicating four times faster than at 300 baud.

This becomes a significant factor from two standpoints, both of which have to do with cost. A 300 baud modem is much cheaper than a 1200 baud modem. The attraction of a 300 baud modem quickly disappears when you consider the cost of telephone and access charges. The faster 1200 baud means less time on the telephone lines. That is a considerable cost savings (even though 1200 baud usually means higher access rates), but that's not the whole story.

Many data bases and information utilities, like The Source and Compuserve, charge access time. While you are hooked into their systems you are paying by the hour. Once again, the faster you can get things done, the less it is going to cost you. So while a 300 baud modem is initially much cheaper, in the long run it is going to cost you a whole lot more. You will usually be charged a higher access time rate at 1200 baud, which you should take into consideration. After you have used both 300 and 1200 baud you will see just how much slower 300 baud is.

Most 1200 baud modems can also work at 300 baud. It's important to have the option of using 300 baud, because many data bases and information services still use 300 baud. Several use only 300 baud, so it's important for you to be able to switch to 300 baud if you need it. If you're looking at a 1200 baud modem, be sure that it will also work at 300 and 120 baud (120 baud isn't used much at all, but you might run across a need for it).

Here's a check list to help you make a better decision when it comes to purchasing a modem:

Find out about the company. What's the background on the company manufacturing the modem you plan to buy? How long have they been around? What other products do they make? You want to be sure that the company will be around two years from now.

Look closely at the manual. Is it readable? Can you easily understand what it? Review the sections on installation and use—are they helpful? Keep in mind that this will be your point of reference once you get your modem installed. Can you live with this manual once you purchase the product?

Who is using this particular type of modem right now? Ask for references and check with them before you buy. Ask friends, PC user group members, and business associates about modems. Have a look at their modems.

Can this modem handle touch tone and pulse dialing? While this might not be a concern for you now, you could possibly move to an area where you need either of these options. Most modems can handle both touch tone and pulse dialing, but you want to be sure to check for this option.

Full- or half-duplexing is an important consideration. Full-duplex means that the modem can send and receive information at the same time. Half-duplex means the modem can either send or receive, but not both at the same time. Your modem should be able to switch back and forth between the two because you will come across both. You can send and receive information at the same time in the full-duplex mode, which is the main reason you want this a feature in your modem. A full-duplex modem can also work in a half-duplex environment.

Is there auto re-dial? This option for a modem might seem like a luxury, but it turns out to be a time saver. To have a number automatically re-dialed for you is a handy feature, because the world of communications is not immune from busy signals. Bulletin boards especially are often busy. No matter where you find a busy signal, it's nice to know that your modem will automatically re-dial until it gets through.

Check into the warranty. How long is the modem guaranteed? What are the details of the warranty? Are there extra costs involved (like for shipping and handling, or even parts)? How much time is involved for the repair? Clear up these questions *before* you buy the modem. That way there won't be any surprises if and when you do have problems.

The Federal Communications Commission (FCC) has three restrictions which apply to modems:

Restriction #1: You are not allowed to connect a modem to any party line or pay telephone.

Restriction #2: The telephone company must be notified that a modem is being used and be given the FCC registration number of the modem.

Restriction #3: Any repairs made to your modem must be done by the manufacturer, if the valid FCC registration is to be maintained.

The procedure for hooking a modem to your PC is outlined below:

STEP ONE: If you are installing an internal modem you must first install the modem adapter card. (See Chapter 2, section 2.6.)

If you are installing an external modem you may proceed to the next step. If you have just completed installation of the internal modem (including putting the PC's cover back on) you may proceed to STEP FOUR.

STEP TWO: You should now connect the RS-232 cable to the modem and to the back of the PC at the serial port (this is for external modems only). Figure 8.3 shows the back of the Hayes Smartmodem 1200 with the connections, the switch, and the volume control knob. The RS-232 connection is in the middle of the back panel. Be sure you have the proper cable for the connection.

Fig. 8.3: Back panel of the Hayes Smartmodem 1200, showing the connections, switch, and knob

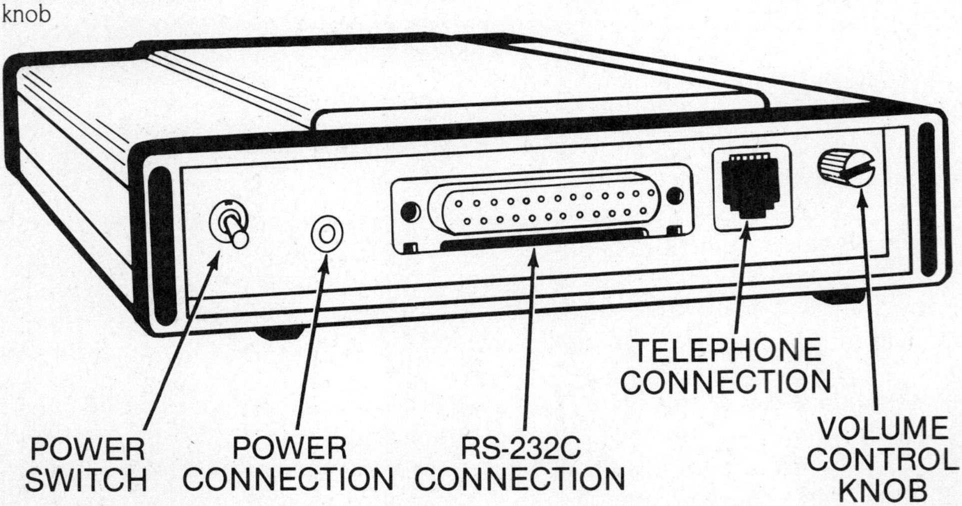

Courtesy of Hayes Microcomputer Products, Inc.

While there will be variations in the different types of modems that can be installed on the IBM PC, Figure 8.3 gives you a good idea of what needs to be done. The user's manual for your modem will cover the differences.

STEP THREE: Connect the AC power cord to the modem (again, this is for external modems only). DO NOT plug that cord into the wall yet. You will do that when you are ready to use your modem. Figure 8.3 shows where that connection is.

STEP FOUR: Connect the modular telephone cable into the wall outlet and into the modem. Refer to Figure 8.3 for the location of the telephone connection for the external modem and to Figure 8.4 for the internal modem.

STEP FIVE: If your modem has a volume control, turn it to the lowest setting. As you use your modem, you might want to hear the numbers being dialed and even the connections being made. However, this can be an irritating series of sounds, so start with it as low as possible and gradually turn it up as you see the need.

STEP SIX: Plug the modem's power cord into the wall. This step only applies to external modems. Your modem is now ready for use.

The only thing you need now is software, through which you control your modem and where in the universe you and your PC go. The next section explains some of the basics of communications software and outlines some of your options.

8.3 You Can't Do Anything without Software

Software is what makes everything work. It's that simple. As with any other program you use with your PC, you have a set of commands and a series of menus to work from. The biggest thing to overcome in communications is the terminology. The only

Fig. 8.4: Back of PC, showing the internal modem's telephone connection

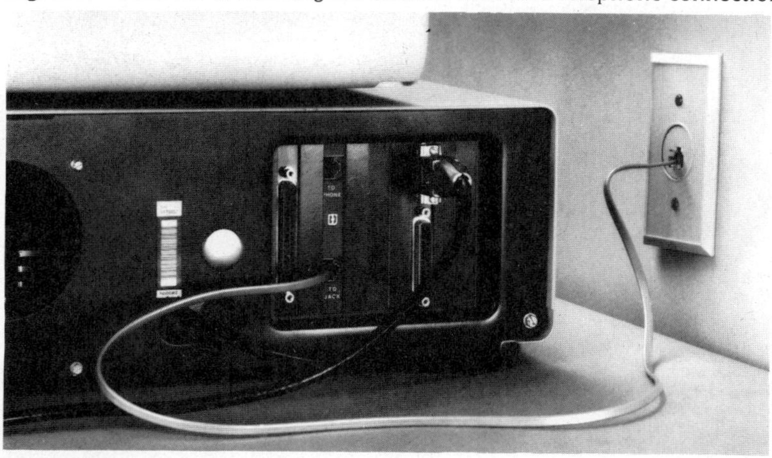

Courtesy of Hayes Microcomputer Products, Inc.

way to learn is just to jump in and get started. It helps to know someone who is currently working with communications, but you can do it on your own.

Much of what you learn about communications as you evaluate modems will also apply to the program which you will use with the modem. Companies like Hayes sell software packages to go with their modems. Hayes even throws in the software when you buy an internal modem. You have dozens of options when it comes to communications software packages. You can buy a modem from one company and the software from another. Some people even write their own software to use with a modem. But don't try that unless you are an experienced programmer.

One of the best software packages for communications, according to many magazine reviews, is PC-TALK III by Andrew Fluegelman which is marketed through the free ware concept. You make a copy of the program and then after using it, you have the option of paying for it. The program is quite inexpensive. The 70 page manual is included as a file on the program disk and prints out very nicely on just about any kind of printer.

PC-TALK III is available from many computer user groups and bulletin boards. It works very well and the manual is written in such detail that it could be used in a course on communications. You do have many other options for communications software. Many companies, including IBM, have such software available.

As you find out what you want in a modem you should jot those points down. The software you buy must be able to match up with what your modem can do or you will have problems. Again, we come back to books and magazine articles. That is where you will get all the details and background on what you need in software.

Communications And Networking For The IBM PC, explains all of the features you might want in the way of software and why. The authors also have put together a very handy software comparison guide.

Some features you will want in communications software:

- Well written manual and user's guide
- Good use of menus
- Auto dialing
- Auto re-dialing
- Option of manual dialing
- Full duplex (the ability to both send and receive information simultaneously)
- Return to operating system (DOS) easily
- Elapsed time of call
- Display of help files
- On-line printer OFF/ON toggle
- Abbreviated menu on line 25 or help screens on call

Ask others what they have and what they recommend. Have a look at a variety of programs before you make your final decision.

Your experience in working with communications in large part depends on the quality of the software package you use. You want to be sure that you get the best possible program to meet your needs, one that is user friendly and offers a wide range of functions.

8.4 Using a Modem

Using a modem and the software to go with it doesn't require any extraordinary skills. If you can use other programs and equipment with your PC, you shouldn't have any problem with communications. Once you begin working with communications you feel like you have been missing out on something by not having discovered it sooner.

***A Word of Warning*:** The use of communications with your PC can be habit-forming. It can even cause you to neglect other work and general duties around the home or office. A lot of time spent accessing distant computers with your PC can lead to rather high (if not outrageous) telephone bills. That's why the built in communications software feature of displaying elapsed time is so important.

Here's how easy it really is to use your modem. PC-TALK III is used as an example here.

STEP ONE: Place the working copy of the PC-TALK III communications software disk in the A drive of your PC. This disk should have the DOS system files, along with the DOS BASIC.COM file.

STEP TWO: Turn on your PC and the modem (if it is an external one).

STEP THREE: You can begin using PC-TALK III with an AUTOEXEC.BAT file or you can just type `PC-TALK` at the DOS prompt.

STEP FOUR: PC-TALK III displays an initial screen, showing the name of the program and other information. After pressing any key, you proceed to the program.

STEP FIVE: To dial a number you have already put in your auto-dialing file, you hold the Alternate Key down and press the letter D. That takes you to the part of the program that will dial your numbers for you. At this point you can add, change or delete numbers. You can store up to 60 different telephone numbers.

STEP SIX: Simply select the number which is next to the telephone number you want and enter that at the cursor prompt you see on the screen. As soon as you enter you will see the screen change. The program will then work with your modem to dial the telephone number you selected.

STEP SEVEN: Once the telephone call has been placed and the connection made you will see the word `CONNECT` displayed on the screen. At this point you are ready to enter whatever data base, service, bulletin board, or information utility you have called.

Once you are linked into another computer through communications you will be even more surprised to see how everything is designed to make it easy for you to find your way around. There are usually plenty of help menus at the services you will be linking into. You can usually get assistance by typing the word HELP. You might have to put a slash or some other character in front of it, but the help menus will explain that to you.

8.5 Bulletin Boards

There are vast sources of information about the IBM PC and other computers in your area and all around the United States. That information is available from services known as Bulletin Board Systems (BBS). A bulletin board is nothing more than a place to call for gaining and sharing information. Most bulletin boards don't cost any more than the price of the phone call.

A bulletin board is simple to use. Once you get connected you'll see what is available on the bulletin board (helpful tips, programs and/or files). You merely choose whatever interests you. You can also leave information for others to benefit from.

You can learn about bulletin boards from computer user groups, computer stores, magazines, and bulletin boards themselves. Magazines and newsweeklies will probably be your best sources for bulletin board listings. Here are three magazines which feature BBS information on a regular basis:

PC World Magazine. The regular column is called "BBS Watch." It periodically lists bulletin boards and pertinent information about them. This column also gives you a lot of useful tips and pointers.

Compute!'s PC & PCjr Magazine. "IBM PC Bulletin Boards" is a monthly feature here, with an up-dated BBS list. This magazine also features another column called "Telecomputing Today" that covers the bulletin boards, information utilities, and much more.

Creative Computing. This magazine's regular column is called Telecommunications Talk. While it isn't totally devoted to the subject of BBS, it does provide you with a lot of helpful information. It covers the spectrum of communications related uses.

If you subscribe to The Source or Compuserve (both of which are information utilities) you will find many bulletin board listings, too. Both of these services also provide you with SIGs—Special Interest Groups. You will find a SIG for the IBM PC in other data base services as well.

Using a bulletin board is like everything else with your PC. You learn best by doing. As you access bulletin boards around the United States remember:

- That you're paying the phone costs, which can add up rather quickly.
- Many bulletin boards operate under the Remote Bulletin Board System (RBBS). Such a system requires that you send three carriage returns after the connection is made. This allows them to adjust for the hookup.
- Some bulletin boards require that you let the phone ring once and then hang up.

- The one term you absolutely must know is SYSOP. That stands for System Operator—the person running the bulletin board.

You'll be surprised at just how much useful information is available on bulletin boards. And when you realize that there are hundreds of them all over the United States . . . well, that is a lot of BBS territory to explore!

8.6 Information Utilities

Information utilities offer a range of services, including business data bases, stock quotes, news on the wire service, and much, much more. You can even store files on an information utility. The way such a service works is that you pay by the hour for connect time and for the amount of storage you use. If you use the service at night—usually after 6 p.m.—you pay less. Daytime service costs more because that is when more people will be accessing it.

There's usually an initial fee to subscribe to information utilities. Most services charge a minimum monthly fee whether you use the service or not. There can be additional charges for accessing special areas of an information utility, (for example, the encyclopedia in the reference section of Compuserve). And of course you pay for the time you use the service.

It takes a while to get to know your way around an information utility, merely because there is so much available to you. Everything is done through menus and plenty of help is available, but still the first few times can be a bit overwhelming. The best way to cope with this is to familiarize yourself with the manual you receive. Compuserve and other services have a GO command you can use to zip around all over the place. By typing GO and a code for the menu or area you want, you can instantly move there. The codes are listed for you in the manual.

Here's how you get into an information utility. Compuserve is used as an example.

STEP ONE: Once you see the word CONNECT on your screen you will be prompted for your ID Number. This is the number that only you have and it must be typed in exactly the way you received it, including punctuation and spacing. A sample ID Number would be 76003,9 . After you type that in and enter it, you will receive another prompt for your password, as distinct from your ID Number.

STEP TWO: When you enter your password you won't be able to see it on the screen (unless your communications software has an ECHO ON feature, which does print out your password on the screen). Again, everything must be typed in exactly the same way as the password was issued to you. An example of a password is: BOAT*TOUCH. You do have the option of changing your password at any time you choose.

STEP THREE: Once your password is verified, you will be permitted access to Compuserve. As you are logged on to the service you will get a message similar to:

```
Compuserve Information Service
```

```
5:54 PDT Monday 15 Oct 84
```

From that point on you are in the system and may choose to go wherever you want by following menus or using the GO command. If you don't live in an area where Compuserve or any other such service can be accessed through a local call, you have other options. There are services, such as Telenet and Datapac, which allow you to dial a local number and then access whatever service you choose. There will be a charge for this, but it will be significantly less than paying for the long distance call. This type of information will be listed in the service's manual.

More and more business information is becoming available through services like Compuserve. You can even store information in the data base if you want. And, yes, there are games and other types of entertainment on these services. There's really just about anything you could ever imagine. They even have electronic mail.

8.7 Electronic Mail

Instead of putting your letter or report in an envelope you put it in your PC and send it off. Actually there's a bit more to it than that, but the concept is exciting from many standpoints. Now you can actually get something to someone else in a few minutes, no matter where they are in the United States and no matter what kind of computer they have—as long as they subscribe to the same electronic mail service you do. What's even more impressive: you can use the technology of electronic mail to send a telegram, a telex, a mailgram or even a computer letter to anyone—whether they own a computer or not.

If that sounds like the future, it is—and you can use your PC to take advantage of it right now, TODAY. Information utilities offer an electronic mail service you can use to send letters, memos, documents, and files to anyone else who also subscribes to the service. It provides instant communications.

Your electronic mail options are expanded with a service like MCI Mail which offers electronic mail along with the Dow Jones News/Retrieval data base package. It doesn't cost anything to subscribe to MCI Mail and there is no minimum monthly charge. Once you subscribe you will receive a packet of information in an MCI Letter, which includes your customer number, ID number, and your password. From that point on you are all set to begin using the service. You can send letters to anyone in the growing MCI Mail system.

If you want to send something to someone who isn't in the system you can send an MCI Letter, either by mail or hand delivery. Hand delivery does cost extra. You can also send a telex. For a nominal fee you can register your letterhead and signature to give your letters a personal look. The letters are all laser printed so the quality of the signature and letterhead is very good.

Using MCI Mail is much like typing a letter—that simple. You first type in the addressee's name and MCI ID number. (If you don't have someone's ID number, just type the name.) When you're done typing the letter and/or including other files, it's as simple as typing the word SEND to post your letter.

Copies of letters you send will be in your OUTBOX for 24 hours, just in case you might want to review them. When you sign on to MCI Mail you will get a message immediately if you have any mail waiting for you. You can SCAN through your INBOX (i.e., electronic mailbox) to read the letters. All MCI Mail documents can be printed out on your printer, too.

There are many electronic mail services available. Evaluate them and choose the one that best suits your needs. MCI Mail was used as an example in this section to illustrate how electronic mail works and how easy it is to use. Imagine the luxury of talking to someone in another city who needs a document you have in your PC files and being able to say, "You'll have it as soon as I get off the phone and send it to you."

8.8 Networking

Networking and LAN (which stands for Local Area Network) mean linking two or more PCs together. Networking has been used for years with mainframe computers, but only recently has come to personal computers. Companies like AST, Corvus, Davong, and Orchid Technology all manufacture networking packages for the PC.

IBM, just this year, announced a cluster package for networking. While this is somewhat limited, it does accomplish the task.

Because the field of networking is changing so quickly you should carefully assess your options and needs. This section is a brief introduction to networking with the IBM PC. For more complete explanations and background information you can refer to books which focus on communications and networking.

Here's what you need for networking:

- A fixed disk (either an PC/XT or a separate fixed disk unit), although you can get by without one.
- Networking adapter cards for each PC in the network. These adapter cards allow your PC to function in the network—sending and receiving information.
- Special cables for connecting the PCs. These cables are limited, depending on the type of network you are installing. These limitations will be covered in the user manual.
- A special software package which allows you to send information back and forth in the network and access a printer or fixed disk that is not directly connected to your PC.

Anything else that you will need will be outlined in the user manual that should be included in the networking package you purchase. While setting up a network is complicated, it isn't impossible to do. However, what you are doing is complex and technical. There can be problems if anything isn't done correctly. Buying a package (like the one from Davong Systems, known as the Starter Kit) with everything in it is the ideal way to go.

With such a starter kit you can do it all yourself. Many people, because of the time and research needed to understand networking, take advantage of the stores and consultants who provide assistance (usually at an hourly rate). While the installation manuals walk you though each step, problems that may develop can be hard to trace.

Often the local computer store has a networking system set up for demonstration purposes. If you don't have the luxury of trying before buying, ask for some references. Before you invest in a networking system it is best to see one already working. More importantly, it is extremely helpful for you to actually try out the networking system to see how the commands work.

Networking expands the potential of your PC and allows two or more PCs to share a fixed disk, a printer, and other devices. Reducing costs and improving efficiency are strong factors in favor of networking. There will be more and more developments in networking, especially now that AT&T has announced the PC Interface (see Chapter 9, section 9.4).

That networking capability from AT&T allows you to use a PC with an AT&T 3B computer. And that means networking with AT&T's mainframe computers and being able to take advantage of the advanced operating system known as UNIX System V.

9

This chapter is a collection of miscellaneous options for expanding the use of your PC. From the mouse to the intriguing Dvorak keyboard, you will discover more ways to get extra power and use out of your PC.

AT&T has entered the computer marketplace in a big way. This chapter will explain how you can now link IBM PCs to the AT&T 3B family of computers. That means you can now use your PC within the UNIX System V operating system and take advantage of the 'C' programming language under UNIX. UNIX has been available for the PC, but now there is a direct connection to AT&T's latest version of this operating system.

Using just about any kind of CP/M or Apple program on your PC is covered in this chapter. Speech synthesis and its uses on the PC, surge supressors, and uninterruptible power sources are also reviewed here.

Finally, windows: what they are, how they work, and why you might want them, are explained in detail.

Most of this chapter comes under the category of add-on devices. With so many add-ons for the IBM PC, it is easy to want it all, succumbing to the hypnotic attraction of EXPAND! EXPAND! EXPAND!

We all find ourselves showing off with our PCs from time to time, but when it comes to expanding the use of your PC you should first look at need versus want. One reason is financial. Other factors, such as how often you will use the items you are installing, and how practical they are for you, must be considered. If you have unlimited funds you can load up your PC to the maximum. The basic question still remains, "What do you really need?" You need to evaluate that yourself, carefully and objectively.

9.1 Adding a Mouse—Step By Step

Talking about a mouse for your IBM PC will, without a doubt, bring a smile to many faces. However, when it comes to getting down to the business, the mouse has many advantages in cursor movement and ease of use.

This section will focus on just what the mouse is and how it works. The Microsoft mouse will be used as an example here, along with the word processing program, Microsoft Word (which uses the mouse). Both are popular and illustrate the variety of uses and advantages of a mouse. Other companies manufacture similar products. Hooking up the Microsoft mouse will be covered at the end of this section.

Figure 9.1 shows a typical mouse, a small unit with a rolling device on the bottom of it. Moving the mouse will take about one square foot of space on your desk. As you move the mouse, the cursor moves on the PC's screen. The mouse also has buttons (one or more), which allow you to communicate with the PC. As a button is pressed a specific command is carried out.

The mouse got its name from its size and from the little black cord connecting it to the back of the PC.

Moving the cursor (effortlessly and quickly) isn't all that the mouse does. Using the mouse you can select menu commands and even create graphics without ever touching the keyboard. It's as simple as pointing to the menu item you want and then clicking one of the buttons on the top of the mouse (see Figure 9.2). Once you click the button your command will be carried out instantly.

The Microsoft mouse has attracted a lot of attention because it was designed not only to run with Microsoft's Word, but to work very well with four of the most popular programs for the IBM PC: Wordstar, VisiCalc, Multiplan, and 1-2-3.

The menus for all of these programs now allow command selection through the use of the mouse. That means hardly any keyboard control and swift, easy, cursor movement with the mouse. Microsoft designed their mouse with an incredible amount of flexibility. You can modify any of those menus and even design your own. You can create mouse menus for programs you write, too. The Microsoft manual takes you

Fig. 9.1: Microsoft mouse, showing the two buttons for clicking

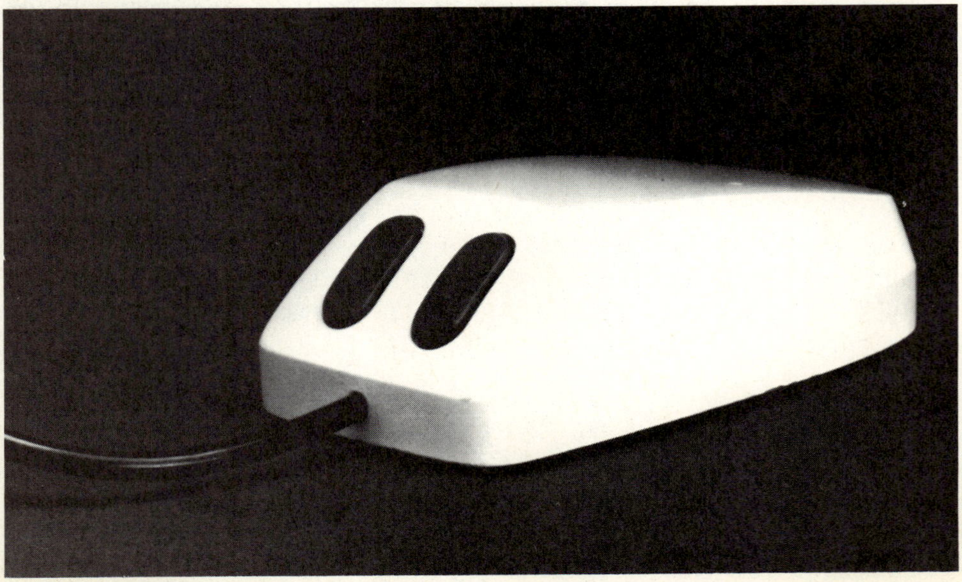

Courtesy of Microsoft Corporation

Fig. 9.2: Top and bottom view of the mouse

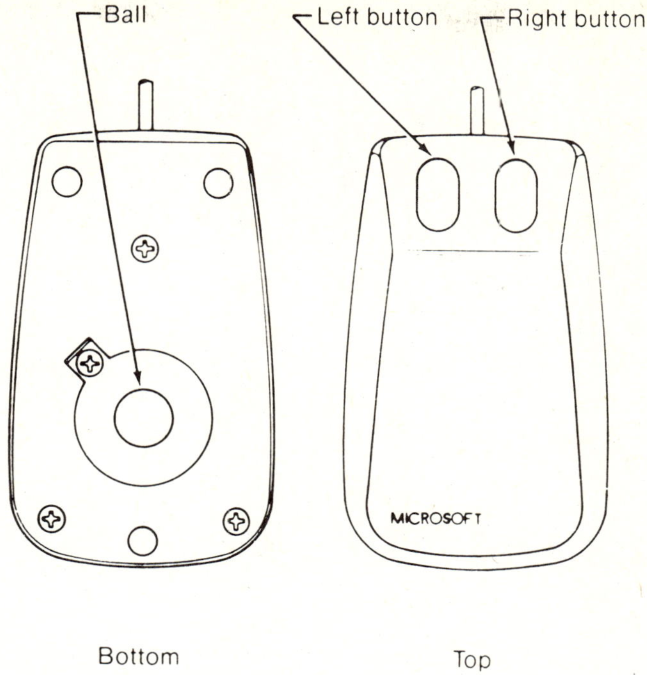

Courtesy of Microsoft Corporation

carefully and slowly through each and every step of modifying and designing programs and using menus.

A mouse lets you point to something in a menu and select it with the flick of a button. Normally, the cursor for the Microsoft mouse is a rectangular box, taking up a space the size of a character. However, when you use the mouse to move the cursor into a menu area, that cursor turns into an arrow. You then use the mouse to point the arrow at whichever item in the menu you want. To get that item, you press a button on the mouse.

The mouse moves the cursor or pointer (i.e., the arrow) to any area of the screen you want. You control what happens by what you do with the mouse. Here's what you can do with the mouse pointer:

- Select text
- Scroll in the document
- Split and close windows (not in Wordstar)
- Move a window border (only in Microsoft Word)
- Turn ruler on and off (only in Microsoft Word)
- Set, clear, and move tab stops
- Change indents
- Request help for a specific topic

Fig. 9.3: Menu showing mouse arrow to select an item

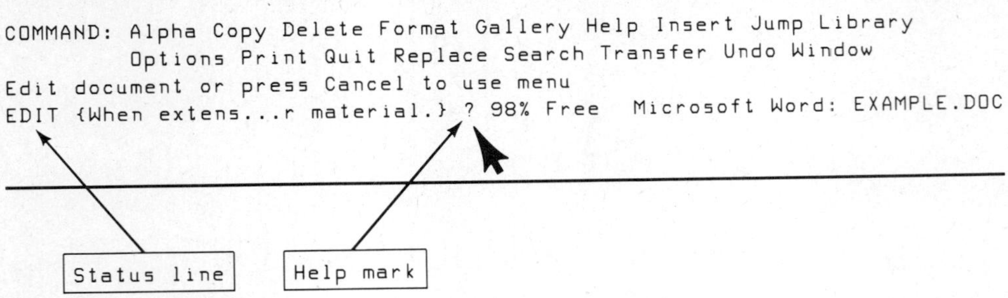

Courtesy of Microsoft Corporation

Fig. 9.4: Microsoft mouse menu for initial menu of Wordstar

```
                       <<<NO-FILE MENU>>>
Cancel menu     Change drive      Print a file  Rename a file  Run a program
Open document   Toggle file dir                 Delete a file  Run Spellstar
Open no-doc     Set help level    Exit to DOS   Copy a file    Run Mailmerge
```

Courtesy of Microsoft Corporation

Microsoft's word processing program not only benefits from the flexibility of the mouse, it also has some merits of its own. Boldfacing, italics, and underlining are all shown on the screen as they will appear on the printed page. You can split the screen into different areas called windows. Using up to eight windows at one time, you can look at different parts of a file simultaneously. You can also view several different files at once and easily copy information from one to the other.

Microsoft Word is an impressive word processing program, enhanced by mouse technology. The new AT&T 3B computers also use mouse technology, as do Apple's Macintosh, Lisa and IIC. Whether you plan to use a mouse or not, you should at least be aware of it . . . and even try it out at some time. The general feeling of the personal computer industry analysts is that you will be seeing more and more programs written to take advantage of mouse technology.

All of those programs, however, will also be written to run without a mouse. Microsoft's word processing program lets you work with or without a mouse. Keyboard controls can still handle everything the mouse does. It's just that in many cases the mouse is faster and easier.

The Microsoft mouse is available either in a package with Microsoft Word or separately. Microsoft made a shrewd marketing decision when it decided to make the mouse available separately and then, as part of the mouse purchase price, to include the necessary software to run the mouse with Wordstar, VisiCalc, Multiplan, or 1-2-3.

Once you have the Microsoft mouse—with or without the word processing program—you are ready to install it. You will need a medium, flat head screwdriver for putting the mouse adapter card inside your PC.

The following steps will explain how to install the mouse adapter card and also how to hook up the mouse:

STEP ONE: Remove the cover from your PC. Be absolutely sure that you have unplugged all power cords and disconnected the cables from the back of your PC.

STEP TWO: The mouse adapter card, which comes with your Microsoft mouse, allows your PC to function with a mouse. Install that adapter card in one of the empty expansion slots on the system board of your PC. The procedure for installing an adapter card is outlined in Chapter 2, section 2.6.

Once you have installed your mouse adapter card, put the cover back on the PC.

STEP THREE: Now you are ready to attach the mouse cord to the mouse adapter card at the back of the PC. Figure 9.5 shows you how the mouse cord is attached at the back panel.

STEP FOUR: You can't begin to use your Microsoft mouse until you have loaded a special program into your PC's memory. To set this software up properly, and to be sure it is done correctly, you must first read the README.DOC file, which is supplied on the Microsoft mouse program disk. Following the instructions outlined in that file you will create a program disk that will always be ready to use the mouse.

Fig. 9.5: Mouse cord attached to the back of the PC

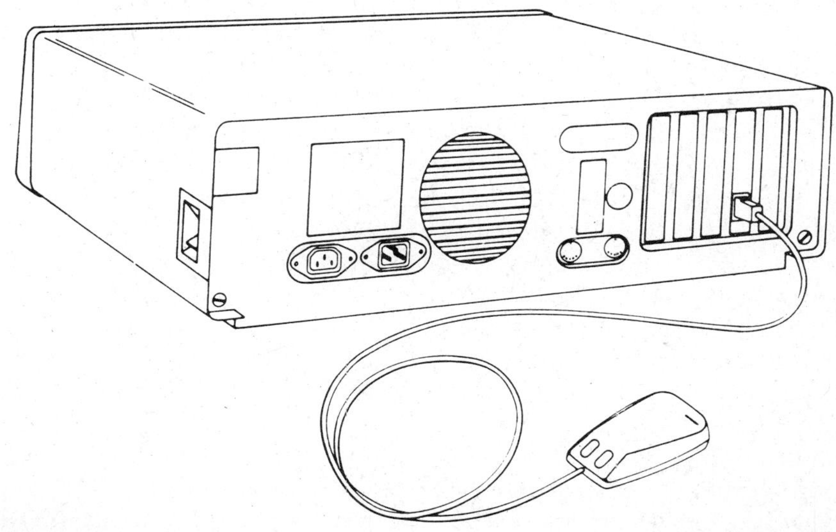

Courtesy of Microsoft Corporation

If you are using DOS 2.0 (or a newer version) you can choose to create a CONFIG.SYS file, which will automatically take care of setting things up for the mouse each time you turn on your PC. A CONFIG.SYS file is always read first by DOS (even before an AUTOEXEC.BAT file), when the system is turned on or when it is re-booted (i.e., by tapping the ALTERNATE, CONTROL and DELETE keys).

After DOS reads that CONFIG.SYS file it will create a device driver. (In this case the mouse is the device.) The CONFIG.SYS file directs DOS to read a specific file on the disk which drives the mouse.

STEP FIVE: Copy the CONFIG.SYS file from the Microsoft mouse software disk to your program disk.

STEP SIX: Now, using a text editor (in the non-document mode), type in `DEVICE=MOUSE.SYS` into the CONFIG.SYS file.

STEP SEVEN: Delete the AUTOEXEC.BAT file from your program disk. You are now ready to use the mouse each time your PC is turned on or re-booted.

Please Note: Once you have made this change to your working program disk there will be one difference from the program disk created by following the instructions of the README.DOC file. No message will appear to notify you that the mouse has been properly installed. This might not seem too important, but a notice on the screen saying, "Mouse driver installed," makes many people feel a little more secure.

If you encounter any problems using the mouse you should retrace your steps—those listed here and the ones in the *Microsoft Mouse Installation and Operation Manual*. For problems beyond that you should check with the store.

9.2 Windows for Your PC!

For the future historian of technology, one of the more significant computer phenomena of 1984 will certainly have been windows. A window is a visible sign of running more than one program at a time. Windows divide up your monitor's screen into sections so that you can look at different programs and files (or several areas of a single file) simultaneously.

Integrated programs mean you can not only run word processing, data base and bookkeeping programs all at once, but move information back and forth between files. That opens up a new dimension of computer power; you can take portions of spreadsheets, charts, or graphs and combine them with the text of a word processor. Many window programs take advantage of mouse technology for quick cursor movement and menu selection.

Figure 9.6 shows one concept of windows in which files are placed on your screen the way papers and reports are placed on your desk—some on top of others. You can easily move a file to the top of the pile—only here it is done with specific commands.

Windows can also be created side by side on the monitor's screen. In other words, there are no overlapping files on the screen. The screen is just proportioned

Fig. 9.6: IBM PC with Quarterdeck DESQ windows on the monitor's screen

Courtesy of Quarterdeck

into areas which border on each other. The windows from Microsoft work this way, but most companies producing windows are overlapping them.

Integrated programs and their resulting window environments require as much as 512KB RAM (i.e., user memory). Here's a brief rundown of the user memory requirements of five integrated programs with windows:

- Concurrent DOS from Digital Research: requires 256KB RAM
- DESQ from Quarterdeck Systems: requires 512KB RAM
- Framwork from Ashton-Tate: requires 384KB RAM
- Symphony from Lotus Development Corporation: requires 320KB RAM
- VISION from Visicorp: requires 512KB RAM
- Windows from Microsoft Corporation: requires 192KB RAM

The concept of dividing the screen into different areas isn't new. Even the original Visicalc provided windows. Programs like 1-2-3 and Microsoft's Word just took it a step or two further. Now, however, the use of windows seems to imply more than one application or program is in use. Instead of (as in the old days) taking out your word processing program disk to run a spreadsheet program, with windows you now have it all in one—sharing information between files without ever changing disks.

One of the best aspects of window environments is that even though you are using several different types of programs simultaneously, the commands you use to control the programs are all the same. This eliminates having to learn different commands for the same tasks. Window environments work from keyboard control, with many of the programs written for a two or three button mouse. Some programs even allow you to access mainframe computers through a window, while still working with other programs in separate windows. You can have up to nine windows in a program like DESQ.

DESQ takes a little bit different approach to windows. With DESQ you can use programs you already own (like Wordstar or VisiCalc) all at the same time, too. Since you already know the commands there shouldn't be any problem using the system. This is significant because it adds a new dimension to your "old" programs.

Symphony, from Lotus Development Corporation, has been the most watched of all window programs. Lotus released this program while its other product, 1-2-3, was still in the number one position on the IBM PC software sales chart. Symphony has enhanced the aspects of 1-2-3 and added new features, such as improved word processing, communications, and what Lotus called open-endedness to allow for add-in programs. In other words, you can tie in any program you currently use to Symphony. As with other window products, you can work with two or more files on the screen at once. Shown in Figure 9.7 are two word processing windows and one data base window. Symphony also supports the operating environments of Microsoft Windows and Quarterdeck's DESQ.

Fig. 9.7: Symphony screen showing two word processing and one data base file

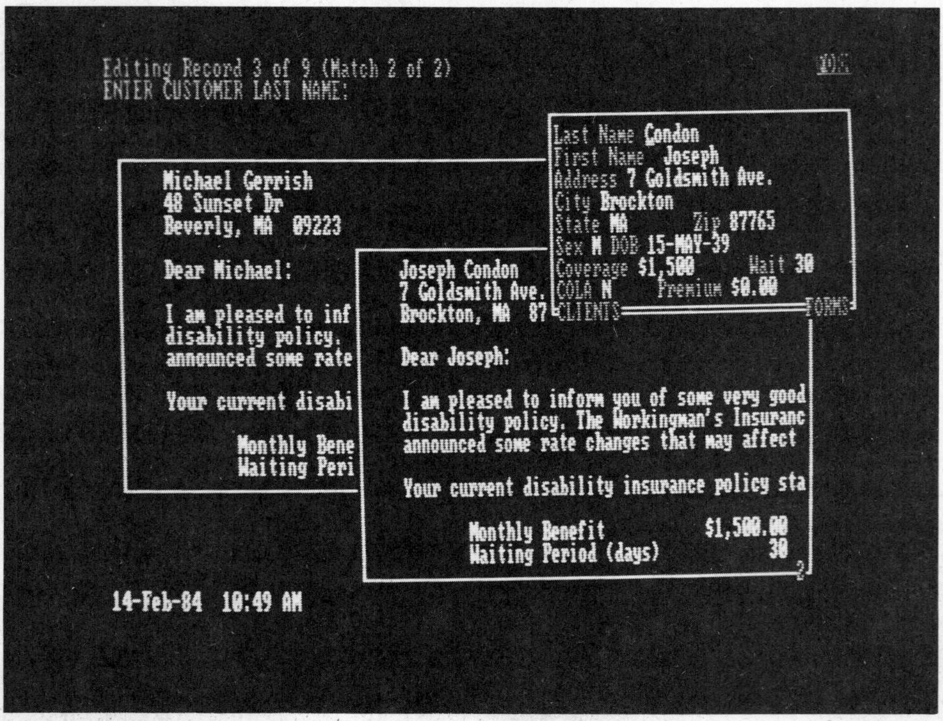

Courtesy of Lotus Development Corporation

While windows and integrated programs are complex, they aren't that hard to learn and adapt to. The luxury of working with more than one type of program at one time will cause rapid growth of integrated programs. Instead of having to learn the commands for three, four, or five different types of programs, you can now do it all at once. Windows can be a bit overwhelming at first, but after working with them for a while you will find yourself wondering why more programs aren't written that way.

If you're interested in windows for your PC, have a look at your options before you make a decision. This is a rapidly emerging technology and you don't want to find yourself locked into a windowing program that is outdated or awkward.

Several dozen windowing integrated programs will be introduced within the next year. When the dust settles that number will be significantly smaller. Carefully evaluate the companies and their products before you put out the cash to work windowing for yourself.

9.3 Using Apple and CP/M Programs

You have several options for using CP/M and Apple program disks in your IBM PC. In most cases, running such programs will be accomplished through the use of specific software adapter card.

What you are actually doing with this software and hardware is making your PC think it is an Apple or CP/M machine. The process is somewhat complex and not quite flawless. Almost all of the Apple and CP/M programs can be used on an IBM PC, but there will be programs that won't run on the PC no matter what you do.

You will also find other little quirks and kinks. Most of these will be minor and not cause any real problems. In some cases you'll be able to run Apple software on a PC/XT, but without the use of the PC/XT's fixed disk.

One of the most useful aspects of a connection between an IBM PC and Apple or CP/M software, is that if you have up-graded from an Apple to a PC, you can easily transfer your old disk files to PC files. Even if you only use such an option when you buy your PC, it is worth it when you consider all the time it would take to have dozens (or hundreds) of files retyped in the PC format. However, many people keep their Apple computers after getting PCs. Now they can use both, knowing the files can be moved back and forth between the two.

From Apple to the IBM PC and Back Again!

There are many products which allow you to run most Apple program disks in your PC. The costs vary greatly for such products but they do provide an important link between the PC and Apple. If you plan to run Apple programs on your PC, you should get the program manuals for Applesoft BASIC and Apple DOS. When your PC is running Apple software you will need to use Apple commands and work according to Apple rules. While there are some similarities in the commands, there are also vast differences. Do yourself a favor and start with the Apple manuals. They will add to your overall costs, but in the long run save you much heartache.

If you only need to transfer files between your PC and an Apple, then you might want to look at the software package offered by Alpha Software Corporation. For under $200 this company offers *The Apple-*IBM *Connection*. With this software you can transfer any file back and forth between an Apple and your IBM. This software will also let you connect the PC to the Apple with a cable or a modem hookup. Then you can transfer information between the computers any time you want. This is all done with a special disk in each computer and is ideal if you still own an Apple and want to use it in conjunction with your PC.

Alpha has designed its software for the non-technical user. It's as simple as turning the computer(s) on and letting the software do all the work. It starts by asking you the name of the file being transferred. After a few other questions (in less than a minute) the file has been quietly moved from one computer to the other.

CP/M for the IBM PC

The IBM PC market place offers dozens of options for running CP/M on the PC. From software packages to adapter cards, the choices are many and varied. There are even special multifunction adapter cards for the PC which allow you to run CP/M programs.

One such multifunction adapter card is the Baby Blue II, manufactured by Microlog, Inc. This card throws in an extra bargain in the form of the capability to run programs written for the CP/M-80 operating system. The Baby Blue II adapter card has a Z-80 microprocessor on it, which allows it to run CP/M-80 software.

The design of Microlog's CP/M emulator allows you to freely mix PC-DOS programs with those written for CP/M-80. You can run whichever programs you choose, knowing the Baby Blue will handle them for you. You can also transfer files back and forth between PC-DOS and CP/M formats. There's even a built in keyfix function on the Baby Blue to set up your keyboard with up to 54 programmable function keys for CP/M programs. Each programmed key can hold up to 80 characters. That means you can save dozens of keystroke commands by assigning them to one specific key.

The Baby Blue II comes with a special diskette which has the files to help you extend PC-DOS; that is, to add new operating commands to the ones you are already working with. You will use these new commands to:

- convert CP/M programs to run under PC-DOS
- transfer files between CP/M and PC-DOS
- provide programmable function keys for CP/M programs

You install the Baby Blue II multifunction adapter card in one of the empty expansion slots on the system board of your PC. (See Chapter 2, section 2.6.) Then you transfer certain files from the Microlog diskette to your working diskette. These files are accessed through specific commands similar to DIR, COPY, and others in PC-DOS. The commands for the Baby Blue II allow you to work with CP/M-80 programs and files.

There was a time when being able to use Apple or CP/M programs and files on the IBM PC was extremely important. That was in the old days when there weren't too many programs at all for the PC. At this point—and from here on out—just about anything you need is written for the IBM PC or at least in MS-DOS.

However, if you do need to use and/or transfer files back and forth between your PC and Apple or CP/M formats, you have plenty of options. Again, check into what others have done. Ask friends and business associates about it. And check with local IBM PC user groups. Don't forget about your local computer store either.

9.4 The AT&T Connection

After many months of rumors and speculation, AT&T announced its line of 3B computers in late March of 1984. That 3B family of computers ranges from super mainframes down to desk top models—all running on 32-bit technology and the UNIX operating system. Much to everyone's surprise AT&T also announced the PC Interface.

The PC Interface, exactly as the name implies, ties together the two most popular operating systems on the market today. PC-DOS (and MS-DOS) and UNIX System V can now work together because of the PC Interface. This move on AT&T's part was viewed as friendly, but was also shrewd in that the hundreds of thousands of IBM PCs already sold can be conveniently tied into an AT&T system.

AT&T's PC Interface is a combination of hardware and software that interconnects the PC to an AT&T 3B computer. Several PCs could be linked to AT&T computers, sharing files and peripheral devices such as printers, fixed disks, and disk drives. Another important factor is that with an IBM PC you can now work in the famous UNIX operating environment. While variations of UNIX have been available for the PC, the UNIX System V operating system is the most advanced and fastest.

9.5 The Dvorak Keyboard

The keyboard that comes with your PC is called a QWERTY, after the first six letters on the second row. The layout of this keyboard dates back to the 1870s, when inventor Christopher Sholes did something about mechanical typewriters that kept jamming. Up to that point there was no standard for typewriter keyboards. Sholes stopped the jamming by spreading out the most used keys to slow typists down. Soon the QWERTY keyboard became the standard and has remained so.

August Dvorak's studies of easier ways for people to use machines led to his development of the Dvorak keyboard in 1936 (see Figure 9.9). Dvorak's keyboard alternates the use of each hand and places the most used keys in a much better location. The result is improved typing speed. On the QWERTY keyboard almost 60 percent of the typing is done by the left hand. Dvorak's keyboard evens out the work load, with a little bit more devoted to the right hand.

Dvorak's keyboard places the vowels and most used consonants on the home, or middle, row of keys. That alone increases typing speed, because 70 percent of all typing is done on the home row. More than 3,000 words can be typed without ever moving your fingers from that row. The next most commonly used letters are placed on the top row. The least commonly used letters are on the bottom row. A typist's rhythm becomes much smoother on the Dvorak keyboard because of the key placement.

There is less fatigue, too, because the work of both hands—the movement from side to side and up and down on the keyboard—is more balanced. The Dvorak

Fig. 9.8: The QWERTY keyboard

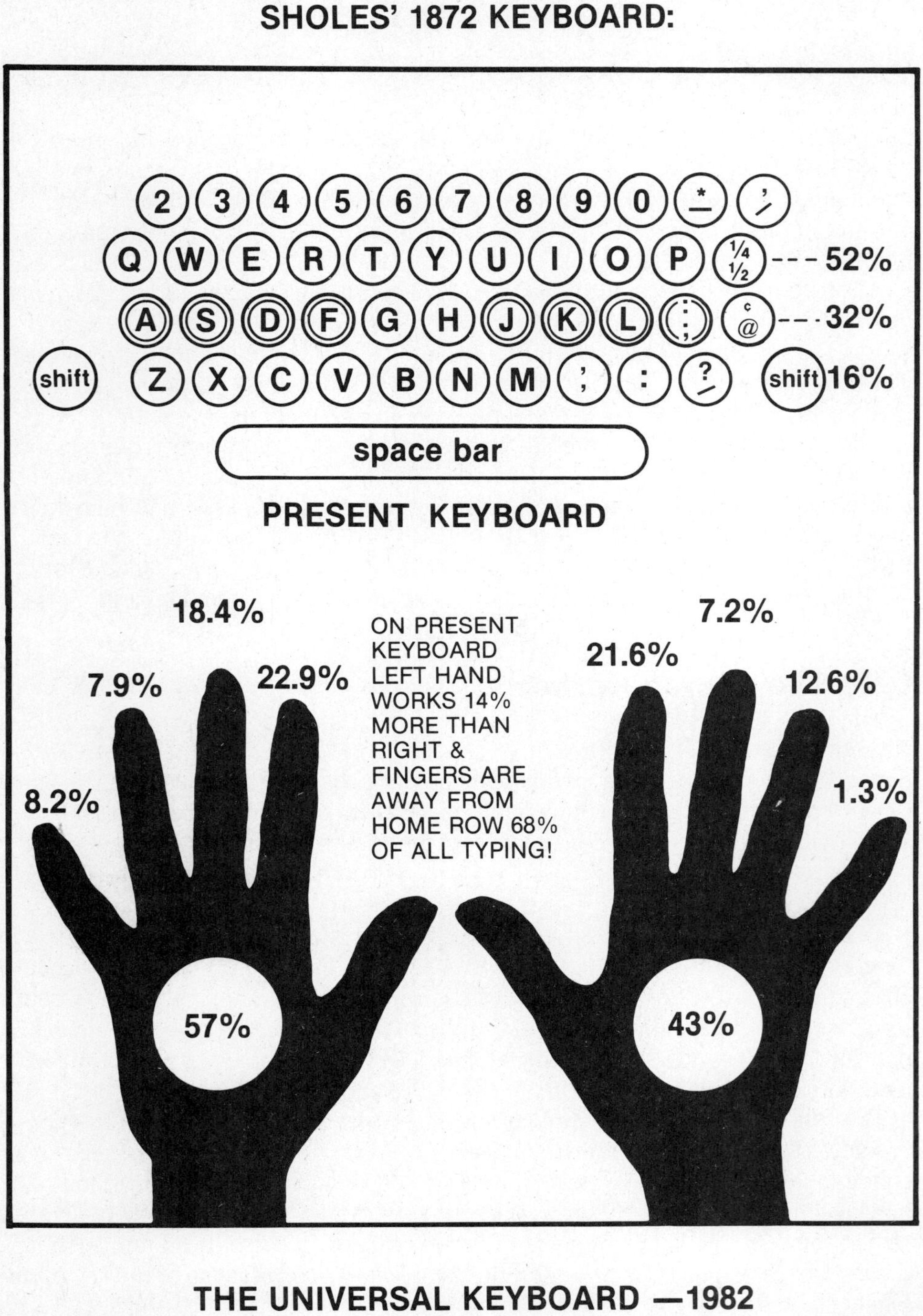

Fig. 9.9: The Dvorak keyboard

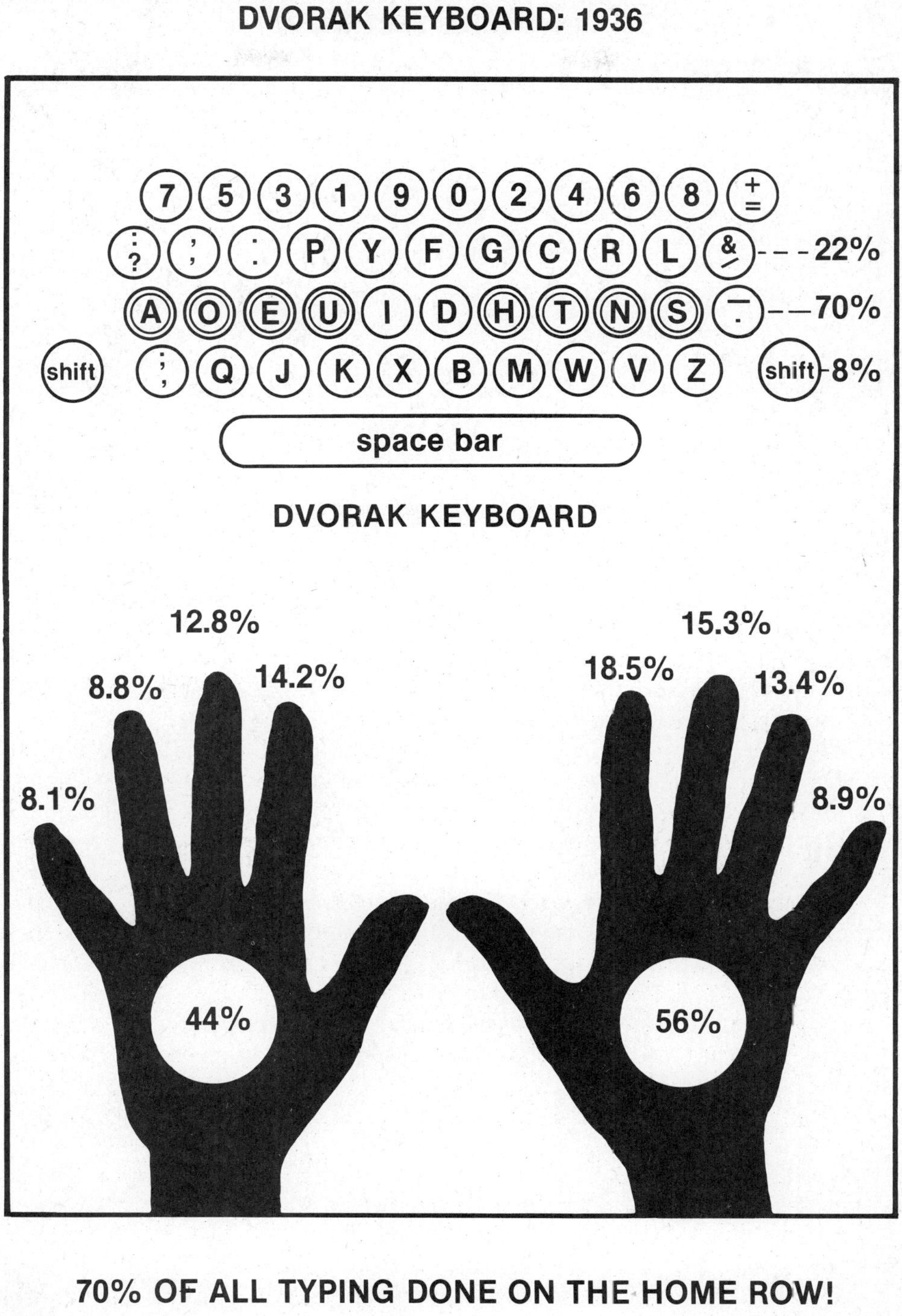

keyboard reduces the number of words typed by just one hand. Dvorak's design creates a shifting of work back and forth between the hands. The number of times that typing a word will require using all three rows of keys has almost been eliminated. Most of the time you will move your fingers from the home row either up to the top row or down to the bottom row—but not both.

The Dvorak keyboard moves most punctuation up to the top row. The order of the numbers has been changed, too. Only the letters A and M remain in the same position on the Dvorak keyboard. Studies show that the Dvorak keyboard is easier to learn and much faster to use.

While the claims that the Dvorak keyboard is more efficient and productive are valid, there is a big question about whether or not it will ever see widespread use. Major corporations have evaluated it for potential, but as of now, use of the Dvorak keyboard has been limited, (though it has been available for many years on IBM typewriters, among others).

The big question about the Dvorak keyboard has to do with the millions of QWERTY keyboards all over the world. Whether we like it or not, the QWERTY keyboard is a very solid standard. However, if the Dvorak keyboard is better it will allow for even more productive use of computers—PCs and others. Once you learn the Dvorak keyboard, you can still use the QWERTY keyboard, but there is definitely some confusion in working with both.

If you want to try the Dvorak keyboard on your PC you have a couple of options. One is a software package called SureStroke from Seasoned Systems, and one is a replacement keyboard from Key Tronic. The Surestroke package sells for approximately $50 and modifies DOS to re-structure your keyboard into the Dvorak setup. It works with DOS 1.0, 1.1 and 2.0. The Key Tronic keyboard sells for approximately $250 and just plugs into the same socket as the standard PC keyboard.

While the Key Tronic Dvorak keyboard is easier to install, it costs more. Seasoned Systems' approach results in the same Dvorak configuration for much less money. Their SureStroke package even comes with a cassette tape to walk you through the learning process. Transfer letters to mark the individual keys without any permanent damage are included with their manual.

The manual also shows you how to pop off the key tops—if you are so inclined—and move them into the Dvorak positions. Seasoned Systems also designed their Dvorak keyboard with an escape feature which allows you to go back to the regular keyboard layout any time you want to.

According to Seasoned Systems, a professional keyboard operator's fingers travel 19 miles a day. The Dvorak keyboard reduces that distance to a mile, greatly reducing fatigue.

Here's how to set up Seasoned Systems' Dvorak keyboard on your PC:

STEP ONE: You will modify the working copy of your DOS diskette first. It would be a good idea to make a copy of your working DOS disk and then use that whenever you want the Dvorak keyboard. You can easily modify the DOS disk on a PC with one disk drive, two disk drives, or a fixed disk.

All you do is place the Seasoned Systems' SureStroke diskette in the appropriate disk drive (following their manual's instructions). Then follow the instructions on the screen to create your Dvorak DOS disk.

STEP TWO: Once you have modified the DOS disk you are ready to use the Dvorak keyboard. However, you must first mark the keys on your keyboard.

Before you do anything—TURN OFF YOUR PC.

The SureStroke package comes with three sets of transfer letters. By following the diagram in the SureStroke manual, you can easily place the transfer letters on the correct keytops. Or, you can place the transfer letters on the front of the keys, instead of on top. That way the transfer letters won't wear out, and your keyboard will have a cleaner look.

To place the transfer letters on the front of each key requires removing the keys. The manual explains how to do that. You just might want to move the keytops into the Dvorak configuration and not bother with the transfer letters. Seasoned Systems designed a lot of flexibility into their package.

Removing the keytops will not hurt your PC keyboard in any way. If you do move the keytops into the Dvorak positions and then decide you like the QWERTY setup better, it's just as easy to pop off the keytops again and return them to their original positions.

STEP THREE: The Dvorak keyboard will not be installed each time you boot up your system until *after* the time and date have been entered. If you have a multifunction adapter card with a clock/timer on it you don't need to be concerned here. If you don't, when the prompt for the time and date come up you face the awkward prospect of typing in that information QWERTY style on a keyboard marked for Dvorak.

You can get around this by just hitting the enter key in response to both prompts. That will solve the dilemma but result in no date/time stamp on your file. That isn't a major problem, but when you enter a DIR command it often helps to know just when a file was created. You can hit the enter key twice, and then, with the Dvorak keyboard, type TIME to enter the current time, followed by DATE to enter the correct date.

Once you get past the time and date by either entering it or hitting the enter key, the Dvorak keyboard goes into effect. You don't need to do anything further to set up the Dvorak keyboard. It is all done automatically.

STEP FOUR: To help you learn the Dvorak keyboard, Seasoned Systems has included a program file called The Coach and a listening cassette tape. The Coach and the cassette guide you through the three stages of learning the Dvorak keyboard:

- Learning the key locations
- Making it automatic
- Rapid all-finger touch stroking

The Coach is extremely helpful because as it gives you exercises it also shows you a Dvorak keyboard on the screen. In the lower part of the screen is a pair of hands. As you come to each letter, the finger needed to enter the letter moves and the letter appears on the fingertip. Then the letter also lights up on the screen's keyboard. As you come to know the Dvorak keyboard, The Coach helps you build up your speed. The Coach can keep track of 12 people—their progress and speeds—as they learn the Dvorak keyboard.

The cassette tape takes advantage of self-hypnosis techniques. Seasoned Systems says that this tape's suggestions are important for those who want to retain their QWERTY skills.

Using the Dvorak keyboard for even a short time can become addicting, mainly because you can type so many words without ever leaving the home row. You also notice the immediate improvement in your rhythm and speed. The best way to decide if it's for you is to give it a try. You'll be surprised by the experience. Learning the Dvorak really doesn't take that long—especially compared to the drudgery of learning the QWERTY keyboard.

9.6 Speech Synthesis

We've all seen talking computers for years on television and in the movies. The science of synthesizing human speech is extremely complicated and involved. It also requires a lot of user memory (RAM), which really wasn't available for personal computers until a few years ago. The technology can now reproduce human speech very close to the real thing. Speech synthesis is accomplished two ways.

Text to speech is the most common form of speech synthesis. Here words (i.e., text) are electronically reproduced through phonetic encoding. The words you type into the computer are spoken by a speech unit inside (or outside) the computer. This method uses the least amount of memory because there are only 50 basic phonemes in the English language which need to be stored for random use. A computer sounds somewhat robotic when text to speech is used and many words need to be mis-typed to sound correct phonetically.

Fixed speech is preferred for closer duplication of the human voice. Through the use of a custom vocabulary for which a person has actually spoken words which were then digitized, the computer calls up words as needed. This form of synthesized speech requires large amounts of user memory and is usually found in more commercial applications like the talking check-out register at the grocery store.

For home and general business use, speech synthesis has largely been generated through text to speech. The actual words are produced as speech in much the same way as output from the PC is printed when it is contained in a PRINT statement. A speaker (beyond the one provided with the PC) is needed for better quality sound reproduction.

While speech synthesis has become associated with computer games, it has many other applications which are quite useful and valid.

People with speech defects can now use their PC to talk—even on the telephone, with the proper setup.

Programs are being developed which allow people who are blind or have limited sight to take advantage of word processing. This new form of word processing has an audible cursor and actually says each letter, number, or space as it is typed. Other programs read to blind people through speech synthesis.

Business and industry are using synthesized speech for training employees. Inventory and even sales reports are now available over the telephone through speech synthesis.

Education is probably the most popular area for speech synthesis and holds the most potential. Children have a lot of fun with computers—so much so that they really don't realize they are learning. A talking computer has much more time to devote to each student than a teacher does, and it allows the teacher to do other things. Easily made corrections, repetition, ease of use, simple selection of answers, bright colors and graphics, positive reinforcement, and fun are the ingredients which make speech synthesis such a winner in education.

The heart of any speech synthesis unit for a computer is the speech chip, which mimics the process of human speech. Tecmar makes a speech synthesis adapter card called the Speech Master for the IBM PC. It comes with a miniature speaker and still fits very well into one of the expansion slots. The Speech Master manual explains how to use speech synthesis and how to develop your own applications.

Here's how to hook up the Speech Master:

STEP ONE: Turn off your PC and unhook all the connections, including the power plugs.

STEP TWO: Install the Speech Master adapter card. (See Chapter 2, section 2.6.) Once the adapter card is installed on the system board of your PC and you have put the cover back on your PC (see Appendix C) you may proceed to the next step.

STEP THREE: Turn on your PC. Load the Tecmar DEMO program by placing the Tecmar software disk in the A drive of your PC and typing `DEMO` at the DOS prompt. Now your PC will make a brief speech.

STEP FOUR: Now load the TALK program by typing `TALK.` This program is designed to say whatever you type on the keyboard. It is at this point you will discover that you must mis-type many words for them to sound correct (because the words are spoken phonetically). With the built-in buffer on the Speech Master you can type up to three lines of text without overloading the buffer.

To use speech synthesis in the BASIC programs you write, you must use the LPRINT statement for whatever you want to be spoken by your PC. At present, the practical applications for speech synthesis are somewhat limited. But it is fascinating to hear your PC talk. In fact, your PC takes on a whole new personality when it can talk.

Speech synthesis is a lot of fun with friends and relatives. The next time someone says, "What can that PC of yours really do?" let your PC answer the question. And voice recognition is on the horizon. Eventually your PC won't just be talking to you, you will enter commands by talking to it!

9.7 Surge Suppressors and Uninterruptible Power Sources

There's a lot of confusion about static electricity, power surges, and power interruptions. While all three are totally different, many people think they are all the same. The best way to explain the differences is to cover each of them separately.

If you are concerned about potential damage to your PC or afraid of losing valuable information and files, you should read this section very, very carefully. This information will prove to be quite valuable to you and others with whom you share it.

Static Electricity All of us build up static electricity when we walk across the room or even while we sit in a chair, making slight movements. Static electricity can destroy memory (and other) chips inside your PC. It can also damage or scramble data on floppy disks. Chapter 11, section 11.7 explains static electricity and how to deal with it in detail.

The most important point to consider is an anti-static mat under your PC. If you touch that mat often you won't have to worry about static electricity.

Power Surges Transient voltage surges (also known as spikes and glitches) appear suddenly and unexpectedly and can cause significant damage to your PC. Voltage spikes can be caused by lightning or power load changes by your utility company. Your PC power supply does have a built-in filter for surge protection (up to a certain point), but printers and monitors don't.

For a minimum investment (usually less than $100) you can buy an AC surge protector (Figure 9.10). A device like this, plugged in between your equipment and the wall power outlet, protects your PC and other equipment from power surges.

You might never need an AC surge protector, but you might want to buy one for the same reason you purchase theft insurance. The cost isn't all that much when you consider that it can save you hundreds of dollars in damage from just one voltage spike or line surge.

Fig. 9.10: AC Surge Protector from Electronic Protection Devices, Inc.

Courtesy of Electronic Protection Devices, Inc.

Power Interruptions While interruptions of electrical power won't hurt your PC, they can cause you to lose significant amounts of information and data. Whatever hasn't been saved to a floppy or fixed disk is lost when the power goes off. If you work with an emulated disk (see Chapter 5) you run the risk of losing all information each time the power goes off.

Power interruptions don't just happen in the winter or during storms: a blown fuse, a circuit breaker shutting off, an overloaded circuit breaker, someone turning off the power by mistake, a power pole being knocked out in an accident, even your PC being unplugged by mistake—all of these circumstances, and many more, show how vulnerable you are to power interruptions.

You can also plan on a power interruption wiping out precious file information just when it's least convenient, too. That's just one of those wonderful laws of nature that somehow seem to always work against us and our PCs.

All hope is not lost, however. With an AC power back-up or uninterruptible power source you can eliminate data loss forever. With such a device as the Datasaver (shown in Figure 9.11) you can have up to 30 minutes to save information to disk once the power goes off.

It usually doesn't take longer than a couple of minutes to save to the disk, so you really don't need too much time in terms of back-up power. Prices start around $400 and go up steeply from there, depending on what you choose in the way of wattage and length of back-up time.

Back-up power units also come in handy for voltage dips. Short term power dips can be just enough to cause your PC either to go off or to work erratically. With a

Fig. 9.11: Datasaver AC Power Back-up Unit

Courtesy of Cuesta Systems, Inc.

back-up power unit you don't have to worry about such problems. The cost is definitely a factor, but what is your time and effort worth in even one instance when the power goes off and you lose whatever was in RAM or on your emulated disk?

Most AC power back-up units recharge themselves and are little trouble to maintain. Installation is simple—just plug it into the wall outlet and then plug your PC into the power back-up unit. Several companies manufacture AC power back-up units and offer a wide variety of choices and models.

9.8 Joy Sticks

A joy stick is a device primarily for playing games on the IBM PC. It is designed for quick movement and rapid response to activities happening on the screen. The joy stick is basically a little black box with a short handle in the center. On the end of the handle is a round knob. Cursor movement on the screen is controlled by moving the handle and pressing a button or two on the black box (sometimes on the handle).

Before the IBM PC came along, joy sticks were almost mandatory if you wanted to play games. The PC changes all of that. While joy sticks are available for the PC, just about all games written for use on the PC can be controlled from the keyboard.

Keyboard control is admittedly a bit slower than a joy stick. However, if you want a joy stick, you need a game card adapter inside your PC. That means you need to use one your precious expansion slots or get a multifunction adapter card that includes a game adapter. Before you buy a game card adapter, closely evaluate your present and future computing needs.

If you plan to add a multifunction adapter card to your PC you will have used up three expansion slots at that point—two are already in use when you get your PC (one for the disk drive controller card and one for the monitor/printer adapter card). Then you might want to add:

- a graphics adapter card
- a fixed disk adapter card
- an internal modem
- a mouse adapter card
- a separate serial port adapter card
- a separate memory adapter card

All of those options illustrate how important that expansion slot you are considering for the game adapter card is. If you do decide to install a game adapter card, refer to Chapter 2, section 2.6 for card installation directions.

To hook up the joy stick you just attach its connector cord to the connection on the game adapter card at the back of the PC. Be sure to read the instructions that accompany the joy stick for any variations in installation or use.

10

The brains behind your IBM PC are located in the 8088 microprocessor chip. This 40-pin chip is made by Intel and was designed as an all purpose processor chip to handle many different functions in computing. The 8088 is an affordable and powerful 16 bit chip, which is just one of the reasons the IBM PC captured so much of the world's attention three years ago when the PC was introduced.

Until the 16 bit chip came along, most computers were running on 8 bit chips. The difference between the two is significant, because the 16 bit does things in multiples of 16 (instead of 8) and so functions more efficiently and quickly. Also, the 16 bit chip means that over one million bytes of memory can be accessed, compared to the maximum of 64,000 bytes from the 8 bit days (unless you did something known as bank-switching).

It's no wonder that the PC and the 8088 have become standards in the personal computer industry. However, the 8088 can't do everything as fast as everyone would like. For most of us, the speed of the 8088 is sufficient.

There are PC owners who do require more speed for math functions and that's where the Intel 8087 Numeric Data Processor comes in. For doing math, the 8087, which is referred to as a coprocessor, enhances the 8088. However, a point of clarification. You can't do anything with an 8087 Numeric Data Processor *unless you have the software to go with it* (which you either buy or write yourself). Many people assume that all you need to do is put the 8087 chip on the system board next to the 8088 chip and you're in business. It just doesn't work that way.

Before you run out and buy the 8087 you need to know about possible installation problems if you have an older PC (one made before mid-1983). If you have a newer PC or a PC/XT you won't have any trouble putting the 8087 in yourself. You can't, however, afford to ignore the problems considered hereif you do plan to use an 8087 math chip in an older model PC. In some cases, it just might be better to let your computer store install the 8087 math chip. Remember, if you own a newer PC or a PC/XT you will be able to install the 8087 almost effortlessly.

10.1 Just What Is the 8087 Coprocessor?

The 8087 coprocessor is a chip which does complicated math at blinding speed. The conservative estimates of how much faster the 8087 does math calculations range from 50 percent up, depending on what is being done. In complex mathematical equations and calculations that makes a significant difference.

IBM didn't do much at first with the 8087, other than to leave room for it next to the 8088 on the system board. Unfortunately the timing on some older PCs is incorrect for the 8087. This is further explained below.

Since the PC's introduction, there has been more and more done with the 8087 in the PC aftermarket, where so much else has happened. IBM's strategy has been to allow for as many options as possible in the design of the PC, and then to take a wait and see attitude. Once the popularity of the 8087 took off, IBM's interest in it intensified.

10.2 Now That the 8087 Is Popular IBM Does More with It

The 8087 is included as standard equipment in IBM's new 370 IX computers, which are beefed up versions of the PC. The 370 IX computers are used primarily to link PCs to mainframe computers. Otherwise they function like regular PCs. The 8087 package costs approximately $260 and is available from computer stores as well as other sources.

10.3 Not All PCs Are Created Equal When It Comes to the 8087

As mentioned in other chapters of this book, there are two versions of the IBM PC. Before you do anything else you need to check and see which PC you have. Figure 10.1 shows the back panel of the PC. If you see the letter 'B' in a circle, stamped between the fan and the expansion slot openings then you have a newer PC and will be able to install the 8087 yourself. If you don't see the 'B' then you have an older PC.

If you have an older PC, installing the 8087 yourself could lead to problems. Some 8088 chips in older PCs aren't timed right for the addition of the 8087. With such chips, no matter what you do, your new 8087 will never work properly.

You might want to consider having your computer store install the 8087. The store will automatically include a new 8088 in the bargain. IBM is making sure that you get an 8088 properly timed to go with your new 8087. The new 8088 is given to you and installed at no extra cost. If you buy an 8087 through the mail, you won't get this deal in most cases.

If you have one of the newer PCs or an PC/XT, you can install the 8087 yourself, because the 8088 the factory installed in them is timed properly for the 8087.

Fig. 10.1: Back panel of IBM Personal Computer, showing the location of 'B'

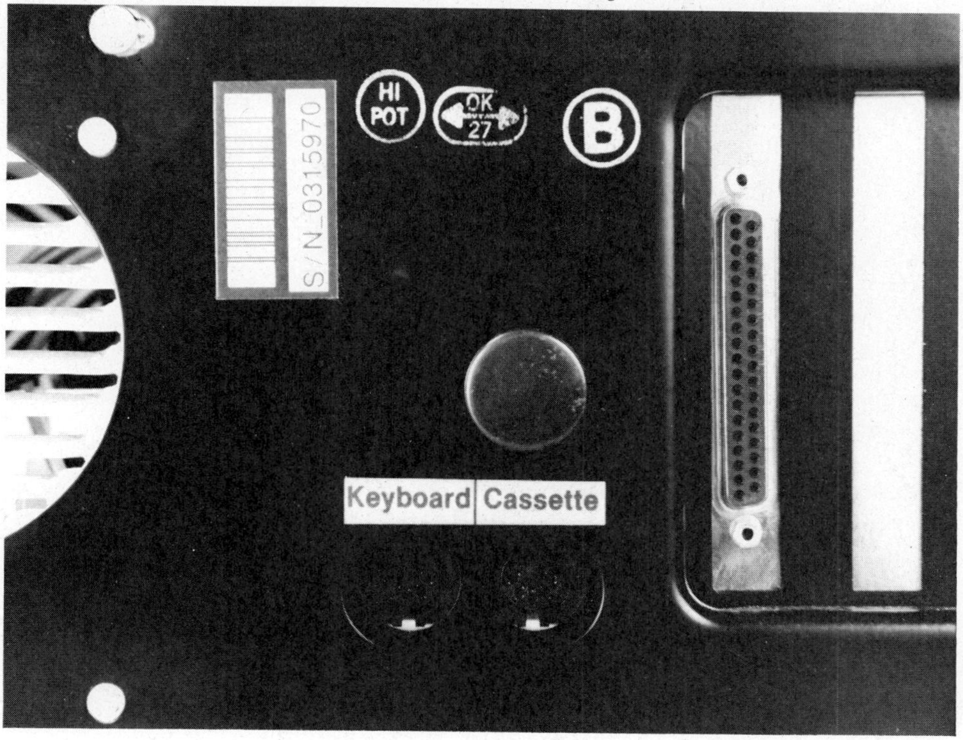

10.4 How To Put the 8087 Coprocessor in Your PC

It doesn't take long to install the 8087 chip. Once you take the cover off the PC you will probably be done in less than five minutes. However, you don't want to be in any kind of hurry. Take your time and carefully work your way through the steps outlined here. Read over any instructions included with the 8087 chip itself.

You won't need much in the way of tools to install the 8087 coprocessor. A pen, for flipping one switch on switch block 1, is about all you will need. You might want to use an insertion tool to hold on to the chip. The 8087 is much larger than memory chips and has 20 legs on each side. You must be extremely careful with it because the legs or pins can be easily bent.

Remember that static electricity can cause serious problems for your 8087 (just as it can for the memory chips). Leave the 8087 in its container until you are ready to install it. Touch it as little as possible. Wear rubber soled shoes and don't wear polyester clothes. Stand on an anti-static mat or spray anti-static spray on the floor where you will be standing. Touch the PC chassis frequently to ground residual charges.

STEP ONE: Remove the cover from the PC. Be sure that all cords and connections are unhooked from the PC.

STEP TWO: Figure 10.2 shows the inside of the PC with the disk drives facing you. The area you are primarily concerned with is between the power unit (which takes up most of the back right hand corner) and the expansion slots.

The 8088 processor is already installed (lengthwise toward you) in front of the black connection for the keyboard. To the right of the 8088 is an open connector. That is where you will place the 8087. Remove the 8087 from the protective wrapping and notice the circular notch on one end of it. See Figure 10.3.

STEP THREE: You will now place the 8087 chip in the connector slot next to the 8088 processor. Be sure that the notch on the 8087 is facing the same direction as the similar notch on the 8088. As the 8087 nestles into place it will make a crunching sound.

You can't be too careful when inserting the 8087. You need to be extremely cautious not to bend any of the 40 prongs or legs. Move the 8087 into position on the connector slot with gentle but firm pressure. Don't force it or hurry. Easy does it.

STEP FOUR: Once the 8087 is in you will need to flip one switch on switch block 1. (If you own a PC/XT you have only one switch block to begin with.)

Figure 10.4 shows which switch you need to set and how to set it. If this is a PC, be sure you are moving switch #2 on switch block 1.

Switch #2 needs to be flipped off (yes, off). If this seems backwards, it is, but that is how it works. If that switch is pressed down in the ON position then the circuit is closed, which means that the 8087 circuits are bypassed. So with the switch in the OFF position the 8087 circuit is open. That then brings in the 8087 coprocessor

Fig. 10.2: System board of the IBM Personal Computer
(Close-up of the area where the 8087 is located)

Fig. 10.3: The 8087 Numeric Data Processor Chip (Note the notch on one end)

Courtesy of Intel Corporation

Fig. 10.4: Switch block 1 on the IBM Personal Computer
(showing correct switch setting for the 8087)

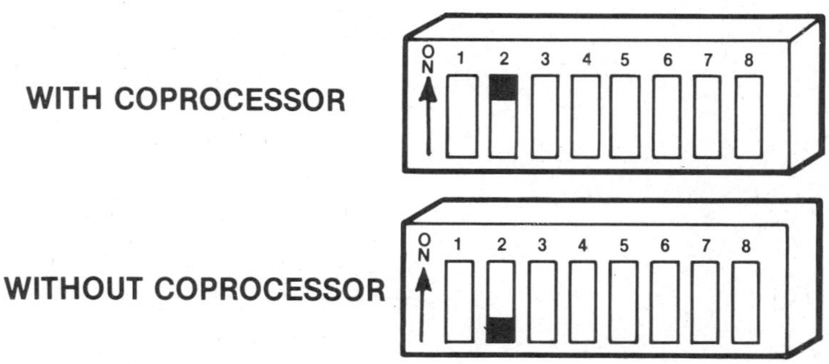

Courtesy of International Business Machines Corporation

functions. At that point the 8087 can work with the 8088. With the proper software, they work as one high powered processor.

STEP FIVE: You are now ready to put the cover back on the PC. Check one more time to be sure the 8087 chip is snugly in place. Press on it gently with your index finger.

STEP SIX: Put the cover back on your PC. Once the cover is on you are ready to start using your PC with the added powers of the 8087. Be sure you have connected all of the cords and cables, including the ones for power, which were removed in Step One.

You shouldn't have any problems as you begin to use the software which has specifically been written to take advantage of the 8087's capabilities. If you feel things aren't working the way they are supposed to, then you have only two areas to check.

First, remove the PC's cover and check that you have Switch #2 on switch block 1 in the OFF position. If that isn't the problem, then it will be with your 8087. Be sure that you haven't damaged any of the legs on the chip or bent them in any way. Be sure the chip is securely in place, not just resting on top of the socket. Be sure that you don't have an older PC (the one without the 'B' on the back panel—see section 10.3). Be sure that you don't have the chip in backwards. Check to be sure the circular notch on the end is facing the same direction as that of the 8088 chip.

After you've done all of your checking, put the PC's cover back on and try the program for the 8087 again. If it's not as fast as you think it should be, check with store that sold you the 8087 chip.

10.5 You Can Get a New System Board

There is a way to upgrade an older PC with one of the newer system boards. It will cost about $400, but it will mean that you won't have any of the timing problems with the older 8088 chip. You will also be able to put 256KB of user memory (RAM) on that new system board. Doing so might affect any maintenance contract you currently have on your PC, so check into that before you do anything.

There are companies which will upgrade your current system board to the new standards and specifications; however, you might be better off sticking with what you have and letting your local computer store add the new 8087 chip for you. Remember, that will include a new, properly timed 8088 chip at no extra cost.

11

There are more factors than you realize involved in expanding the use and potential of your PC. Physically adding things (i.e., devices) to your PC comprises most of those factors, but there's more you need to know. The rest of this book will cover many points which, unfortunately, get overlooked. They don't have anything to do with connections or interfaces. In a way this chapter has to do with making things easier for you. Organization and efficiency will allow you to take full advantage of the IBM PC without fighting limitations you might have created. There are checklists and steps to help you think a little more objectively about what you're doing and how you're doing it.

That's not to say there is anything wrong with what you are doing now or are planning to do. The point here is to give you tips that you might not have thought about. Those of us who own PCs are part of the computer revolution, and much of what we do is just learned as we go. We think we know exactly what to do, but sometimes miss certain things. That's what this chapter is all about.

We'll take a look at everything, from furniture to keeping track of disks, files, magazines, and manuals. Organization is the key to efficiency and productivity . . . and all of that leads to expanding your use of the PC.

11.1 It All Starts the First Day

From the minute you bring your PC home, whether you know it or not, you're doing some very important long range planning. If you haphazardly set up your PC, you could easily set up everything to work against you instead of for you. You will either build in convenience of use or obstructions to hamper work.

Ideally, before you bring your PC home you have thought a lot about where you will put it, how you will use it and how all of that will affect the rest of the members in the household. If the noise from your printer drives everyone nuts each time it runs, then you are building in a problem right from the beginning.

If you don't give much thought to where you place your PC or how you will work with it, then you can plan on rearranging things several times through trial and error until you find out what works best. This will probably happen anyway, but it can be minimized with a little forethought.

11.2 Steps to Setting Up Your PC System

This section will guide you through the entire setup for the PC. Even if your PC is already set up you should take a look at the steps listed here. They are designed to lead you through a very careful thought process.

You want the setup of your PC to be organized for your convenience. After all, you're the one who will be working with it all the time. Working with your PC should be a smooth flow of ideas and concepts formulated into work and projects through the use of a computer as a tool. The keyboard should function as a natural extension of your mind.

STEP ONE: Consider your PC (and everything that goes with it) as a system. Don't just look at the PC as a computer to put somewhere. Think about it in terms of something you will be working with.

It's more than a typewriter, so think of it as a system for completing tasks. You will need room for the keyboard, the system unit (also known as the CPU—the place where you insert the floppy disks), monitor, and a printer. That's not all, either. Your PC system also includes supplies (like disks, labels for disks, paper for the printer, manuals and magazines. And, *don't forget about all the cables*!

Approach the setup of your PC system from the perspective of having an area for the complete, uninterrupted processing of the work you want to accomplish.

STEP TWO: Where will the system be most effective? When you objectively look around your house or apartment you want to pick the best spot for your PC system. It should be out of the mainstream and there should be enough room for the entire setup.

Some people make the mistake of displaying their PC where the most people can see it (this borders on tripping over status consciousness). Actually, you want just the opposite. The PC should be in as quiet an area as possible to allow for full concentration when working with it.

To have the most effective setup for your PC you should consider future expansion plans, too. Will you be getting a second printer or a second monitor? Many times people get a color monitor and keep the green screen working. Will you be getting a fixed disk? Remember that you will probably add to your PC system. Be sure you have enough room.

Consider this checklist:

- Are there enough electrical outlets where you want to set up your PC?

Extension cords should be avoided if at all possible. However, power strips (with more than one electrical outlet on them) work very well. A surge suppressor should be used to protect your monitor and PC from electrical spikes. The importance of surge suppressors is covered in Chapter 9.

- Consider the glare from windows.

This can be a real problem. You should arrange your screen so it is not directly across from a window. In other words, as you face the screen you don't want a window behind you. This will eliminate much eye strain.

- What about proper lighting?

You don't want to be always squinting to line up paper in the printer or when reading from a manual or program guide. You want plenty of light (and remember that means at least one more electrical outlet). Special antiglare lamps are available through most office supply stores.

If you have bifocals, you will want to pay close attention to the position of your screen. Many people with bifocals are crimping their neck upward each time they work on the PC. This can be resolved by either elevating the screen to a certain height or having the screen at an angle (see section 11.3).

- Noise and interruptions are a two way street when it comes to the PC.

You can be bothered and bother others if you don't properly plan your PC setup. Most use of the PC won't cause much more noise than the clicking of the keyboard and an occasional beep or two. But again we come back to the printer.

It doesn't matter whether you have a dot matrix or letter quality printer, **A Printer Will Make Noise.** Even if you have it encased in a sound proof cabinet it will make noise. The location of your printer (and, in effect, the location of your PC system) is important from a habitability standpoint. Some people just print when it's convenient for everyone else, which keeps the printer from becoming an irritating interruption.

Besides being conscious of your printer and the noise it will make, you need to look at the noise and interruptions coming your way. If your PC is set up right next to the television, you've got a distraction. Having the PC next to a telephone has certain advantages (especially if you want to hook in to the outside world with a modem). However, listening to someone talk on the telephone while you're trying to work on the PC can be difficult.

The more you are out in the open with your PC setup the more susceptible you are to interruptions. This might not sound too important, but each time your train of thought is broken, the progress on your work is stalled. The easiest way to avoid interruptions is to have the PC set up in an area away from common activities.

- If you already have a study or den that you have been using as a work area then the PC should fit right in.

Of course, there will be some adjustments and rearranging, but it's important that the PC be blended into your lifestyle from the beginning. You might find that another room or area will be better for using the computer. It all depends on what best suits your needs and how you plan to work with the PC.

STEP THREE: Obviously, you will need to put your PC system on some type of table or desk. This can be an expensive proposition, if you believe the advertisements.

An IBM PC will work just the same on an older desk as it will on a "new and improved solid oak computer work station."

Your desk or table top must be big enough for the keyboard, the system unit and the screen. Then, if you have a printer or will be getting one (or even two) you need to make room for it. Often the printer sits separate from, but next to, the desk or work area of the PC.

The desk drawers will be helpful for storing supplies and printed files. The computer tables you see all nice and neat do not accurately portray reality. You will need a place to put many items—disks, paper, ribbons, pens, manuals, magazine articles, reference books. Having shelves right next to your PC system will be extremely helpful, too.

STEP FOUR: Setting up your printer isn't too complicated, unless you end up with the wrong cable or find out you don't have the right port (i.e., connection on the PC). Making the connection between your PC and a printer (or two) is covered in Chapter 7.

What you do need to consider in setting up your printer is leaving enough room. You will need working room for changing paper (even putting in checks and other types of forms). If the printer is jammed in next to the PC and close to a wall, you will need gymnastic expertise each time you change paper. And give yourself room enough to read the printer's output while it's still on the printer. That way you will be able to spot mistakes as they are being printed.

In most cases your printer will be set up on a separate table or stand. Leaving a little bit of extra room will pay off many times over. There are printer stands available for as little as $15.00 which allow you to put the paper right under the printer.

STEP FIVE: Are you right or left handed? The disks should be within close reach of the hand you use the most. Your reference books and other such materials can be within reach of the other hand, but be aware that the more you can do to complement your most used hand, the smoother things will go.

You shouldn't have to get out of your chair (except occasionally) when working with your PC. Place your commonly used disks right in front of you—on top of or next to the PC itself. Labels for the disks and other items you use on a regular basis should be in drawers or shelves in easy reach.

STEP SIX: The chair you will be sitting in while working with your PC is extremely critical to your PC system. Your chair should be comfortable while supporting your lower back. Don't cut corners when it comes to a chair. A good chair isn't cheap, but since you're going to be planted for hours on end in front of your PC you want a good chair to sit in.

Many people feel they really don't need a good chair, but they are just outsmarting themselves. Lower back pain will result. Secretarial chairs are specifically designed to support the lower back and also move nicely on rollers.

Since you will probably be spending more time at your PC than you did at your typewriter (studies show this to be a fact) you ought to seriously evaluate the chair you have been using up to this point. It just might be time to get a new, high quality chair. Money is better spent for a new chair than for that new oak computer work station. If you choose not to buy both, get the chair first—it's much more important.

STEP SEVEN: Disks, diskette labels, paper, ribbons for the printer, print wheels, mailing labels, and dozens of other items can be killers when it comes to eating up time and efficiency. Your PC work area can be set up perfectly, but when it comes to finding and using supplies, you can find yourself in the middle of a nightmare.

You can be right in the middle of printing a report when the ribbon runs out. If you can't remember where you put the ribbons then you just might spend over an hour trying to find them, or you might never find them. You might have forgotten to order them. The easiest way to avoid such heartache is to organize your supplies from the very beginning—before anything gets out of hand.

Try to keep everything in one area near the computer (at the very least in the same room). Keep items for the printer together and maybe even right near the printer. Disks and labels should be in one of your desk drawers.

The disks which already have information on them should ALL be labeled and in some kind of order. Keep a log of which file is on which disk. Any form letters (or agreements, contracts, and other such documents) should all be printed out and kept in a binder for reference, indexed to the disks on which they are located. If this sounds like a lot of work, it is; but unless you keep track of your disks you will quickly find yourself buried under piles of disks. That will lead to endless searching each time you want to find a particular file and can't remember which disk it's on.

The labels for disks should be right in the back of the tray or holder you keep your disks in. Those labels are the key to quick access. If you make enough changes on a disk, put a new label on it or write the new file names on the old label with a felt-tip pen (a ball point tip can damage your disk). The minute you let things go, you're lost whenever it comes to retrieval of information. So why fight yourself? Organize things from the first day you set up your PC and take the time on to keep things up to date.

STEP EIGHT: Don't get rid of your typewriter yet! If you hide your typewriter away in some closet you'll find yourself seeking it out over and over again. You will still need your old typewriter for certain tasks, so you might want to keep it handy.

The obvious question is, "With this marvelous PC, why would I ever need a typewriter?" The typewriter certainly won't be used that much, but you will find out that it definitely serves a purpose, supplementing what you do with the PC.

Some tasks which a typewriter can knock out quickly:

- Forms. Tax and insurance forms are probably at the top of the list of the kinds of things a typewriter can still be used for. More and more forms are on continuous form feed paper, but if you have just one form to fill out, it's much simpler to do it on a typewriter.
- Envelopes. Doing a single envelope in a printer requires removing the paper and going to a lot of effort.
- Labels. If you're doing hundreds of labels, the printer is the way to go. However, if you're going to do a label for that new disk or file folder you just started using, then the typewriter is faster.

- Checks. Many organizations still do checks by hand or on the typewriter, even though through their computerized bookkeeping they can print checks. The paper in the printer has to be removed and replaced with form feed checks (which cost more, too). Then the checks need to be lined up in the printer. This is a time consuming process and often the task of writing checks is more quickly accomplished on the typewriter or even by hand.
- Memos and Notes. Responding to reply form memos or writing your own quick notes can be done more quickly on a typewriter. You can do such memos or notes while the printer is running something else.

All of this is not to say that the typewriter is here to stay or that it should be used as a crutch. It's just that at this point in the computer revolution the items listed above are better done on a typewriter. This will all change over time. For now, however, make a place in your PC work area for your typewriter.

STEP NINE: More than likely you will be using reference books when you work with your PC. The dictionary, a spelling dictionary, a thesaurus, a synonym/antonym finder, and any other books you refer to regularly should be close at hand to your PC.

There's a lot of precious, *productive* time wasted whenever you have to stop what you're doing, get up, and go to find a reference book. Set up all of the reference books you use on a regular basis as close to your PC as possible. Consider a shelf on the wall near or behind your PC set up, or buy a free standing book case. With your reference books as part of your work area you won't miss a step looking something up.

STEP TEN: Don't forget about paper files. Somewhere in the middle of your PC work area you should leave some room for paper and files. Being computerized doesn't mean that you totally eliminate the need for paper and a way to keep track of it. You will still be getting letters, reports, forms, documents, and contracts on paper. Those all need to be filed (not piled) somewhere, in some kind of logical order.

You should keep paper files of all your form letters and even general correspondence. Having hard copies comes in handy when you're reviewing what you have or when you want to find out what a particular form letter looks like. It starts piling up fast, so it's important to deal with this right from the very beginning.

11.3 Different Ways to Set Up Your PC System

You have one more task at hand before you actually set up your PC system. Just how will the PC sit on your desk or work table? Will you be doing other work there? Is there room for the PC?

Figure 11.1 shows what is probably the most typical and basic setup of an IBM PC. The screen sits on top of the system unit with the keyboard in front of it. The printer can be set up on either side.

With this arrangement, the ridge across the top of the keyboard (just above the row of numbers and symbols) can be used to hold manuals or books, while using

Fig. 11.1: Basic setup of PC with screen sitting on system unit and keyboard in front

the PC. This makes it very easy to refer to something while working. You can work on the keyboard, look at the screen and read from a manual, book, or magazine.

You have several other options for setting up your PC, but before we go into those let's look a little closer at the options you have even with the basic PC setup. It doesn't even have to sit right in front of you. That's one of the nicest features about the detachable keyboard. It can be stored off to the side of the PC or even on top of it and then brought out to the center of your desk only when you need it. The screen can still be seen very well, too, when the PC sits off at an angle on the corner of your desk.

Using the basic PC setup still eats up a big chunk of desk space. You do have other options because of products which are designed to help you free up precious desk space. Curtis Manufacturing makes a line of products not only to help you better organize your work area, but specifically designed to make using the PC much less painful for those who wear bifocals.

One of the most creative ways to use a PC is with the system unit on the side. See Figure 11.2. Curtis' Systems Stand in effect moves the biggest part of the PC out of your way and allows you to conveniently place it by the side of your desk. The stand even comes with two stickers to mark the disk drives A and B so there won't be any confusion. The stand can even be placed on top of the desk (and still save space). This does, however, require an extension cord for your monitor and one for your keyboard. Curtis makes those too.

For people who wear bifocals, a tilt/swivel pedestal for the monitor will be heaven sent. Figure 11.3 shows this base, which allows you to tilt the screen to the proper angle for painless viewing swivel it so that two or more workers can share it.

Info Devices makes a handy tray called a a TUCK-IT!, which allows you to store your keyboard under the system unit. This keeps the keyboard out of sight when not

Fig. 11.2: Curtis' Systems Stand, with the system unit resting in it

Courtesy of Curtis Manufacturing Company, Inc.

Fig. 11.3: Curtis Tilt/Swivel Pedestal

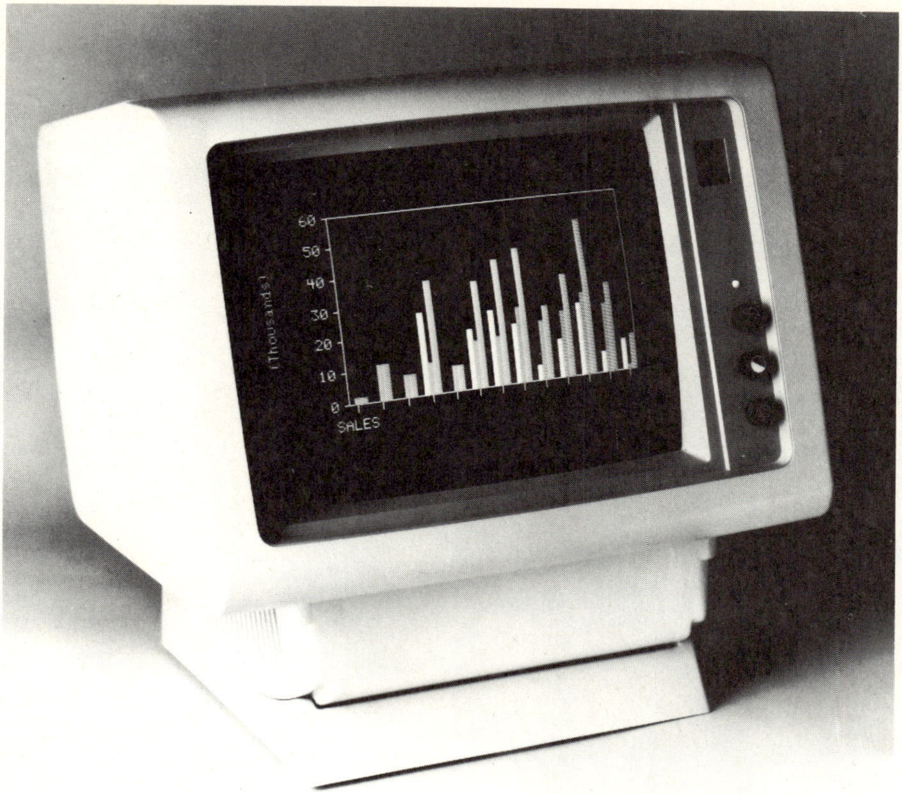

Courtesy of Curtis Manufacturing Company, Inc.

in use (and dust-free, too). When the keyboard is in use, you have a handy tray behind the keyboard for pens, pencils, paper, and even disks.

The more you add to your PC system (like fixed disks, printers, and disk filing boxes) the more you will need to effectively manage your work area. The items mentioned in this section are just a sample of what is available in the marketplace. Look around and see what is out there to help you set up a better system.

11.4 Files, Disks, Manuals, and Magazines

We've already talked about keeping track of reference books. However, we need to go into specifics which will help you do a better job of keeping track of files, disks, manuals, magazines. You need a reliable, simple system to manage information you will need and use daily. What good are magazine articles or reference manuals if you can't find them when you need them? The same goes for disks and files. It's not so much extra work to organize, organize and organize.

Fig. 11.4: TUCK-IT! drawer for storing keyboard under system unit

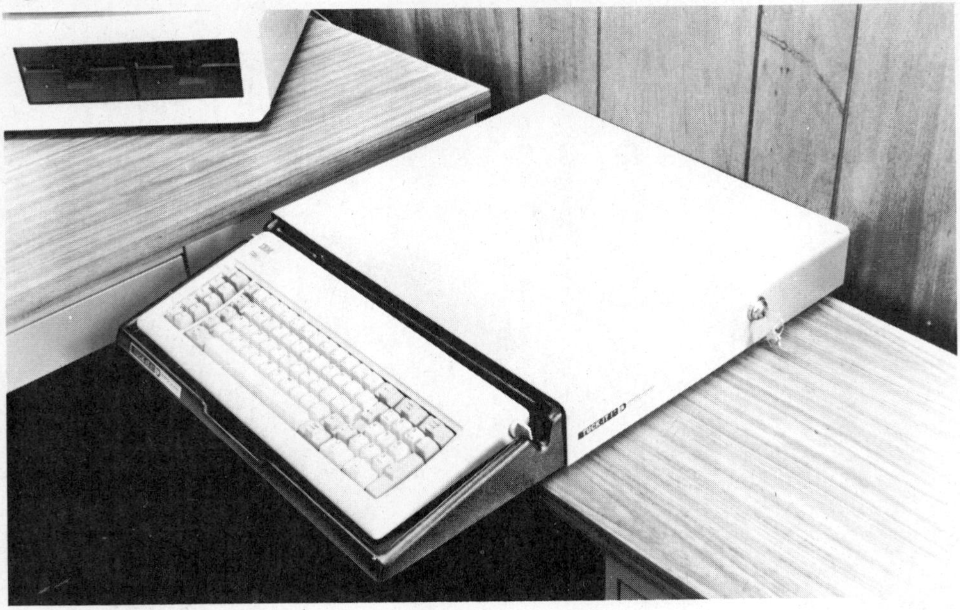

Courtesy of Info Devices

Files Anything you do with your PC is going to require a file name. Once again, if you don't put much thought into this you can quickly find yourself with a mess on your hands. Ultimately you want to use a system of file names which will allow you to find what you want when you want it, without searching through disk after disk and file and after file.

DOS (the Disk Operating System) finds files by their names. Each time you open a file (in other words, do something like a letter, report, or spreadsheet) you must come up with a file name. If you haven't put much thought into this you could end up with something like this:

BODRPTD1—Board of Directors Report, draft 1

BUDPLN84—Budget Plan 1984

ARPTFPLN—Associated Report for the Planning Department

When you have dozens of these on the screen, the file you want tends to get lost in all the rows of capital letters.

Another problem with long file names is that it is easy to transpose letters when opening a file to edit it. When that happens you find that you have opened a new file (at this point many people panic, thinking they have lost their original file).

If you're comfortable with long file names and they work for you, then use them. But before we close the case here, let's look at some alternative ways of naming files which will help you better organize and categorize what you're doing.

File names can be up to eight characters long. You can use letters of the alphabet and the numbers 0 thru 9. You can also use the following special characters:

! @ # $ % ^ & ( ) - _ ' ` ~ {}

A file name can also be followed by what is called an extension. The extension starts with a period (following the file name with no space in between) and can have up to three characters.

REPORT.DEC

Since you can use special characters in file names, you now have a whole new way of naming files; you can use codes. Here are some suggested codes, to help better organize your files and, at the same time, make them easier to find

Type of File	*Code*
Letters	}
Reports	^
Forms	#
Spreadsheets	$
Data Bases	~

Other categories can be assigned one of the 11 other special characters, or you can use them in combinations. If you preface every file name with your codes, then when you look for a letter your eyes will quickly find all the } codes. You want to be sure that the codes you pick are easily distinguishable from each other.

You should keep file names as short as possible. Say you correspond with someone named Bernie Shepard on a regular basis. Your files to Bernie could be something like this: }B315

That file would mean letter written to Bernie Shepard on March 15th. There wouldn't be a need for the year if you set up your disks properly. We'll get to disks in a minute. If you felt more comfortable spelling out BERNIE, you could do that. Your files must be set up the way you think. So whatever works for you is what you should do. Perhaps what you have read here will help you modify how you name and keep track of files.

There are two other special characters that you need to be aware of. If your files are named properly, these characters can save you time, espeically when you're working with a lot of files. They don't actually name a file, but they can help search for specific files.

The question mark ? and the asterisk * are called global filename characters. They will help you find the exact series of files (especially reports and letters) and group them together for your review with the DIR (Directory) command or the COPY command.

Below is a list of reports and inventories you want to find which are on a disk with over 60 other files.

80STOCKS.AVG
81STOCKS.AVG
82STOCKS.AVG
82STOCKS.FEB
82STOCKS.JUL
83STOCKS.AVG
82INVEN
83INVEN
84INVEN

If you type `dir ??stocks.???` you will get a listing on your screen of all the files except the ones for inventory. If you use the copy command `copy *stocks.avg` you copy the stock files for 80, 81, 82, and 83. The significance of these global file name characters is in saving keystrokes. Not only can you find files with the dir command much more quickly, you don't have to search through rows and rows of file names.

Disks After you have had your PC for a while you can suffer from a case of diskette madness. It's like the game hide and go seek. You are always it as you try to find a particular disk that you just know you had your hands on a couple of days ago.

That might be an exaggeration, but unless you systematically keep track of your disks and label them properly (and sufficiently) you are building in long term problems and headaches. Disks can be reformatted by accident (especially the ones you forgot to label), wiping out many files. The law of averages aside, chances are the files you lose will be the ones you need most.

You can avoid most problems if you organize your disks into categories. You can eliminate lost files if you religiously make back-up copies of your disks and files. Back-up copies are important from several standpoints. If you reformat a disk by mistake, the back-up copy is a life saver. However, that's not the only reason to make back-up copies.

Floppy disks are just that—floppy. They are not indestructible. Just about the time you say that's never happened to me, or "I'm more careful than that" the dog chews up a disk or you poke a pencil through one or your son comes to show you his new magnet. There are dozens of ways disks (and the files on them) can be damaged, destroyed, or eliminated. Don't let it happen to you. Take the extra minute or so each day and make back-up copies.

Well, suppose you haven't wiped out a disk, but still can't find your file. Where could it be? Chances are that in searching for it you have looked at it several times and didn't recognize it.

You can save yourself these frustrations if you keep track of your disks the way you keep track of papers and file folders. Your correspondence should be on a separate disk. You might want to use such diskettes on a quarterly or monthly basis, depending on your volume. Label the disks as follows:

CORRESPONDENCE
LAST QUARTER 1984

This way you won't need to put the year on the individual file names. You might even have your correspondence disks divided into subcategories; again, depending on your volume.

Keep your reports, spreadsheets, databases, forms and letters on separate disks. Use little plastic library cases (they even come in colors) to keep your disks from getting mixed together. The last thing you want is a pile of disks on your desk to wade through for this month's budget report. Make sure each disk and each case has a label on it. And keep those labels current.

Anyone who has a fixed disk also needs to be careful to organize files and make back-up copies. Some fixed disks even have tape back-up capabilities. If your fixed disk crashes (i.e., ends up needing to be reformatted) you will certainly be thankful for those back-up copies. Backing up fixed disk files to floppy disks isn't too much work, but we quickly get spoiled and tend to look for ways to cut corners. Don't outsmart yourself—make back-up copies every day!

Manuals The simplest way to organize your manuals is to keep them all together. This includes the following kinds of manuals:

- DOS Manual
- Guide to Operations Manual
- Program Manuals
- Hardware Manuals (this includes any adapter card manuals)
- Printer Manual

If you know that your manuals are all in the same location it will be easy to find them and put them away when you are through with them. The place you select for storing all of your manuals should be as near to your PC as possible. If you keep your manuals in another room you will find that you tend not to look things up when you really should. From a practical standpoint you should have your manuals, especially the ones you use regularly (like the DOS and program manuals), within reach. The most you should have to do is stand up to grab whatever you need.

Manuals should be tools which you use to help solve problems and answer questions. You will be surprised how much you learn each time you pick up a manual and look through it. Unfortunately, most of the time we discover things in a manual while we are looking for something else.

Magazines If you don't read at least a couple of the monthly magazines devoted to the IBM PC, you are missing out on valuable resources. Those magazines, as well as general computer magazines, have tips, pointers, and helpful hints—many of which are submitted by readers.

You will find that often the problem you are currently experiencing with a program, or in using the PC itself, is discussed in one of these magazines. Even the advertisements provide a good way to keep up with what's new. There are also sections in these magazines devoted to new product announcements.

Once you start getting a magazine or two (or three, or four, or more) each month you face the same old problem of data organization. With all of this useful information presented in such quantity in the magazines, you need to develop a special system for keeping track of it all. If you don't, you will end up with stacks of magazines and not know where any particular article is. That means you're going to spend a good deal of productive time searching through hundreds of magazine pages.

Here are some suggestions for organizing your magazines, which you should keep somewhere near your PC. Initially, they might spend some time at your bedside, but eventually all magazines should fall into some order. This is no small feat when you consider the size of each issue.

First we need to talk about how to read computer magazines. Don't be afraid to mark them up. Fold the top corners of pages down or use paper clips to mark the articles you're interested in. As you read the articles use a red pen or a highlighting marker to underline or circle those phrases, paragraphs and figures you know you will want to refer back to.

Computer magazines only become reference tools once you've marked them up. How else will you find what you want in a month (or even six months to a year from now)? Once you've marked the magazines up the next step is to keep track of everything.

Using a Data Base If you have a data base program it isn't much of a problem to set up a data base for magazine articles. Decide on the categories you want to keep track of and then, on a regular basis (as you read the magazines) plug in the information. Don't make it too detailed or you will defeat your own purposes. Keep everything brief, but enough to the point so you will be able to find things effortlessly.

If you don't want to go through all the trouble of setting up such a data base, a company called LETUS A-B-C, marketing a data base overlay of the same name, has already done it for you. The data base contains abstracts of articles (and even letters to the editors) from several of the major PC-related computer magazines—PC *Magazine*, *Softalk*, the PC *Tech Journal*, PC *World*, and PC articles in *Byte Magazine*. LETUS A-B-C is designed to be used with the data base program PC-FILE III.

LETUS A-B-C contains every article from those magazines, going back to 1982. Each abstract is three lines long, summarizing the essence of each article, review, letter or tip. You can search by keyword, subject, title, or author. Annual subscription to the service is $80, with new data disks issued quarterly. You can pay for LETUS A-B-C on a quarterly basis also.

3 × 5 *Cards* Some people who have a data base program still use 3 × 5 cards in a little box to keep track of articles. It works like this: Any article on the subject of BASIC programming is listed on a card labeled BASIC. You would list each article by the name of the magazine, the date, the author, the starting page of the article and perhaps a note or two about it. If you fill the card up, turn it over and write on the back or attach another card to it.

You can get as complex as you want with a data base system or 3 × 5 cards. The point to remember is that you just want to keep track of the information in a painless and trouble-free way. It's better to keep everything simple, because the minute your system for keeping track of magazine articles becomes too cumbersome, you just won't use it or keep it up to date.

The 3 × 5 cards do have an advantage over the data base (even though the data base offers the luxury of fast sorting, while allowing you to enter the information in the order you wish). The cards are always accessible. If the computer is off, in the amount of time it would take to turn it on and get into your data base you could have used the 3 × 5 card to find what you wanted.

Something else to consider is that if you are in the middle of a program and have a question related to that program, the 3 × 5 cards are handy to look through. To use the data base would mean exiting that program and calling up the data base. Again, the 3 × 5 cards would be quicker and more realistic.

For managing large amounts of information easily and quickly a data base is unbeatable. If you wanted all of the articles written by Peter Norton about BASIC, you could easily and quickly sort through your entire data base. Another advantage of the data base over cards is that it is much easier to cross-reference articles which fit into three or four areas. You could do that by using codes—B for BASIC, D for

DOS and so on. With 3 × 5 cards you would need to use more than one card for the proper filing.

Tearing the Articles Out This is what a lot of PC users have done after a year or so of trying to faithfully keep up a data base or 3 × 5 cards. Physically tearing out the articles you want and putting them in file folders works very well. It almost seems sacrilegious to rip apart a magazine, but once you do, you find that over sixty percent of it was advertising. However, a word of warning: If you throw away the rest of magazine, then you might one day want to find an article (on a subject you never thought you'd be interested in) in a journal you throw away.

It all comes back to developing a system which works best for you. Everyone has different preferences and different ways of doing things. The key factor here is in developing a system for keeping track of magazine articles, which will become an important part of your reference library. You will be amazed at how often you find yourself referring to those magazine articles.

A final word on keeping track of information. While the magazine articles are going to be important, don't forget about your computer books. As you come across helpful items or sections in books you should keep track of them too. Tearing pages out of books is wasteful, so you might want to choose either the 3 × 5 cards or the data base.

After a while you will have many books and several armfuls of magazines. There is no way you can retain everything you read, either as you read it, or after reading it more than once. What you must decide, before things get out of hand, is how to manage all of that information so you can use it all as a resource to help you get more from your PC (and from your abilities to use it).

11.5 Find Out What Others Have Done

Make it a point to see how others have set up their PC systems. You might improve the way you do things. If you keep your mind open about this you will learn a lot, while sharing what you know with others. You can always take ideas and modify them to suit your particular needs. You will find that, as a rule, people with PCs (or any computer) love to show off.

Someone who has had an Apple or Radio Shack computer for seven or eight years probably has more ideas on computer setup than you could possibly use. More than likely, that person has tried many of the actual setups you're considering. Don't overlook a valuable resource just because the person doesn't own a PC.

Computer users share a lot of the same concerns and problems, no matter what make of computer they own. You should definitely try to learn as much as possible (even beyond the initial setup or physical configuration) from anyone who has a computer. Remember that this is a two way street, so you should be sharing your experiences too.

A good way to share information is to get involved with a *computer user group*. It is through such groups that people can get together on a regular basis to discuss problems and share tips. There are groups devoted to specific computers, like the PC, but there are also general computer user groups.

With such groups it doesn't matter what kind of personal computer you own; if you own a computer you can be a member of the group. Many groups have members who don't own computers. In fact, it's a good idea to get involved with a computer user group *before* you buy a computer.

Computer user groups are organized in several ways—through computer stores, through individuals, and even through associations and employers. The whole idea is to share knowledge and information with each other. Because you know people from the group you can work out your problems, as well as their's.

There are other reasons to be involved in a computer user group. It is through such groups that you can get public domain software. The programs can be good or bad, but will only cost you the price of a diskette to find out. There are many good public domain software programs currently in circulation.

A computer user group can often arrange group purchase plans and ongoing discounts for its members. The group can also bring in monthly speakers to talk about everything from programming to specific uses of the computer. You can work with the computer stores to have product (software and hardware) demonstrations for the group. This isn't just for groups organized through the computer stores, either; the stores welcome the opportunity to show new products to potential users.

There are many advantages in an active computer user group. Membership doesn't require a lot of time or effort, either. To get the most from your PC, you can't afford *not* to get involved with a user group. At the very least, make it a point to see what other PC owners have done and are doing. The more you do, the more you'll learn.

11.6 From Dust Covers to Antiglare Screens

Okay, so now you have your PC all set up and ready to go. What about glare from the windows? Or dust? Or hitting the wrong keys while getting used to the PC's stretched out keyboard? And how will you ever remember all of the commands for the program you're learning?

Here are some things to consider:

Dust Covers There are two schools of thought on dust and the PC. One says, "Who cares?!" The other says, "Better safe than sorry."

At some point most of us will see floppy disks with a thick coat of dust on them, or a PC running just fine without a dust cover. A large number of computer users never worry about dust or what it can do—and most of the time they have no problems. However:

Dust can build up on the reading head of the disk drive, preventing it from reading information from the floppy disk. Even the slightest build-up of dust can create disk reading errors. Disk drive head cleaners (sold in most computer and office supply stores) help cut down on many potential problems.

When dust accumulates in your PC it can conduct electricity to vulnerable areas inside of your PC. Dust covers don't totally eliminate the dust problem, because dust is moving around as you work. However, during the large amount of time your PC isn't being used, the dust cover keeps most of the dust out. There are plastic dust covers, designed to fit separately over the keyboard and snugly in front of the disk drives. There are also fabric and film plastic dust covers for the monitor (See Figure 11.5). Be aware that some dust covers create static electricity (see section 11.7) which can generate enough voltage to destroy disks and memory chips.

You can choose a fabric or film plastic dust cover for your printer, too, or or you can take care of dust and noise at the same time. A sound cover (or acoustic enclosure) costs a lot more than a dust cover, but does kill two birds with one stone. See Figure 11.6.

Sound covers for printers still allow the paper to feed to the printer. Everything works the same, except that the sound is deadened (not quite eliminated) while the dust is pretty much kept out, too.

Your floppy disks should be protected from dust also. The disks should always be kept in their protective envelopes when they aren't being used, and they should be stored in covered trays or holders. Figure 11.7 shows some typical storage units for diskettes. Besides protecting the disks from dust, these units allow you to better organize your disks (i.e., mini-filing cabinets).

Keytop Enhancements Going from a typewriter to the IBM PC takes some adjusting, to say the least. The PC's keyboard is 25 percent wider than a typewriter's (even the IBM Selectric's). Most people like the PC keyboard once they get used to it; but, when it

Fig. 11.5: Dust covers for keyboard, disk drives and monitor

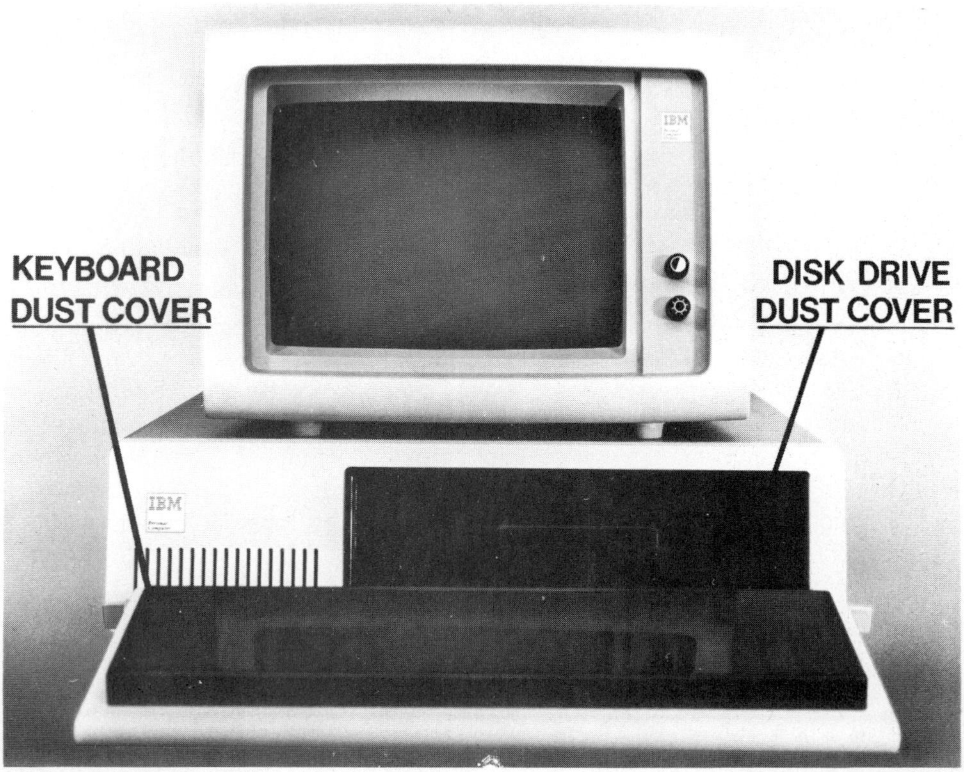

Courtesy of CompuCable Corporation

Fig. 11.6: Sound cover or acoustic enclosure for printers

Courtesy of Eagle Data Products, Inc.

comes to hitting the shift key and the special keys, it takes a while not to miss the mark. This problem is compounded because the *enter key* is only marked by an arrow with a tail pointing upward.

The Hooleon Company seems to have solved this problem of finding certain keys with Touchdown Keytops (see Figure 11.8). While some people might not want to mar the look of the PC keyboard, these keytops, which fit tightly over the existing keys, make the use of the keyboard practically trouble-free. You won't have a problem feeling your way to any key.

Keyboard Templates Many people are overwhelmed by all the commands of popular programs like Lotus 1-2-3, Wordstar, VisiCalc, dBASE II, and Easywriter. Templates, like the ones made by Creative Products (in Figure 11.9), show which keys to use for which commands, and they give helpful tips. You don't have to look anything up.

Much of the information you need for properly operating the program is right at your fingertips and easy to read. This offers a better alternative to putting stickers on your keytops. Stickers present a problem when you use more than one program, because they usually don't mean anything for other programs.

Antiglare Screens The glare from computer monitors can cause eyestrain and tension. The green screen of IBM's monochrome monitor for the PC is easy on the eyes, but it is the glare from windows and lights that make any screen hard to take. You can position the screen away from light, but that doesn't always solve the problem.

For some the glare problem is really no problem at all. But for those who want to do something about a glaring screen, there is a product made out of a fine black

Fig. 11.7: Storage trays for floppy disks

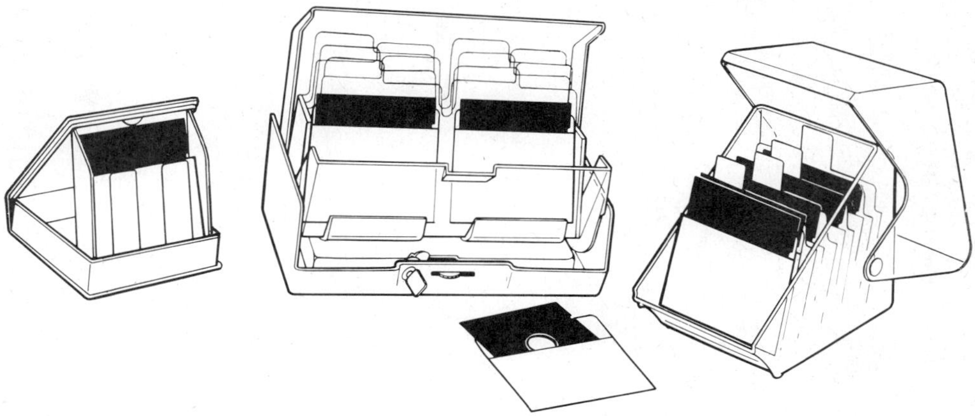

Fig. 11.8: Touchdown Keytops on the PC keyboard

Courtesy of Hooleon Company

Fig. 11.9: Keyboard templates on IBM PC keyboard

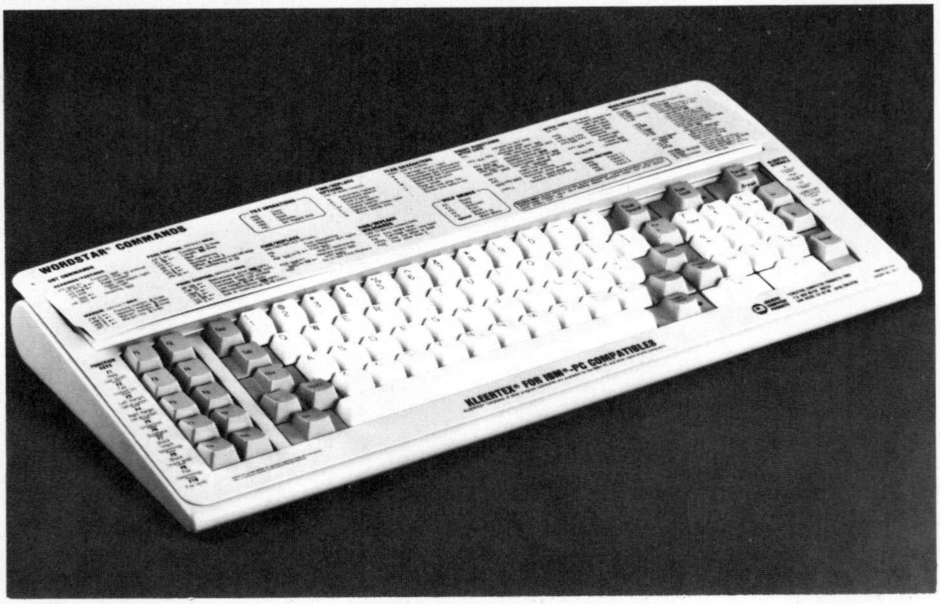

Courtesy of Creative Computer Products

Fig. 11.10: Antiglare screen on IBM monitor

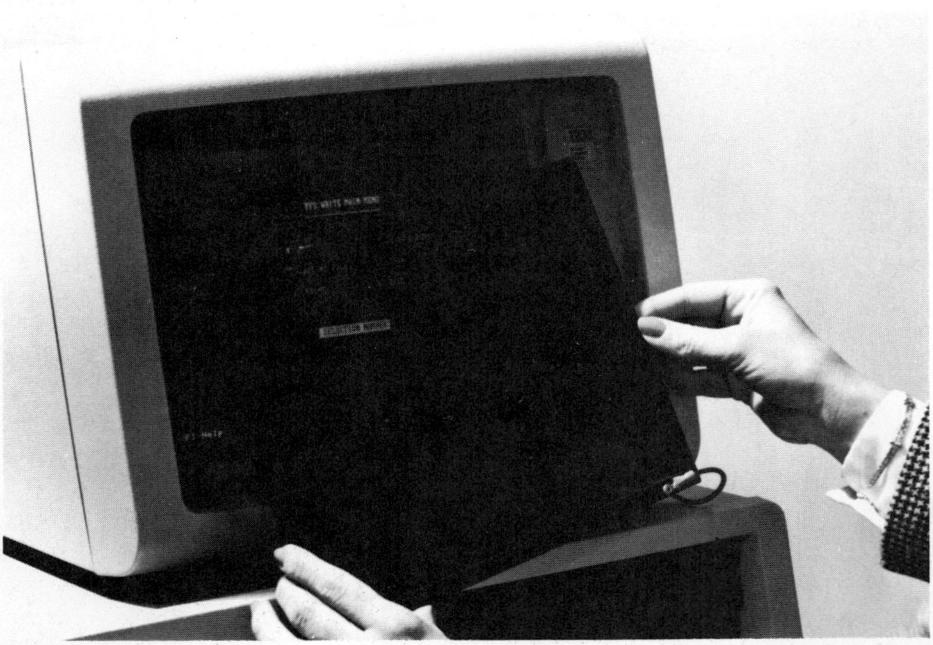

Courtesy of Screen Data Corporation

mesh, which fits right on to your monitor. It works for both color and black and white screens. See Figure 11.10.

The best way to decide whether or not you need one is to look at an antiglare screen in your local computer store or at one of the computer trade shows. In most cases, the screen (usually under $40.00) sells itself. Though you can still see the light source after you put the antiglare screen over your monitor, the glare is gone and the text being displayed is definitely clearer.

11.7 Static Electricity and Why You Should Be Concerned about It!

Electrostatic discharge. That's what it's called. Most of us know it as static electricity. Don't confuse static electricity with voltage or power line spikes from the electricity used to run your PC. That is something much different and is covered in Chapter 9.

Most of the time you can't feel static electricity, but it is always there. It's an ever-present danger for the PC and all computers because of the damage it can do. Static electricity is like a miniature bolt of lightning which can:

- Blow holes in the the circuitry of computer chips (memory chips and others);
- Fuse together the microscopic circuitry in the computer chips;
- Damage or scramble data stored on disks;
- Cause components of a computer to fail;
- Create unexplained quirks and glitches in your PC system.

Static electricity is measured in terms of voltage, but it's important to remember that we are talking about very low amperage. High voltage and low amperage won't hurt *you*, but you need to be concerned about your PC. Static electricity is really a static charge which builds up in many ways. Static charges accumulate on:

- The human body
- Ungrounded work areas
- Floors (all types, from cement to wood)
- Carpets and floor coverings
- Chairs (wood, fabric, plastic and metal)
- Clothing (both synthetic and natural fibers)
- Plastic bags, packing materials, and styrofoam.

Much static build-up happens in a non-conductive way. That means the charge builds up and is stored until it is released by touch. That's where the shock comes and where the damage is done.

Walking across a room can generate as much as 30,000 volts of static charge. Even moving in a chair can create up to 2,000 or more volts. A nylon work smock, before you touch it, can have up to 20,000 volts of static charge. You don't feel anything until 4,000 or 5,000 volts, but as little as 100 volts can cause problems for your PC and floppy disks. As more circuitry is crammed into computer chips (especially the newer ones) they become more sensitive to static electricity. The higher the humidity, the less of a chance for problems with static electricity. However, it's still present.

Chapters 1 and 2 discussed static electricity in precautions for installing memory chips. Your concern shouldn't stop there. Since static electricity is always present and you are constantly generating it, you need to look at your PC work area from the perspective of eliminating as much static discharge as possible. You don't want your PC or any of your floppy disks to be casualties of static electricity.

There are many options for fighting static electricity. Anti-static floor mats or rugs have been around for quite some time, but they have become popular only recently. One drawback to this approach is that rubber and synthetic soled shoes act as insulators between the static charge on your body and the anti-static floor mat. Dust and dirt also insulate, so the mats and rugs need to be cleaned regularly.

You can buy anti-static spray for floors, chairs, and work areas. While it is effective, you run into problems of deciding when and how often to spray. How long will one spraying be effective? It varies. It does work well, however, so it just might meet your needs.

One of the most effective ways to combat static while working at your PC is to have an anti-static mat underneath your PC. (See Figure 11.11.) The mat can be used

Fig. 11.11: Static Stopper anti-static mat, underneath IBM PC

Courtesy of Static Handling, Inc.

when you are installing memory chips, too. It allows you to work at your PC and discharge any static charge by just touching it with your hand.

If you have a metal lamp near your PC you can touch that and effectively release all static electricity, too. You can even buy an anti-static wrist strap, which is grounded and constantly releases static electricity. It all depends on what you feel most comfortable with and how you want to address static electricity on an ongoing basis.

The real problem with static electricity has been the difficulty of proving any damage it done by it. There are specific tests to determine when static electricity has caused damage, but those aren't done too often and require special equipment. The best thing to do is take some precautions and save yourself the hassle of lost data or destroyed memory chips.

12

This final chapter does a little of everything. It shows you how to get more out of your PC from tutorials, covers customizing your programs, setting up AUTOEXEC.BAT files, and using device drivers. There are also sections on mail order buying and insurance.

12.1 Tutorials Are Uplifting

In the early days of the PC (two or three years ago) there was no such thing as a tutorial program. You bought the PC and some programs to go with it. Then you painstakingly worked your way through the manuals, trying to learn how to use the programs. Sometimes the simplest command would take hours to figure out. In the process there were times when you really felt like trashing the PC and going back to the typewriter (if you could find which closet it had been relegated to).

This went on for quite some time, until courses on using the PC and all the programs to go with it began to sprout up here and there. The courses were good, but they cost a lot and wereusually taught in the evening or on weekends. By the time you finished a long work day or a hectic week you weren't up to knuckling down for two or three hours of intense learning and concentration.

The courses did serve to fill a void. Computer user groups also helped in sharing information about use of the PC and all of the programs. Then someone came up with the idea of putting training sessions on disk so a PC owner could study, train, and learn whenever it was convenient and at his or her own pace. The tutorial programs caught on quickly and actually spawned a growing industry under the PC's very large umbrella.

A tutorial program walks you through each step of learning a program or more about using your PC. The keyboard is even displayed on the screen at different points to show you which key to press. In working your way through a tutorial program you learn far more than you would trying to read all those manuals.

Tutorials have stayed reasonably priced (under $75.00) and sold well. Once you invest in a tutorial you have it forever. Others can then use it and benefit from it. Many tutorial programs have consistently sold in the top thirty of software nationally. Tutorial training programs have taken the mystery out of using Wordstar and many other programs. Tutorials have been easy to use and efficient. A new employee, for example, can learn much more effectively and without too much assistance from other workers.

The tutorial programs have also been used for teaching people how to type. IBM's Typing Tutor program is still one of the top selling programs in the nation. It sells for under $50.00. Figure 12.1 shows a sample page from a CDEX Corporation tutorial.

Fig. 12.1: CDEX tutorial training program—sample screen

```
B3: 500                                                                    MENU
Worksheet  Range  Copy  Move  File  Print  Graph  Data  Quit
Global, Insert, Delete, Column-Width, Erase, Titles, Window, Status
ƐƐƐƐƐƐƐƐƐƐA         B         C         D         E         F         G          HƐƐƐ
1ƐƐƐƐDept. #           Sales Forecast By Month
2ƐƐƐƐ          Jan       Feb       Mar       April     May       June
3ƐƐƐƐ      1   ƐƐƐƐƐ500Ɛ      750       750      1000      1500      1750
4ƐƐƐƐ      2       1000      1250      1250      1750      2000      1750
5ƐƐƐƐ      3       1250      1500      2000      2500      2750      2750
6ƐƐƐƐ  Total       2750      3500      4000      5250      6250      6250
:ƐƐƐƐ

ƐƐƐƐƐƐƐ Lotus  ƐƐƐƐƐƐƐƐƐƐƐƐƐƐƐƐƐƐƐ Lotus  ƐƐƐƐƐƐƐƐƐƐƐƐƐƐƐƐƐƐ Lotus  ƐƐƐƐƐ

    Section 1      3 From the Main Menu, you start the
     Defining      3 operation by pressing G, Bil..  Try it
       Graphs      3 now.
                   3
                   3
                   3
                   3  ENTER  G
                   3
                   3
```

Courtesy of Cdex Corporation

The following list will give you an idea of the tutorials available for many of the popular programs.

- Using Your IBM PC
- Using DOS
- Wordstar
- Lotus 1-2-3
- Multiplan
- Visicalc
- Visiword
- TK! Solver
- Multimate
- SuperCalc
- dBASE II

- EasyWriter
- BPI General Accounting
- Peachtree General Ledger System

This is just a sampling of what is available, so there's bound to be a tutorial for the program(s) you are currently using or thinking about buying. Now the software houses are putting out their own tutorials.

All of the tutorials start with one basic perspective—you need a lot of help when you first get your PC and each time you get a new program. That's just one of the realities of this computer revolution.

If you want to go it alone, like in the early days of the PC, you're free to do that. However, with so many good tutorials on the market (and more being developed all the time), you really should consider taking advantage of the tutorial programs. They will save you much time, frustration, and heartache.

12.2 Taming the DOS Beast!

There are tutorial programs for DOS (your disk operating system), but many people want more than that. With everything a person needs to know to use all of the different programs, DOS can be just one more computer beast to endure. Sometimes DOS is friendly, many times it is not.

For those who would prefer a tamer DOS there are many programs. One such program is 1DIR (by Bourbaki Inc.) through which the essence of DOS is always displayed on the screen (see Figure 12.2).

This program, like several others on the market, makes working with DOS much easier—and you don't have to memorize too much either. To copy, erase, or rename a file, you just use the numeric keypad to move the command cursor to the command you want, with the file name which is also displayed on the screen. Then you press the enter key to execute the command. It's that simple.

You save a great deal of time and eliminate mis-typed file names. You know how much room you have left on the disk and all the details about the files on the disk too. You can easily tell if the CAPS LOCK or NUMBER LOCK is on. The date and time are displayed. And if you run a program 1DIR disappears like the A> always did, returning when you exit the program.

There are a few drawbacks to such programs. While they are convenient, they are sometimes slow and cumbersome. The best way to decide if you want to use such a program is have a look at it in your local computer store or see if anyone you know is using it.

12.3 Retrieving Files and a Whole Lot More

When you first get your PC you will wipe out some files in the learning process. Even when you start feeling comfortable with the PC and using your programs—especially your word processing program—you will still unintentionally erase or delete files

Fig. 12.2: 1DIR screen display, showing a typical screen with commands and files.

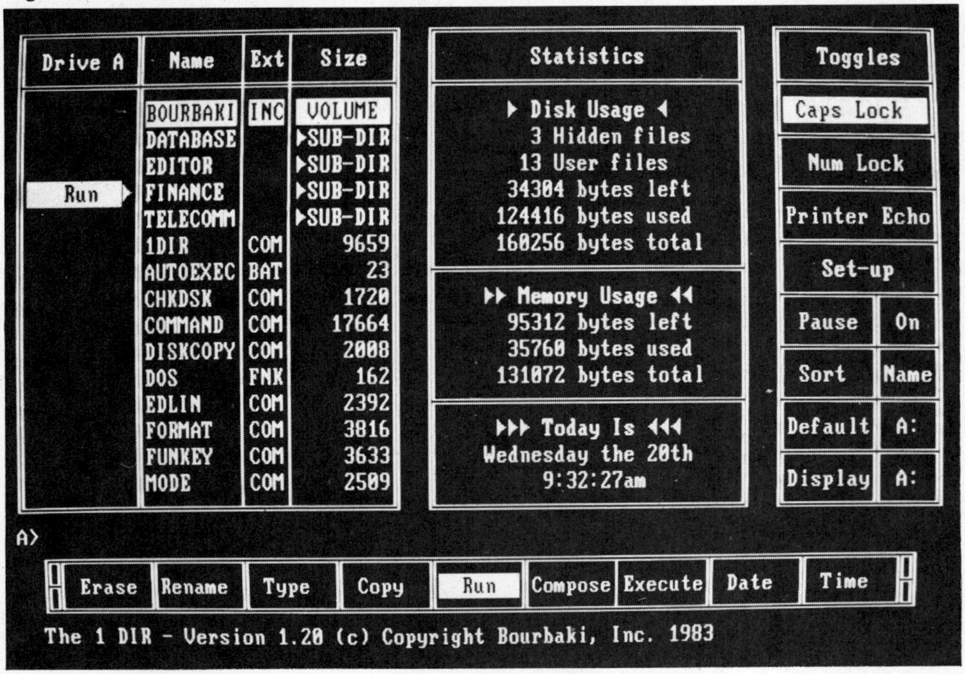

Courtesy of Bourbaki, Inc.

occasionally. All hope is not lost if you erase a file, because it is still on disk—you just can't get to it.

That's where programs like The Norton Utilities* come in. There are amazing things you can do with your PC that many people aren't even aware of. Knowing how to "unerase" a long report you've spent hours on and accidentally erased is extremely important.

Actually there is no magic involved at all. Information is magnetically stored on a floppy disk in tracks and sectors. When you erase a file all you are really doing is taking that file out of the DOS directory. In other words, the file is still there, but its space on the disk has now been allocated as empty and ready to be re-used by a new file. A program like Unerase (in the Norton Utilities) allows you to recover that file before something else is recorded over it. If something is recorded over it, it really is lost.

The process of recovering a file involves just two steps.

- find the file's location on the disk;
- use Unerase to put the file back in the DOS directory.

It takes less than three minutes to retrieve an erased file.

---

*Peter Norton. *The Norton Utilities* (Robert J. Brady Co.) 1983.

The Norton Utilities have become popular because of easy to use programs like Unerase. You hope you won't need a program like Unerase too often, but when you do, it is a marvelous tool.

The complete package of The Norton Utilities sells for $80.00 and includes programs for:

- Recover from damaged disks
- Recovery of scrambled data
- Exploring disks to see program structure
- Hide and unhide files
- Disk labeling
- File printing

There are other programs like this on the market, but The Norton Utilities were among the first and have been selling in the top 30 of software nationally for over a year. The most refreshing part of all is that the manual for these programs is simple to use and quite readable. It all helps you understand more about how the PC works and in the process you'll have useful tools that might turn out to be lifesavers.

12.4 Customizing All of Your Programs

There is no such thing as a perfect program. Everyone has different needs and preferences so there are bound to be adjustments you want to make in using programs. Each program has little quirks and twists, many of which are unexplained—they're just there.

It didn't take long for programs to be developed which make it easier to use Lotus 1-2-3, Wordstar, and just about any other program. Through special enhancement programs like ProKey you can save time and keystrokes while actually customizing all of your programs. Another way to describe ProKey is that it is transparent.

Let's use Wordstar as an example here to explain how ProKey works. ProKey is loaded (or installed) into the memory (RAM) of your PC, before you load Wordstar. To use ProKey, hold down the ALTERNATE key and press another code key on the keyboard (which can be any key, including function keys). Now insert a string of commands or text. A string of text can be anything from your signature block on a letter to a standard paragraph (or more) you use on a regular basis.

ProKey has a special file from which it draws the commands and strings. You can add to that file any time you want, and it is easy to modify it. The ProKey manual is a little intimidating at first blush, but ProKey (as well as similar programs) comes with a tutorial built in, which covers use of ProKey with programs like Wordstar and VisiCalc. In fact, the files provided give you a head start in creating your own ProKey files. The ProKey program diskette contains files already set up for the use with Wordstar, VisiCalc, 1-2-3, and dBASEII.

The ProKey tutorial shows you how to mark a sentence for moving from one part of a file to another by tapping one key. ProKey also reformats the paragraph after you've moved the sentence. Ordinarily, this would take several commands. ProKey makes your work easier and makes your PC, with all of the programs you have for it, friendlier.

One other handy feature of ProKey is variable and fixed fields. If you have a memo format you use on a regular basis, you can store it in ProKey's file. Then, with one keystroke you can have ProKey type out the memo, stopping at the spot where you want the date and again stopping wherever you need to fill in the blanks. The blanks are the variable or fixed fields. A variable field allows you to type in any number of characters, while the fixed field is restricted to a number of characters you select. Dates and zip codes work well in fixed fields.

Cutting down on errors and saving time are probably the two biggest selling points for programs like ProKey. Why do all that tedious, repetitive work if you can have ProKey do it over and over again—swiftly, effortlessly, and without mistakes?

Once you start using a program like ProKey you'll wonder how you ever got along without it. You will also find more and more uses for it. From data bases to spreadsheet programs, hundreds of keystrokes can be saved.

12.5 A Primer on Saving Time with AUTOEXEC.BAT Files

Sooner or later you will hear about an auto-execution batch file. It will become one of your best tricks in using the PC. When you use a batch file you are simply having the computer, through DOS, do what you would otherwise have to do, step by step. This is especially handy when turning the computer on or going from one program to another. In effect, an AUTOEXEC.BAT file lets the computer automatically start up a program.

Say you are using Wordstar with ProKey. Without an AUTOEXEC.BAT file you would need to first load ProKey and then load Wordstar—two separate steps, which really turn out to be more if you examine it closely. First of all, DOS comes up on the screen and asks for the date and time. That's two steps, even if you bypass both by hitting the enter key. Next you would install ProKey by typing in `prokey`. After that you would type in `ws` to get into Wordstar. That's four steps you had to do, one at a time.

An AUTOEXEC.BAT would do all of that without you ever so much as touching the keyboard (unless you had hit the ALTERNATE, CONTROL, and DELETE keys to re-boot the system). The AUTOEXEC.BAT file looks like this:

```
prokey
ws
```

It automatically goes to work installing Prokey and then Wordstar, having bypassed the prompt for you to enter the current date and time. If you want the date and time you can exit Wordstar and enter the date and time by first typing DATE at the DOS prompt of `A>`. Then type TIME before going back into Wordstar. You also have the option to make DATE and/or TIME part of your AUTOEXEC.BAT file so you will be prompted to enter them.

If you have a clock/calendar on an adapter card to keep track of the date and time, then you can make that too part of the AUTOEXEC.BAT file. If you want to set up an electronic disk (see Chapter 5) you can use an AUTOEXEC.BAT file to copy your program files from the A drive over to the electronic disk.

You can add whatever you want to an auto-execution batch file. You can have an AUTOEXEC.BAT file close out your work for you, copying files from that electronic disk to the B drive, after you exit Wordstar. That gets a little complex, so for now let's just examine the ways to set up an AUTOEXEC.BAT file.

Many programs come with AUTOEXEC.BAT files. However, if you want to modify those, or set up your own, you have three options:

1) You can use just about any word processing program to set up a batch file. With Wordstar, you want to be sure you do so in the Non Document mode—that means you will hit the letter N instead of D to open the file.

2) DOS comes with EDLIN, an editor for programming that can be used to set up AUTOEXEC.BAT files. EDLIN stands for Line Editor and the DOS manual has a complete section on how to use it.

3) You can create an AUTOEXEC.BAT file directly from the keyboard (sometimes referred to as the console).

The steps below will show you how to set up an AUTOEXEC.BAT file by copying information from the keyboard. We'll assume that we want to set up that AUTOEXEC.BAT file for Wordstar. If you are using another program, just substitute it for Wordstar. Also, you may add any other commands you like to your batch file.

STEP ONE: Turn on the PC with your DOS diskette in the A drive. Once you see the `A>` on the screen (this is after you have entered the time and date), take out your DOS diskette.

STEP TWO: Place the program disk, onto which you want to create the AUTOEXEC.BAT file, in the A drive of the PC.

STEP THREE: Type: `COPY CON: AUTOEXEC.BAT` and press the enter key.

You are telling your PC to copy from the console (or keyboard) directly into the disk file AUTOEXEC.BAT. At this point the file is created and kept open for you to enter whatever commands you want DOS to execute each time you use the program.

STEP FOUR: Now type: `ws` and press the enter key. That means ws now has been entered into the AUTOEXEC.BAT file. Each time you turn your PC on it will automatically go right into Wordstar. If you had any other commands at this point you would enter each of them separately, followed by pressing the enter key. In other words, you would have one command to a line.

STEP FIVE: You're not quite done yet. You need to end this copying process. To do that you will press Function Key 6 (it's the key marked F6 in the two rows of darker colored keys on the far left hand side of the keyboard), and then press the enter key.

When you do that a ^Z will appear on the screen. That signifies the end of the copying process. Now your AUTOEXEC.BAT file is all set up and ready to run.

12.6 Device Drivers for a RAM Disk, a Mouse, and More

If you have DOS 2.0 (or any newer version) you will no doubt be hearing about device drivers. While you probably won't have too much to do with device drivers, you should know a little bit about them. When you set up an electronic (or RAM) disk in the extra memory of your PC, you are actually using a device driver. The same holds true if you are using Microsoft Word with a mouse.

A device driver is nothing more than a means by which DOS makes a device (something you add to your PC, like a mouse) work. For example, you install the definition and attributes of an electronic disk. Once a device driver is installed DOS knows how to work with it and coordinate what it does with the rest of the PC's activity.

Through a CONFIG.SYS file, device drivers can be installed when the system is booted up. DOS then reads and processes the device options (i.e., sets up the format to work with whatever device is being used). This is done even before the AUTOEXEC.BAT file is activated. That way your electronic disk drive will be installed as the C drive before your AUTOEXEC.BAT file copies files from the A drive over to it.

Chapter 5 and Chapter 9 both cover device drivers in detail and explain how to set them up. Chapter 14 of the DOS 2.0 manual explains device drivers and includes the actual code listing for the program to install an electronic disk drive with DOS 2.0.

12.7 Mail Order—A Place To Save Money and To Be Careful

This section was developed to help you work your way through the maze of options, opportunities, and open manholes of mail order buying. Doing business with a mail order house can mean cost savings as high as 50 and 60 percent. That by itself is sufficient reason to make purchases through the mail. Many times you can get things faster through the mail, too. But before you drop everything you're doing and rush to your phone to place an order, you need to know a little bit more. There are some drawbacks to mail order buying.

You can face delays (sometimes long delays); and sometimes companies aren't around too long. If you return something it means more time and possible re-ordering, too. Orders can get mixed up. Do your homework and be a wise consumer.

Mail order houses sell everything: printers, disk drives, memory chips, software, and even cables. The bigger mail order houses have knowledgeable staff to help you pick out the right products for your needs. This service is sometimes even better than that available from your local computer store.

It almost seems too obvious to say that buyers need to be careful when making mail order purchases, but you hear the horror stories over and over again. Most of those stories involve not getting products or getting the wrong ones. In some cases the products didn't work and replacements just never seemed to show up. You can avoid becoming one of the horror story tellers by taking your time and being cautious.

Step By Step Through the Mail Order Maze: These steps will help you work your way through mail order buying. If you think you already know what to do, read all of these steps anyway. It's a good idea just to review them from time to time. The minute you overlook a step you might be tumbling right down that open manhole.

STEP ONE: Make a list of what you need. Leave room by each item to make notes.

STEP TWO: Look through the computer magazines. Read the ads and mark those pages with good prices on the items you want.

STEP THREE: After you've gone through what you feel are enough magazines and ads, you can narrow down your choices. *Make sure you read the fine print at the bottom of the ads*, because many of those good deals turn out to cost more than you think. The reason some prices aren't as good as they look is that the fine print lists service charges for credit cards, shipping, and other items. Sometimes the printed price reflects the bulk purchase discount, and, if you are buying less, you pay 10 to 15 percent more!

STEP FOUR: Once you've narrowed down your choice, you should make a few phone calls. Not to place an order; just to get a feel for whom you will be doing business with. Many mail order houses will have toll-free numbers, but even if they don't, call them anyway. Tell them you're about to make a purchase and you want to know how long it takes to receive orders. Find out what their return policy is and how problems are handled. Ask about their credit card policy, too.

You also ought to find out if they include "how to" instructions with the products they sell. This is important, because many of the instruction manuals that come with products are poorly written. More and more mail order houses have been putting together their own instruction manuals, which are quite helpful. This is another extra service you want to be sure you receive.

Calling mail order houses will help you narrow your choice even further. After talking with each mail order house, ask yourself if you would feel comfortable spending your money there. Remember, those are the people you will be working with if any problems develop.

STEP FIVE: Ask friends and members of computer user groups which mail order houses they have worked with.

STEP SIX: You can send a check with your order or order over the phone, charging your purchase. If you use a credit card, you not only get your order faster (having called it in), but you are protected through the bank that issued the credit card. If a problem develops, or your products aren't delivered, you have more legal options than if you had used a check. Credit card orders have two other advantages: you usually aren't charged for the items you ordered until they are shipped, and you can have as much as 30 to 45 days (or more, if you don't mind the interest) before you have to pay for the order.

STEP SEVEN: Circle all of the items you plan to order and add up the cost. Add sales tax, if applicable, and don't forget about shipping and delivery charges. *Read all of the fine print.* If there is a credit service charge, add that too.

STEP EIGHT: Now, on a separate piece of paper, write the following:

- The name of the company you are calling
- The telephone number you are calling
- The date and time you made the call
- Expected delivery date
- Total cost of order
- The credit card number you plan to use

Write down how much user memory (RAM) your PC has and other details, like dual disk drives and double sided disks.

If you have any questions, write them down here, too. This is going to become your record for this transaction and will come in handy whenever you want to refer to this telephone order. As you talk to the person taking your order, fill in each item on your list. Using a red pen makes it easier to be sure you have an answer for each item on your list.

STEP NINE: Get your credit card out and you're ready to place your order. Placing your order will be quite simple, and that is what causes so many misunderstandings. If you don't have a list to go by, you might forget to ask a question. You or the person taking the order might assume something about your order that isn't right. The point here is not to leave out one single detail.

Before you give your credit card number, check their total with yours. If there is a difference, get it cleared up then and there. If you think something is wrong, don't complete the order. There might have been some price changes or your addition might have been wrong, so don't automatically think you're being taken to the cleaners. Discuss the matter to find out where the problem is. And remember that you might have added an item or two to the order because of their monthly specials.

STEP TEN: Before hanging up, check over your list of items and questions. Be sure every one of them has been addressed, especially the expected delivery date. Clarify whether or not you want the mail order house to substitute items or back order what you want. Many times the substitute items are just as good (even better) as what you had ordered, but it all depends on what you want to do. Find out how long the wait is for back ordering. You can always order that item from someone else. Write the name of person taking the order on your list.

12.8 Is Your PC *Really* Insured Or Do You Just Think It Is?

The time to find out that your PC isn't insured *is not* after something horrible has happened! The point of this section is to make you double check the kind of insurance coverage you have on your PC—if you have any at all. Some insurance policies can cover a PC under your regular homeowners policy—others won't. There are policies that clearly define the acceptable use of your PC for proper coverage; some companies require special clauses or even separate policies.

Sometimes the coverage is limited and is not for replacement value (i.e., paying the total cost in today's dollars to get a new PC). You need to look into all of this now, before you have a problem and before you are told, "Sorry, that computer of yours isn't covered under this policy."

Insurance policies vary from company to company and from state to state. Find out what your options are and if necessary pay the extra cost for *complete replacement coverage*. It will be well worth it the extra premium. If you currently don't have any coverage at all on your PC, you should quietly put this book down and run right out to get that PC insured!!!!! After the considerable investment in your PC, you really can't afford to NOT have it insured.

You will see ads in magazines for personal computer coverage, but check with your own insurance agent first. Chances are the PC can be included under your present homeowner or business policy, and without much (or any) premium increase.

APPENDIX A

8087 Numeric Data Processor A coprocessor which works with the PC's 8088 microprocessor. The 8087 Numeric Data Processor is used for complex math and scientific calculations. Working in tandem with the 8088, the 8087 does all of the complicated math at blinding speed. The 8087 needs software specifically written for it before it can function.

8088 Microprocessor This is the PC's brain. This 16-bit chip from Intel is what controls everything on the system board of the PC. The 8088 is the CPU (Central Processing Unit) through which the PC does all of its work.

A

AC Surge Protector Device which connects between the PC (and other computer equipment, too) and the electrical outlet for protection from power spikes and surges.

Acoustic Modem Modem into which the telephone receiver is placed. The receiver is cradled in an acoustic modem once the telephone number has been dialed.

Adapter Cards A circuit board placed into one of the expansion slots of the PC to connect the system board to other devices, add memory, or do graphics.

Add-On Devices Computer equipment and items attached or connected to the PC.

Aftermarket All of the industries, products and devices designed for working with and around the PC come under the category. The market for products—and services—developed after the release of the PC. This aftermarket is a multi-million dollar industry. The aftermarket is a phenomenon with computers in general.

Antiglare Screen This device (usually made from a fine wire mesh or coated surface) is placed in front of the monitor's screen, cutting down on glare from lights and windows.

Anti-Static Floor Mat A grounded mat placed under the chair on which the PC user is sitting. It provides some protection from static electricity.

Anti-Static Mat This term usually refers to a grounded mat which is placed directly under the PC. Touching this mat periodically dissipates static charges.

Anti-Static Spray A spray which counteracts electrostatic discharge.

AUTOEXEC.BAT File A file set up to have specific DOS commands executed automatically each time the PC is turned on or rebooted. Such a file can be used to go directly into a program when turning the computer on (or whenever the system is rebooted).

B

Bar Charts In graphic displays and printouts, bar charts are a good way to show comparisons, through a series of vertical or horizontal bars representing different figures—depicted in a variety of colors, shades, or patterns.

BASIC A programming language that is on the DOS Program Diskette, along with BASICA (the advanced BASIC). BASIC is known for its ease of use and is one of the most popular programming languages for beginners.

Batch File A non-document file used to execute DOS commands. Such a file can even be used to call up programs.

Baud The number of bits per second which are transmitted in communications. The higher the number, the faster the transmission of information.

BBS Abbreviation for Bulletin Board System.

Bit Binary DigIT abbreviation. The smallest unit of information within a computer. The value of a bit is either 0 or 1. A string of 8 bits make up one Byte.

Boot Up Starting the PC by turning on the power switch; or rebooting it by pressing the ALTERNATE, CONTROL and DELETE Keys simultaneously.

Brightness Control Knob on most monitors for adjusting the intensity (brightness) of the screen.

Bulletin Board Systems Throughout the United States (and the world) there are hundreds of services to call for gaining and sharing information. Such services are called Bulletin Board Systems. Most Bulletin Board Systems (also known as BBS) don't cost any more than the price of the telephone call and have no user fees.

Byte Represents one number or character and is made up of a string of eight bits.

C

C Drive This term is used for referring to both emulated disk drives (RAM drives) or fixed disks. It is the label for a particular drive—beyond the A and B drive (the two floppy disk drives in the System Unit. An emulated disk drive or a fixed disk can also have other letter designations such as D, E and F.

CAD Computer Aided Design; special software packages for architectual and engineering design.

***Central Processing* Unit (CPU)** The microprocessor which runs the PC. For the PC that is the 8088 chip made by Intel (now also made by IBM). The term central processing unit is sometimes used to refer to the system unit.

CHKDSK The file on the DOS Program Diskette that is used to *check disk*. It analyzes the File Allocation Table and directories on any disk. CHKDSK disk can be used to see how much space is left on a disk and how the files have been allocated.

Clock/Timer This feature on many multifunction adapter cards automatically puts the correct time/date stamp on all files.

Color Graphics Adapter Card This is the adapter card needed to use a color monitor with the PC.

Color Monitor A monitor with a color screen, which is especially desirable for graphics. To use a color monitor a color graphics adapter card is needed.

Communications Using the PC via telephone connections to tie directly to information utilities, bulletin boards, and other computers. A modem is required for this communications link.

Composite Monitor A color monitor for the PC. Color monitors all use much the same technology to produce colors. There are still three individual beams, but the signal is combined so that it can be sent on one pair of wires between the PC and the monitor. The electron beams are flashed or sprayed from an electron gun at the back of the monitor to the screen. However, just how that is done determines the clarity of the images on the screen. With a composite monitor, which provides sharper color, the signals that drive the electron beams which hit the screen as colored dots are combined in a composite video signal—thus the name composite monitor.

Computer User Group An organization of computer owners. (Some groups are devoted to the PC, while many have representation from people using a variety of computers.) Ideas, tips, and pointers are shared through such groups. Groups provide speakers and seminars, as well as access to public domain software. Group purchase discounts are also available through many groups.

CONFIG.SYS *File* File used for installing a Device Driver with DOS 2.0 (or new versions).

Connector Cable Used to connect devices to the PC. As more is added to the PC there will, obviously, be more connector cables. A connector cable is also known as an interface.

CP/M An operating system, which preceded PC-DOS (MS-DOS), and is still in use today. CP/M can be used on the PC, with the proper CP/M operating disk or peripheral device.

CPU Abbreviation for Central Processing Unit.

Crash What happens to a fixed disk when a sector, track, or the disk itself is damaged.

Cursor The screen pointer marking the position on the monitor's screen at which information (i.e., a letter, character or space) will be entered. The cursor will usually be either an underline figure or box (one space in width), flashing at a specific point on the screen.

D

Daisy Wheel Print Element Many letter quality (impact) printers use this kind of interchangeable print element. The element is nothing more than a wheel with dozens of tiny spokes. The letters, numbers and symbols are at the end of each spoke and strike the page as they are pushed forward by the printer mechanism.

Data Base Information (large and small amounts) stored in a manner which allows the user to retrieve it.

Device Driver A .COM file containing the code (i.e., instructions) needed to implement a device like a mouse or emulated disk drive (RAM drive). This only applies to DOS 2.0 (and newer versions).

Direct Connect Modem No telephone receiver is needed with this kind of modem, because there is a wire connection from the modem to the phone outlet in the wall.

Disk Drive The device which holds disks and has a read/write head to retrieve from, and store data on, them. This phrase is sometimes used to refer to a fixed disk.

Disk Drive Controller IBM's term for this is Diskette Adapter. The disk drive controller does what the name implies—it controls disk drives like a traffic light, allowing the user to work easily between the disk drives.

DOS Disk Operating System. The software that directs the PC functions—interpreting the programs and commands, storing and retrieving information from the disks (floppy, emulated, and fixed). Microsoft developed PC-DOS which is tied very closely to MS-DOS.

Dot Matrix Printer This type of printer produces letters, numbers, and characters (including graphics) with a series of pins in a matrix pattern which strike the page through a ribbon at high speed. Though it has been considered by many to be a secondary or draft quality printer, the dot matrix printer today has become commonplace and accepted. In fact, many people use dot matrix printers because they want their clients and customers to know that the work was done on a computer.

Some dot matrix printers can produce text so close to letter quality that a magnifying glass is required to tell the difference. You can now get both draft quality (along with the speed) and letter quality with such dot matrix printers—and at a very affordable price.

Double Sided Disks Floppy disks upon which information can be stored on both sides. Capacity, with DOS 2.0 is 360K (320K under DOS 1.1).

Dvorak Keyboard A keyboard designed for greater speed and ease of use than the more common QWERTY keyboard (the one that comes with the PC).

E

EDLIN Text editor that comes on the DOS Program Diskette. Can be used for limited word processing but is somewhat primitive. Edlin is also used for some programming and special applications.

Electronic Mail Letters, documents, and files sent through the telephone lines by a PC setup for communications. Electronic mail offers convenience and instant delivery seven days a week. Such mail can also be used for sending computer letters to those who do not own computers. Such letters are usually delivered in the following day's regular mail. Electronic mail also offers other options, which include telex and mailgrams.

Electronic Spreadsheets VisiCalc started it all in the late 1970s and today Lotus 1-2-3 carried on the tradition. An electronic spreadsheet is nothing more than rows and columns of numbers into which budgets and hundreds of financial calculations can be placed, with what if changes computed quickly. The newer spreadsheets (and revisions of older ones) offer word processing, data base functions, graphics, and even communications.

Electrostatic Discharge Commonly known as static electricity. It can ruin computer chips and even scramble or damage data stored on disks.

Emulated Disk Drive An emulated disk drive is created from extra space in the RAM (Random Access Memory) of your PC and works just like a regular disk drive. In other words, a portion of the internal memory in your PC can also be used to duplicate electronically what a mechanical disk drive does. A minimum of 256KB user memory is needed for an emulated disk drive. However, since an emulated disk drive is created in memory it exists only while the PC is on.

Expansion Slots The system board in the PC has expansion slots for adapter cards. The PC has five such slots and the PC/XT has eight (three for short adapter cards). The adapter cards slip into the expansion slots for the connection to be made.

Expansion Unit Another chassis for the PC, an expansion unit brings with it up to eight extra expansion slots for adapter cards. Expansion units have their own built-in power supplies and some even have a fixed disk.

External Fixed Disk This fixed disk is not physically inside the PC, but is attached by a cable to a special adapter card and functions with appropriate software (supplied with the fixed disk).

External Modem Modem attached to, but not inside the PC. External modems usually have indicator lights which show particular functions as the modem operates.

F

Face Plate Face plates are found on no drive PCs or on PCs with only an A drive (the B drive covered with a face plate). A face plate is removed from the inside by loosening a screw.

Fixed Disk A fixed disk, also known as a hard disk or Winchester disk, is a mass storage device.

Fixed Speech Fixed speech is the preferred form of speech synthesis (i.e., a computer synthesizing speech—talking) for closer duplication of the human voice. Through the use of a custom vocabulary for which a person has actually spoken words which were then digitized, the computer calls up words as needed. This form of synthesized speech requires large amounts of user memory and is usually found in more commercial applications like the talking check-out register at the grocery store.

Floppy Disks Also known as diskettes, these thin, circular pieces of magnetic plastic are used for storing information such as files, reports, letters and documents. The floppy disk spins in the disk drive while the disk drive's read/write head retrieves or stores data.

Function Keys Two rows of light grey keys on the far left hand side of the PC's keyboard are known as function (programmable, memory) keys. They are used for saving keystrokes and executing commands.

G

Game Adapter Card Adapter card used to hook up a joy stick for playing games on the PC. Some multifunction cards have game adapter ports on them, allowing for the joy stick connection.

Global Filename Characters The ? (question mark) and * (asterisk) are global filename characters and can be used with such DOS commands as DIR and COPY. These two characters allow you to copy and list several files by only using part of the file name. Thus `DIR *84` would provide a listing of all files in the directory ending with 84.

Graphics Picture creation. Animation on the screen and full-color printing of images is possible. Graphics can be done on color or monochrome screens.

Graphics Adapter Card Both for color and monochrome screens this card is needed, because it is what allows the PC to actually do graphics.

H

Half-Height Disk Drives Disk drives which are half the size of the regular floppy disk drives.

Hard Disk Also known as a fixed disk or Winchester disk.

I

IBM PCjr IBM's home computer, which is compatible (to a degree) with the PC.

Impact Printer This printer, long known also as letter quality, produces a fully formed character like that of a typewriter.

Information Utilities Data bases and information reference services. Service is by subscription and access is through communications.

Ink Jet Printer Sprays the ink on a page; best printer for graphics reproduction.

Integrated Programs Programs which permit the use of several programs at once. Integrated programs allow more than one program file to be displayed on the screen at the same time (in windows). Files can also be copied back and forth.

Interface Any connection between a device and the PC, two devices, hardware and software, or computer and user. This term can also mean the cabling which is used to link devices together.

Internal Fixed Disk A fixed disk contained inside the PC, as in the PC/XT.

Internal Modem Modem housed on an adapter card, which fits into one of the PC's expansion slots. This type of modem pulls power from the PC's power supply.

J

Joy Stick A device used for playing games on the PC. A joy stick provides an alternative to playing games from keyboard control.

K

K *or* KB Kilobyte. Means 1,000 bytes, but actually it is 1,024 bytes.

L

LAN Networking. LAN stands for Local Area Network.

Laser Printer Laser printers work in the same way as dot matrix printers, only the matrix pattern is greatly condensed.

Letter Quality Printer Term normally used when referring to an impact printer, which strikes a fully formed character onto the paper in a way similar to that of a typewriter.

Light Pen A light pen does nothing more than sense the beam of light from the screen. A timing circuit lets the PC calculate where you are on the screen, as marks are made wherever the pen is touching the screen.

M

Memory Chips The RAM (Random Assess Memory) of the PC is made up of memory chips.

Memory Disk A memory disk, also known as an emulated disk drive, is created from extra space in the RAM (Random Access Memory) of your PC and works just like a regular disk drive.

Memory Sockets The sockets on the system board of the PC where the memory chips are placed. There are also similar sockets on adapter cards which allow for additional memory chips. The memory chips must be placed carefully into these sockets so the pins on each chip don't get bent or broken.

Modem A modem is a device which, when hooked up to your PC, permits the transmission and reception of information for your PC over telephone lines.

Monitor The monitor is the screen viewed while using the PC. A monitor can be either color or monochrome.

Monochrome Monitor Also known as the green screen, this monitor is a standard item on a PC starter system. Now that graphics can be done on this monitor, it has gained new life. Some monochrome monitors are amber instead of green.

Mother Board Everything inside the IBM PC rests on the Mother Board (also known as the system board). It is from the Mother Board that the PC is controlled. The initial user memory is also found on the Mother Board. There are two versions of the Mother Board—one holding 64KB user memory (made before March 1983) and one holding up to 256KB user memory.

Mouse The mouse is a small unit with a rolling device on the bottom of it (however, there are some mouse units without rollers). The mouse moves the cursor as it is rolled.

Mouse Adapter Card The mouse will need a connection to the PC. This is accomplished with the mouse adapter card, which goes into one of the PC's empty expansion slots.

Multifunction Adapter Card These adapter cards have become extremely popular because you get several things in one—and that saves expansion slots. You can get more user memory, a print spooler, graphics, a clock/calendar, a serial port, and more on just one multifunction adapter card.

N

Nanosecond One billionth of a second.

Networking Networking and the term LAN (which stands for Local Area Network) mean linking two or more PCs together. Networking has been used for years with main frame computers and recently has come to personal computers. Several companies, including IBM, currently manufacture networking packages for the PC.

No Drive IBM PC It is possible to purchase an IBM PC without disk drives and diskette adapter. Doing so (then installing all of that yourself) means a significant cost savings.

NS Abbreviation for Nanosecond.

P

Parallel Port Connection at the back of the PC for a parallel interface.

Password Control Through password control, access to the PC or specific programs can be restricted.

PC Abbreviation for IBM Personal Computer.

PC/XT, *also* XT This is a version of the IBM PC, with a fixed disk and eight expansion slots. It also comes with a serial adapter card. Programs will run just the same on the PC/XT as they do on a regular PC. The fixed disk, however, does add much speed.

Phantom Disk Drive Emulated disk drive.

Pie Charts A circle divided in slices to show percentages and other figures. Used in graphic presentations to depict allocations and profit margins.

Plotters Plotters are actually special printers which are dedicated to doing graphics—in black and white and in color. What sets plotters apart from any kind of printer is that plotters actually draw with pens.

***Portable* IBM PC** In the Spring of 1984 IBM released a portable version of the IBM PC. Though different in many ways (i.e., 512 RAM on the system board and eight expansion slots) the portable PC runs just about all of the programs which run on the PC.

Printer A device for transferring computer data onto paper. Printers range from dot matrix and impact printers to laser printers.

Printer Adapter Card This is the adapter card through which the PC is connected to the printer.

Public Domain Software This represents a great wealth of programs that virtually cost nothing more than the disks (and phone charges if you're using communications to access a BBS) used to copy them onto. Public domain software is available through bulletin boards, user groups, and individuals.

Q

QWERTY *Keyboard* The standard computer (and typewriter) keyboard. The name comes from the top row of letters on the left hand side of the keyboard.

R

RAM Random Access Memory. This is the user memory of the PC (also called the internal memory). Programs are loaded into this memory to work. RAM can also be used to create print spoolers and emulated disk drives.

RAM *Drive* Also known as an emulated disk drive.

README.DOC A file on a program diskette which contains instructions (sometimes even a program manual) for using the program, as well as other information.

RF *Modulator* A device used to hook the PC to a television set. The output from the color graphics adapter card in the PC will then actually transmit—in much the same way that a radio station does—signals to the television set. The result is computer graphics on the television screen.

RGB Monitor The RGB stands for Red, Green and Blue. An RGB monitor, like the one made by IBM for the PC, provides the highest resolution and sharpest clarity.

S

Serial Port Connection at the back of the PC for a serial interface. Connection is made via an RS-232 serial port.

SIG Special interest group. These types of groups are similar to computer user groups, in that people with a common interest share information.

Signal Cable Cable inside the PC linking the disk drive(s) to the diskette adapter (which is also known as the disk drive controller).

Single Sided Disks Floppy disks upon which information can be stored on one side only. Capacity, with DOS 2.0 is 180K (160K under DOS 1.1).

Software Programs, either to control computer operations (DOS) or a particular application, like word processing or graphics.

Sound Covers Acoustic enclosures to deaden much of the sound from printers.

Speech Chip This is the computer chip which allows a computer to synthesize human speech.

Speech Synthesis Electronic reproduction of words through phonetic encoding.

Spooler A storage area set up in RAM (user memory) that allows printing or other computer work to take place while something else is being done. It usually comes as part of the package with multifunction adapter cards. Acronym for Symultaneous Peripheral Operations On Line.

Static Electricity Electrostatic discharge.

SYSOP Abbreviation for System Operator of a bulletin board.

System Board Mother Board.

System Unit This is the largest part of the PC—in fact it is the PC. The disk drives, as well as just about everything else (except the keyboard, the monitor and printer) is contained inside the system unit.

T

Templates Plastic or paper cards which lie over the keyboard to make program commands easier. This term is also used in relation to program overlays which are used with electronic spreadsheets and other programs.

Text To Speech Text to speech is the most common form of speech synthesis, in which words (i.e., text) are electronically reproduced through phonetic encoding. The words you type into the computer are then spoken by a speech unit inside or outside of the computer. This method uses the least amount of memory because there are only 50 basic phonemes in the English language which need to be stored for random use. A computer sounds somewhat robotic when text to speech is used and many words haveto be mis-typed to sound correct phonetically.

Thimble Print Wheel A print element which works much like a daisy wheel, but spins horizontally, instead of vertically, as it prints.

Tutorial Program This type of program walks the user through the difficult period of learning how to use other programs. Tutorial programs are available for just about any major program on the market today, including DOS.

U

Uninterruptible Power Source Really an AC power backup unit. With such a device you can have up to 30 minutes to save information to disk, once the power goes off.

UNIX *System* V The operating system from AT&T which is used in the 3B family of computers.

W

Windows A viewing area on the screen. Through windows several program applications can take place simultaneously, with information easily transferred back and forth between files.

Word Processing The creation, storage, and retrieval of text—letters, memos, documents, reports, books.

APPENDIX B

Use this appendix in two ways to find the products, programs, companies, books, and magazines mentioned in this book. You will find an alphabetical listing for all of the companies and magazine publishers in section 1. In section 2 you will find specific products and magazines listed under major headings. Next to the name of each product or program you will find the company which manufactures it. The name of the publisher will be listed next to each book and magazine. If you want an address, telephone number, or a brief description of a company or a publisher, just refer to section 1.

1 Manufacturers and Publishers

Advanced Systems Concepts,Inc.
435 N. Lake Street
Pasadena CA 91101 (213) 793-8971
With the switching devices made by this company more than one peripheral can be hooked up to the IBM PC without using additional expansion slots. This company also manufactures switching boxes which allow up to four PCs to share a printer. The units come in both serial and parallel models.

Amdek Corporation
2201 Lively Blvd.
Elk Grove Village IL 60007 (312) 364-1180
Manufactures color monitors for the IBM PC, plus other computer- related products.

American Ink Products Company
527 Howard Street
San Francisco CA 94105 (415) 982-0161
This company provides ribbons at discount prices for just about any make of printer and refills used ribbon cartridges at considerable cost savings. Two unique services that this company

specializes in are : (1) Providing dot matrix type ribbons for do it yourself refilling of cartridges. (2) Providing ribbons in color for both dot matrix and letter quality printers such as Diablo and NEC.

Alpha Software Corporation
6 New England Executive Park
Burlington MA 01803 (617) 229-2924
Has a line of software products for the IBM PC which includes the Apple-IBM connection.

Apple Computer, Inc.
20525 Mariani Avenue
Cupertino CA 95014 (800) 538-9696
Produces personal computers and the devices and software to go with them. Apple was the first company to popularize and successfully market personal computers world wide.

AST Research, Inc.
2372 Morse Avenue
Irvine CA 92714 (714) 540-1333
Makes adapter cards and other products for the PC. Has complete line of adapter cards, from multifunction to special purpose, including communications.

Ashton-Tate
9929 West Jefferson Blvd.
Culver City CA 90230 (213) 204-5570
Develops and markets programs for the IBM PC, primarily from a data base perspective; their product, Framework, represents data base management, word processing, spread sheets, graphics and other applications all within a windowing atmosphere.

AT&T
222 Broadway
New York NY 10038 (212) 669-2584
As of January 1, 1984, and the resulting divestiture of the old AT&T, the new AT&T was allowed to start selling and marketing its own computer operating system and computer related products to the general public. The 3B series of computers from AT&T represent a broad range of computer power from super minis to desk top micros—all of which the IBM PC can be tied into through AT&T's PC Interface.

Bourbaki, Inc.
P.O. Box 2867
Boise ID 83701 (208) 342-5849
Produces software 1DIR, which makes it much more convenient to use DOS, including versions 2.0 and higher. 1DIR allows the user to perform most functions of DOS (like COPY, ERASE and others) without much effort or confusion. Files on the disk are much easier to get to with this program.

BPI Systems
3423 Guadalupe
Austin TX 78705 (512) 454-2801
Markets software in accounting, bookkeeping, and other areas—both for business and personal use.

ButtonWare
P.O. Box 5786
Bellevue WA 98006 (206) 747-4578
Company through which the easy to use data base program PC-FILE III is marketed and distributed. You can actually make a copy of this program and then pay for it after you have used it.

California Micro Computer Company
17791 Jamestown Lane
Huntington Beach CA 92647 (714) 847-4141
Makes a device to turn an electric typewriter into a printer for your IBM PC.

Cdex Corporation
5050 El Camino Real—Suite 200
Los Altos CA 94022 (415) 964-7600
Producer of program training disks which carefully walk users through each phase of learning and using many of the popular programs on the market today. Also has tutorial programs for learning more about the IBM PC itself and DOS.

CompuCable Corporation
1440 S. State College—Suite 6-J
Anaheim CA 92806 (714) 635-7330
Makes dust covers for the IBM PC keyboard, disk drives, and monitor. Also makes antiglare screens.

Compuserve
2180 Wilson Road
Columbus OH 43228 (800) 848-8199
Information utility offering everything from an Electronic Mall and several data bases to programming aids, SIGS, and games. Through Compuserve's Executive Information Service the world of practical business information is available. Stock quotes, electronic mail, electronic conferencing, Standard and Poor's information about companies, historical market information, and dozens of data base retrieval systems (including statistical reports and studies) can be accessed—as well as all of Compuserve's Consumer Information Services.

Control Data Corporation
(800) 232-6789
(612) 853-8065 in Minnesota
Manufactures computer related products, from disk drives and fixed disks to floppy disks.

Corvus Systems
2029 O'Toole Avenue
San Jose CA 95131 (408) 946-7700
Products include networking systems, fixed disks and other computer-related items.

Creative Computer Products
P.O. Box 85152
San Diego CA 92138 (619) 268-0793
Makes templates for the IBM PC keyboard.

Cuesta Systems, Inc.
3440 Roberto Court
San Luis Obispo CA 93401 (805) 541-4160
Makes the Data Saver, a back power unit for the IBM PC and other computers. This back up power unit will prevent loss of data when there is a loss of electric power.

Curtis Manufacturing Company Inc.
28 Birch Road
Peterborough NH 03458 (603) 924-7803
Antiglare screens, tilt/swivel bases for monitors, extension cables for the keyboard and monitors, along with other items are made by this company.

Davong Systems, Inc.
217 Humbolt Court Drive
Sunnyvale CA 94089 (408) 734-4900
Makes fixed disks, networking systems and other products for the IBM PC.

Diablo Systems Incorporated
1510 Trimble Road
San Jose CA 95131 (408) 946-9574
Manufactures one of the standard letter quality printers. Several models of the Diablo printer include serial as well as parallel interfaces, and graphics capabilities. Supplies and service are also available.

Digital Research, Inc.
160 Central Avenue
Pacific Grove CA 93950 (408) 649-5500
The company which developed CP/M. This company also has software for business, education, and the home. Also has operating systems for the PC and several other program languages.

Eagle Data Products, Inc.
P.O. Box 247
Northville MI 48167 (800) 874-5368
Manufactures acoustical enclosures (sound covers) for printers. Other products, too.

Electronic Protection Devices, Inc.
217 Bearhill Road
Waltham MA 02154 (617) 891-6602 (800) 343-1813
Markets surge protection devices which keep electrical spikes and glitches form harming the PC.

Epson American, Inc.
3415 Kashiwa Street
Torrance CA 90505 (800) 421-5426 in CA (213) 539-9140
Best known for one of the most popular dot matrix printers in the world. Epson printers have been around for quite some time, are seen just about everywhere and also do graphics.

Freeware
P.O.Box 862
Tiburon CA

Company through which you can get PC-TALK III, the communications software package. This is another of the use first-pay later programs.

FTG Data Systems
10801 Dale Suite J-2
Stanton CA 90680 (714) 995-4787
Manufactures and markets light pens. Some software is available for the products.

Genie Computer Corporation
31117 Via Colinas #402
West Lake Village CA 91362 (818) 991-6210
Makes fixed disks, including removable fixed disks.

Hayden Publishing Company, Inc
10 Mulholland Drive
Hasbrock Heights NJ 07604
Publishes Personal Computing magazine.

Hayes Microcomputer Products, Inc.
5923 Peachtree Industrial Blvd.
Norcross GA 30092 (404) 449-8791
Makes Hayes Smartmodems, the most popular of the modems on the market today—and the software product to go with them.

Hercules Computer Technology
2550 Ninth Street Suite 210
Berkeley CA 94710 (415) 540-6000
Manufactures a graphics adapter card which allows you to run graphics on a monochrome screen.

Hewlett Packard Company
16399 West Bernardo Drive
San Diego CA 92127 (619) 487-4100
From computers to plotters, this company seems to do it all. HP has been around a long time and makes a variety of products to meet just about any computer need—including the impressive new ink-jet printers.

Hooleon Company
P.O. Box 201
Cornville AZ 86325 (602) 634-4503 634-4507
Makes the keytop enhancements for the IBM PC, which make it easier to find and use certain keys on the keyboard.

Houston Instrument
8500 Cameron Road
Austin TX 78753 (512) 835-0900
Manufactures and markets plotters, digitizers and other products which can be used with the IBM PC; also produces some popular software.

IBM Corporation
Boca Raton FL 33432
(800) 221-1490 in Alaska and Hawaii (800) 447-0890
The IBM PC, as well as main frame computers, and much, much more.

I-Bus System
8863 Balboa Avenue
San Diego CA 92123 in CA (619) 569-0646 (800) 382-4229
Makes an expansion unit for the PC which allows you to use more adapter cards than a normal PC will hold.

Info Devices
78 East Industry Court
Deer Park NY 11729 (516) 242-1365
Desk accessories, like the Tuck-It for the keyboard, are made by this company.

Information Unlimited Software, Inc.
2401 Marinship Way
Sausalito CA 94965 (415) 331-6700
The popular word processing program EASYWRITER comes from this company. They also have other software products.

Innovative Software
9300 West 110th Street Suite 380
Overland Park KS 66210 (913) 383-1089
Software, such as FAST GRAPHS (and other programs, including a data base), for the IBM PC is produced and marketed by this company.

Intel Corporation
3065 Bowers Avenue
Santa Clara CA 95051 (408) 987-8080
Makes computer chips (especially the 8088 micro processor—the heart of the IBM PC), as well as other computer-related products.

Keytronics, Inc.
P.O. Box 14687 Dept.E
Spokane WA 99214 (800) 262-6006
Provides an alternative to the standard keyboard for the IBM PC (and even the PCjr). Their products have many features the PC's keyboards don't have.

LETUS A-B-C
3790 El Camino Real, Suite 2006
Palo Alto CA 94306 (415) 493-4306
Has developed and now markets a magazine data base overlay for PC-FILE III. This data base contains short abstracts of magazine articles, letters, reviews, and tips from most of the major PC- related magazines, going back to 1982. Sorting is done on keyword, subject, author, and title. Quarterly circulation.

Locus Computing Corporation
3330 Ocean Park Blvd.
Santa Monica CA 90405 (213) 452-2435

Company which developed the PC Interface for AT&T. This product allows you to use an IBM PC with the AT&T 3B family of computers.

Lotus Development Corporation
161 First Street
Cambridge MA 02142 (617) 492-7171
1-2-3 says it all about this company, which has now released Symphony.

MA Systems Incorporated
2015 O'Toole Avenue
San Jose CA 95131 (408) 943-0596
Tutorial programs on DOS, as well as other programs, are produced and marketed by this company.

Maynard Electronics
430 East Semoran Blvd.
Casselberry FL 32707 (305) 331-6402
Fixed disks and other products for the PC are made by this company. Their fixed disks can be installed internally in the PC.

McGraw-Hill Inc
1221 Avenue of the Americas
New York NY 10020 (212) 997-1221
Publishes Byte Magazine.

MCI Mail
2000 M Street, NW
Washington DC 20036 (202) 293-4255
This product allows mail—including files—to be sent to just about anywhere, whether the person has a personal computer or not. Requires a modem and communications software. No minimum monthly charge, with reasonable rates charged for each letter or file sent.

Microlog Inc.
222 Route 59
Suffern NY 10901 (914) 368-0353
The multifunction adapter card known as BABY BLUE II is made by this company.

Microsoft Corporation
10700 Northup Way
Bellevue WA 98004 (206) 828-8080
Products include software, languages, and hardware. Developed the operating system for the IBM PC (PC DOS) and MS DOS. Popular products include Multiplan, Microsoft WORD, and the Microsoft Mouse.

MicroPro
33 San Pablo Avenue
San Rafael CA 94903 (415) 499-1200
Most famous for its word processing success with Wordstar. Other programs include MailMerge, InfoStar, and StarBurst (for controlling several programs under one umbrella).

NEC Information Systems, Inc.
1414 Massachusetts Avenue
Boxborough MA 01719 (617) 264-8000
Printers and computers are what this company is best known for.

The Norton Utilities
2210 Wilshire Blvd.
Santa Monica CA 90403 (213) 399-3948
Produces a series of utility programs. Programs like Unerase and Disk Look allow you to do much more with your PC.

Oasis Systems
7907 Ostrow Street—Suite F
San Diego CA 92111 (619) 279-5711
This company makes products that pick up where word processing leaves off, developing programs that check spelling, punctuation and style. This company has also started marketing games under the new concept of SUNDOG.

Orchid Technology
47790 Westinghouse Drive
Fremont CA 94539 (415) 490-8586
Networking and other computer-related products are made by this company.

Paradise Systems, Inc.
150 N. Hill Drive Suite 10
Brisbane CA 94005 (415) 468-5320
Manufactures the Paradise MultiDisplay Card, which makes it easy to externally switch back and forth between a color and monochrome monitor.

PC Connection
6 Mill Street
Marlow NH 03456 (800) 243-8088
Mail order house for purchasing just about anything needed for the IBM PC. The PC Connection prides itself on fast, reliable service and offers solid guarantees.

PC World Communications, Inc.
555 DeHaro Street
San Francisco CA 94107 (415) 861-3861
Publishes PC *World* magazine.

PennWell Publishing Company
119 Russel Street
Littleton MA 01460 (617) 486-9501
Publishes *Business Computing Magazine.*

Peachtree Software, Inc.
3445 Peachtree Road NE 8th Floor
Atlanta GA 30326 (404) 239-2045
Software products for the IBM PC—from accounting to word processing.

Popular Computing, Inc.
1060 Marsh Road Suite C-200
Menlo Park CA 94025 (414) 328-4602
Publishes *InfoWorld*, the computer news weekly.

Princeton Graphics Systems
1101-1 State Road
Princeton NJ 08540 (800) 221-1490
Color monitors and other products are made by this company.

Printacolor Corporation
5965 Peachtree Corners East
Norcross GA 30071 (404) 448-2675
Makes ink jet printers, which can be used with the IBM PC.

Quadram Corporation
4357 Park Drive
Norcross GA 30093 (404) 923-6666
Makes a complete line of adapter cards for the IBM PC, from multifunction cards to other special cards. Also makes fixed disks.

Quarterdeck
1918 Main Street Suite 240
Santa Monica CA 90405 (213) 392-9851
Produces window environment software for the PC which allows you to run more than one program at a time. You can also see more than one program file at a time on the screen's windows.

RoseSoft
4710 University Way NE-Suite 601
Seattle WA 98105 (206) 524-2350
Makes Prokey, software which allows you to save keystrokes and customize just about any program.

Seasoned Systems
Box 3036
Chapel Hill NC 27515 (919) 967-5818
Through this company's software you can convert you current PC keyboard over to the Dvorak keyboard. Training is included in this package through a tutorial and a cassette tape (enclosed with the manual).

Screen Data Corporation
240 Cedar Knolls Road
Cedar Knolls NJ 07927 (201) 285-1212
Makes anti-glare screens for the IBM PC monitor—color and monochrome—and other computers. A grounding device is attached to the anti-glare screens to combat static electricity.

Siemans Communications Systems, Inc.
5500 Broken Sound Blvd.
Boca Raton FL 33431 (305) 994-8800 Ext. 2127
Makes ink jet printers for the IBM PC.

Softalk Publishing, Inc.
11160 McCormick Street
North Hollywood CA 91603 (213) 980-5074
Publishes Softalk magazine.

Software Arts, Inc.
27 Mica Lane
Wellesley MA 02181 (617) 237-4000
Produces and markets the program TK! Solver, as well as other software. Software Arts created Visicalc and is presently selling it directly to the public at a very competitive price.

Softword Systems, Inc.
52 Oakland Avenue North
East Hartford CT 06108 (203) 282-0131
The word processing program MULTIMATE comes from this software house.

Sorcim
2310 Lundy Avenue
San Jose CA 95131 (408) 942-1727
SuperCALC and other software products come from this company.

The Source
1616 Anderson Road
McLean VA 22102 (703) 734-7500
Information utility, providing data bases and information on an around-the-clock basis. Accessed through a PC with a modem and communications software.

Static Handling, Inc.
21 Franklin St.
Dayton OH 45402 (513) 222-1272
Manufactures the Static Stopper mat, which eliminates static electricity around your PC.

Sysgen Incorporated
47853 Warm Springs Blvd.
Fremont CA 94539 (415) 490-6770
Manufactures fixed disks for the IBM PC and other computer-related products for business and industry. Products include tape backup.

Tecmar, Inc.
6225 Cochran Road
Cleveland OH 44139 (216) 349-0600
Produces a complete line of adapter cards and fixed disks, communications, multifunction, and specialty cards. Also offers networking systems.

Texas Instruments Incorporated
P.O. Box 75240
Dallas TX 75240 (800) 527-3500
Besides its own personal computers (which are PC compatible), it makes printers which run with the IBM PC—providing both draft and letter quality printing in one affordable printer.

Unitrace Corporation
3350 Scott Bldg. #20
Santa Clara CA 95051 (408) 727-7573
Makes and installs up-dated system boards for older version PCs.

VisiCorp
2895 Zanker Road
San Jose CA 95134 (408) 946-9000
The marketing company behind Visicalc and the creator of VisiON.

Vista Computer Company, Inc.
1317 East Edinger Avenue
Santa Ana CA 92705 (714) 953-0523 (800) 854-8017
Makes expansion chassis units for the PC.

Wayne Green Publications Group
80 Pine Street
Peterborough NH 03458 (603) 924-9471
Publishes *jr Magazine*.

Ziff-Davis Publishing
One Park Avenue
New York NY 10016 (212) 725-4694
Publishes the following magazines:

Creative Computing
39 East Hanover Avenue
Morris Plains NJ 07950 (201) 540-0445

PC *Magazine*
One Park Avenue
New York NY 10016 (212) 725-4694

PC *Tech Journal*
The World Trade Center Suite 211
Baltimore MD 21202 (301) 576-0770

PC *Week*
15 Crawford Street
Needham MA 02194 (617) 449-6520

2 Products, Books, and Magazines

ADAPTER CARDS

Color Graphics—IBM Corporation
Speech Master—Tecmar, Inc.

ANTI-GLARE SCREENS

Anti-glare screen—Screen Data Corporation

COLOR MONITORS

Color monitor—Amdek Corporation
RGB color monitor—IBM Corporation
RGB color monitor—Princeton Graphics Systems

BOOKS AND MAGAZINES

Byte Magazine—McGraw-Hill, Inc.
Business Computing—PennWell Publishing Company
Communications And Networking For The IBM PC
Robert J. Brady Company 1983
Graphics Programming On The IBM *Personal Computer*
A Spectrum Book, Prentice-Hall, Inc. 1983
InfoWorld—Subsidiary of CW Communications
jr Magazine—Wayne Green Publications
MS-DOS & PC-DOS *User's Guide*—Robert J. Brady Company 1984
PC *Magazine*—Ziff-Davis Publishing
PC *Tech Journal*—Ziff-Davis Publishing
PC *Week*—Ziff-Davis Publishing
PC *World*—PC World Communications, Inc.
Softalk—Softalk Publishing Company

COMPUTERS

AT&T 3B Computers—AT&T

DATA BASES

dBASE II—Ashton Tate
PC-FILE III—Buttonware
Letus A-B-C—Letus A-B-C

DISKETTE ADAPTERS

Sandstar Disk Drive—Maynard Electronics

DIGITIZER

Houston Instrument Hipad—Houston Instrument

ELECTRONIC SPREADSHEETS

Multiplan—Microsoft Corporation

FURNITURE AND ACCESSORIES

Antiglare screens—Screen Data Corporation
Curtis Tilt, Swivel Pedestal—Curtis Manufacturing Company, Inc.
Dust covers- CompuCable Corporation
Inked ribbons for printer—American Ink Products Company
Sound cover for printer—Eagle Data Products, Inc.
Static Stopper—Static Handling, Inc.

Systems Stand—Curtis Manufacturing Company, Inc.
Templates—Creative Computer Products
Touchdown Keytops—Hooleon Company
Tuck-It—Info Devices

EXPANSION UNITS

Dynaframe—Vista Computer Company, Inc.
SIX-PAC—I-Bus Systems

FIXED DISKS

Genie fixed disk—Genie Computer Corporation
MicroScience 2—Maynard Electronics
Sysgen II-20—Sysgen, Incorporated
Sysgen Image—Sysgen, Incorporated

FLOPPY DISK DRIVES

Full height disk drive—Control Data Corporation

GRAPHICS CARDS

Hercules Graphics card—Hercules Computer Technology

INFORMATION UTILITIES

Compuserve—Compuserve Information Service
MCI Mail—MCI Mail
The Source—The Source

KEYBOARD

Dvorak—Seasoned Systems
Keytronic Dvorak—Keytronic, Inc.

LIGHT PENS

FTG Lightpen—FTG Data Systems

MODEM

Hayes Smartmodem 1200 (and 300)—Hayes Microcomputer Products, Inc.

MOUSE

Mouse—Microsoft Corporation

MULTIFUNCTION CARDS

Baby Blue II—Microlog, Inc.

PC Interface—Locus Computing Corporation
Paradise MultiDisplay Card—Paradise Systems, Inc.
Tecmar PC-Mate Captain—Tecmar, Inc.

NETWORKING

ASCI Switch—Advanced Systems Concepts, Inc.
PC Interface—AT&T
Starter Kit—Davong Systems, Inc.
UNIX System V—AT&T

OPERATING SYSTEM

MS DOS—Microsoft Corporation
PC DOS—Microsoft Corporation
Concurrent DOS—Digital Research
UNIX System V—AT&T

PLOTTERS

Hewlett Packard 7470—Hewlett Packard Company
Hewlett Packard 7475—Hewlett Packard Company
Houston Instrument DMP-40—Houston Instrument

POWER BACKUP UNITS

Datasaver—Cuesta Systems, Inc.

PRINTERS

CMC 5060—California Micro Computer Company (makes printer out of a typewriter)
Diablo Printers—Diablo Systems Incorporated
Epson RX-80FT—Epson American, Inc.
Printacolor TC1040—Printacolor Corporation
Siemans PT 88—Siemans
Spinwriter—NEC Information Systems,Inc.
Texas Instruments TI 855—Texas Instruments

PROCESSORS

8087 Numeric Data Processor—Intel Corporation

PROGRAMS

1-2-3—Lotus Development Corporation
1DIR—Bourbaki, Inc.
The Apple-IBM Connection—Alpha Software Corporation
Applesoft—Apple Computer, Inc.
BPI General Accounting—BPI Systems
The Coach—Seasoned Systems
dBase II—Ashton-Tate

DOS Tutorial—MA Systems Incorporated
Easywriter—Information Unlimited Software, Inc.
Fast Graphs—Innovative Software
Letus A-B-C—Letus A-B-C
Microsoft Word—Microsoft Corporation
Multimate—Softword Systems, Inc.
Multiplan—Microsoft Corporation
PC-File III—Buttonware
PC-Talk III—Freeware
Peachtree General Ledger System—Peachtree Software, Inc.
Prokey—RoseSoft
Punctuation + Style—Oasis Systems
Supercalc—Sorcim
Supercalc 3—Sorcim
SureStroke—Seasoned Systems
Symphony—Lotus Development Corporation
The Word Plus—Oasis Systems
TK! Solver—Software Arts, Inc.
Unerase—The Norton Utilities
Visicalc IV—Cdex Corporation
Visicalc—VisiCorp
Visiword—VisiCorp
Wordstar—MicroPro International Corporation
Wordstar Tutor—MicroPro International Corporation

STATIC ELECTRICITY

Static Stopper—Static Handling, Inc.

SURGE PROTECTORS

AC Surge Protector—Electronic Protection Devices, Inc.

WINDOWS

Windows—Microsoft Corporation
DESQ windows—Quarterdeck

WORD PROCESSING

Word—Microsoft
Wordstar—MicroPro

APPENDIX C

C.1 It's Not as Bad as You Think!

Even the most enthusiastic of PC owners has been known to wilt at the thought of taking apart the PC. However, once the cover comes off it becomes obvious there was nothing to fear at all. The big step (obstacle) is actually getting around to taking the PC's cover off.

The best way to do it is to take a deep breath, let it out slowly and then follow the steps listed below. If it's any consolation, everyone has fears about working on his or her PC in the beginning. By the third or fourth time you've done it you'll be a pro and won't even think about what you're doing.

C.2 First Things First

You will need to unplug and unhook everything first. Before you start un-doing all of those connections you might want to mark where all the connections are made. This can be easily done with masking tape. If you use matching pairs of letters or numbers to mark each cable and its plug, you won't have any problem putting everything back together again when you are through working inside your PC.

You especially don't want the power cord still plugged in while you are poking around your PC. You will be ready to start once the System Unit (which is also known as the Central Processing Unit and is the biggest part of your PC, with the disk drives in it) sits by itself, minus the monitor and all connections, including the keyboard.

Before you do anything you need to determine which version of the IBM PC you have. There are two versions of the PC. The differences are only minor, but you do need to know about them.

An IBM PC made before mid 1983 has only two screws to loosen—both on the bottom of the back panel, in each corner. The PCs produced since then have five screws to loosen, with the three additional screws at the top edge of the back panel. Figure C.1 shows which screws to loosen on each model.

C.3 Removing the Cover from Your PC

It will take less than five minutes to remove the cover. You will need only one tool:

- a flat-blade screwdriver or 1/4 inch nutdriver

STEP ONE: With everything disconnected from the PC you are ready to begin. Move the keyboard and everything else out of your way so you will have plenty of room. You will be working on the back of the PC first, to loosen the cover mounting screws.

Remove the cover mounting screws. You will be loosening either two of them (which would be on the bottom corners of the back panel) or five of them (in which case, there would be an additional three screws along the top of the back panel). Refer to Figure C.1 as to the specific location for the screws. Keep all of the screws together so you won't have a problem finding them when it comes time to put your PC back together again.

STEP TWO: Now face the front of the PC. Grab the sides of the PC's cover with your hands as shown in Figure C.2. Gently slide the cover toward you, pulling away from the back panel where you just removed the screws. *This must be done cautiously.*

STEP THREE: When it is almost all the way off, the cover will reach the point where you can't slide it any further. At that point tilt the cover up and pull it away from the chassis. Figure C.3 shows how to do this. Set the cover down carefully, out of your way. You are now ready to proceed with adding memory, a disk drive, or anything else.

C.4 Putting Your PC Back Together Again

Putting the cover back on your PC is just a simple matter of following the steps listed above in reverse order. However, there are some things you need to be aware of for it to go smoothly.

The two screws at the bottom outer edge of the back panel are a little tricky to get into place. The problem is that the PC's cover naturally bends outward. What you have to do, as you slip each screw into place, is hold the cover of the PC by the side, pushing inward toward the chassis. It's not that hard to do and it will make it much easier to put both screws back in place.

The cover must be pushed all the way back to the rear panel of the chassis. You can check to be sure the cover is all the way on by looking at the ON-OFF switch,

Fig. C.1: The back panel of the IBM Personal Computer

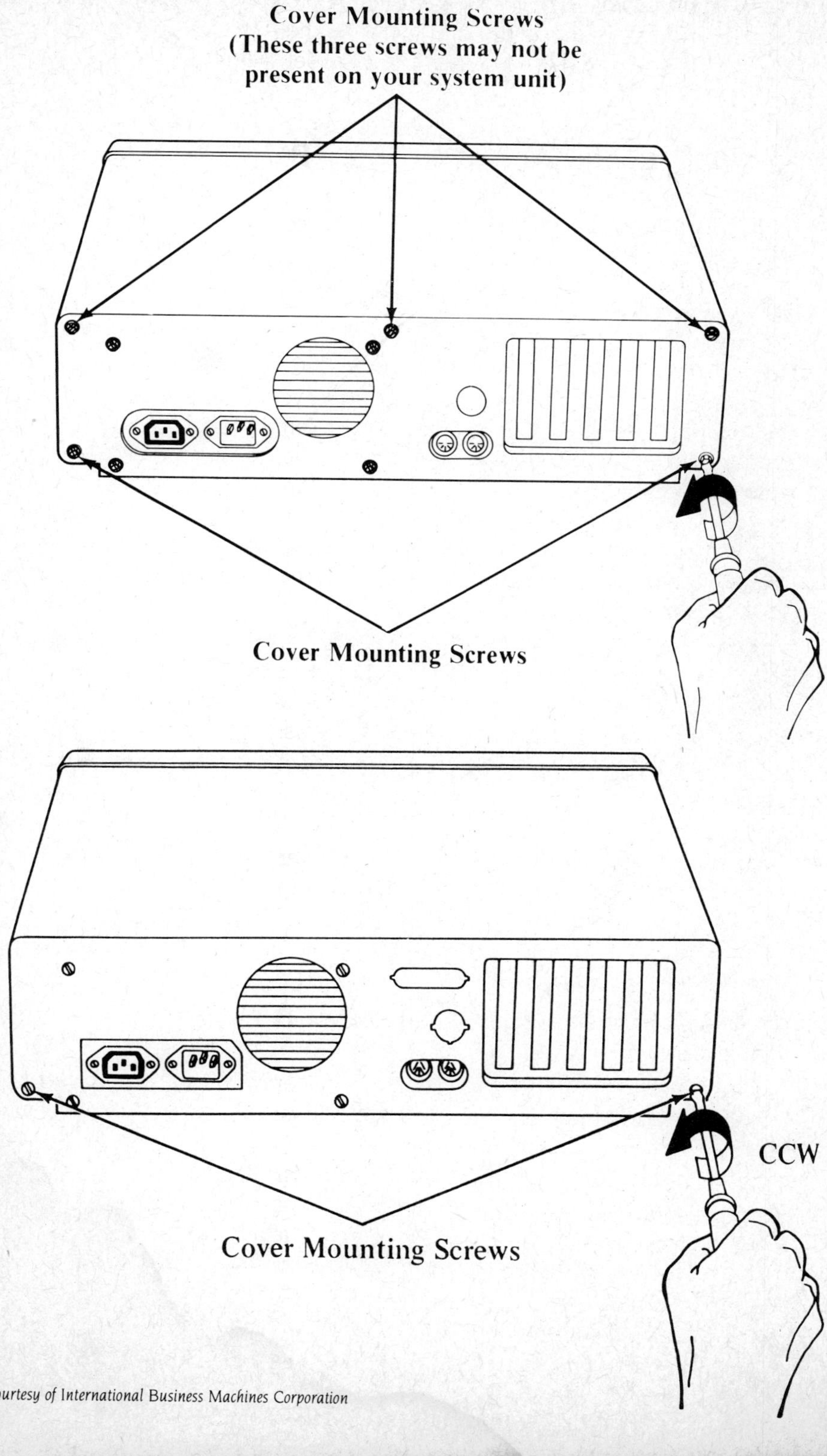

Courtesy of International Business Machines Corporation

Fig. C.2: How to grab and remove the cover from the PC

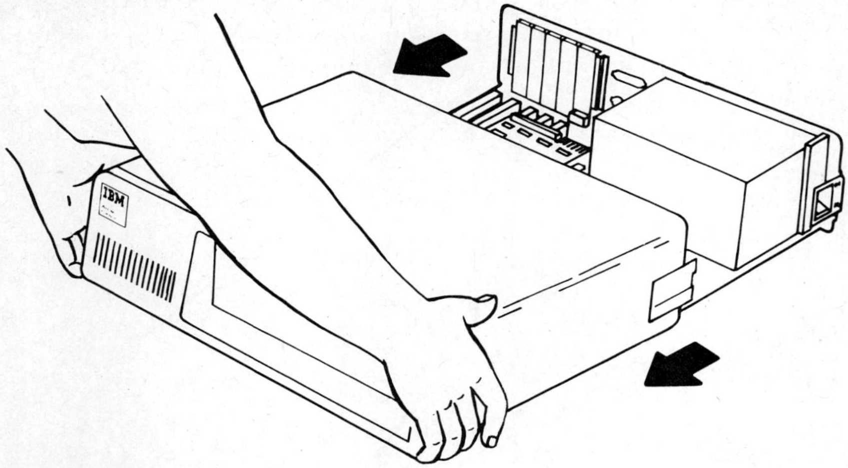

Courtesy of International Business Machines Corporation

Fig. C.3: How to lift cover off IBM PC

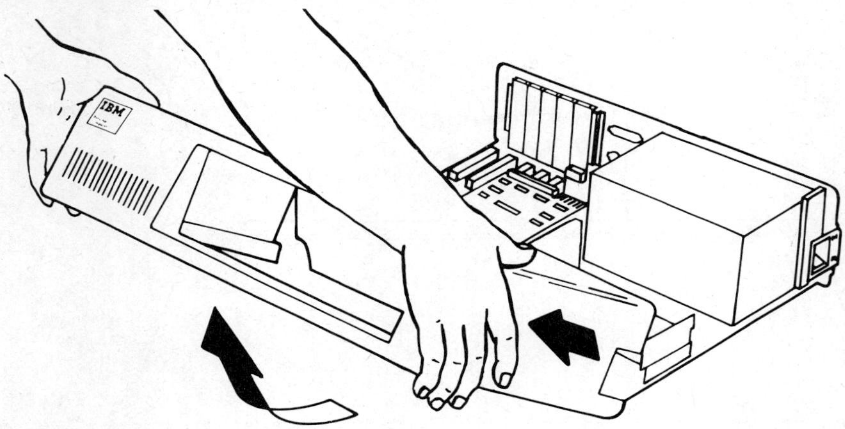

Courtesy of International Business Machines Corporation

located on the right hand side of the PC at the very back. The cover should fit snugly around the black switch unit.

You should make sure that all screws go in tightly. Don't tighten them to the point of stripping, because more than likely you will be taking your PC apart more than once.

INDEX

This index was compiled by Diana Alvernaz, *using a special program developed by* Peter Norton.

About the Author

Bil. Alvernaz is an active freelance writer, concentrating on personal computers. He writes on a regular basis for PC *Magazine*, *Business Computing*, and *jr Magazine*. His computer-related feature articles have also appeared in USA *Today*.

Bil. Alvernaz syndicates a weekly newspaper column, "The Computer Column," to newspapers in the United States. If he isn't writing about computers or his PC, Bil. Alvernaz is actively using his PC for two of his favorite pastimes—communications and programming. He markets and distributes his own software program, *The* UFO *Adventure* (a 45,000 word novel on disk which makes the reader the main character in the story), through his company, Sanctuary Software.

Bil. Alvernaz teaches computer seminars on word processing, and how to use computers. As a computer consultant, Bil. works with corporations, businesses and individuals. He is currently programming a new novel on disk, *The Computerist*, for the IBM PC and the Apple Macintosh. More book projects are in the works, too—all while Bil. actively pursues his other computer-related activities. Bil. Alvernaz Computing is the combined efforts of Bil. and his wife, Diana, who works closely with him in all of his projects.

Bil. enjoys spending time with Diana and their eight-year-old son, Ian, along with wood working, tennis, and the beach. He is an accomplished origamist, having taught paper-folding classes for over fifteen years.